361.7
G56 Goldin, Milton.
Why they give.

WHY THEY GIVE

ALSO BY MILTON GOLDIN

The Music Merchants

WHY THEY GIVE

American Jews and Their Philanthropies

MILTON GOLDIN

Macmillan Publishing Co., Inc.
NEW YORK
Collier Macmillan Publishers
LONDON

TO THE MEMORY OF MY PARENTS,

Ida and Hyman Goldin

Macmillan Publishing Co., Inc.
866 Third Avenue, New York, N.Y. 10022
Collier Macmillan Canada, Ltd.

Library of Congress Cataloging in Publication Data

Goldin, Milton.
Why they give.

Bibliography: p.
Includes index.
1. Jews in the United States—Charities—History.
2. Jews in the United States—Politics and government.
3. United States—Social conditions. I. Title.
HV3191.G66 361.7 76-17655
ISBN 0-02-544560-X

First Printing 1976

Printed in the United States of America

Contents

Acknowledgments

THE INCREDIBLE SCOPE of American Jewish philanthropy during a 322-year period makes a definitive study of the subject impossible, unless a voluminous work is planned. My purpose in this book has been to portray philanthropic responses to crises within as moderate space as was possible.

For help in separating important from (relatively) unimportant events and trends, I spoke with scores of people. One endearing trait of Jewish organizational life is that, whereas nearly everyone is convinced he has an inside track on happenings, few permit themselves to be identified in print as a source of information. Thus I am particularly grateful to the following individuals for their help: Michael Abramoff, Samuel Abramson, William Adalman, Rehaveam Amir, Uri Bar-Ner, Nathan Belth, Peter Bergson-Kook, Robert Bernhard, Nahum Bernstein, Lawrence Buttenwieser, Paddy Chayevsky, Ben Epstein, Ephraim Eshel, Chaim Even-Zohar, Rabbi Louis Finkelstein, David Finn, Edward Geffner, Bertram Gold, Rabbi Joshua Goldberg, S. P. Goldberg, Fred Grubel, Rabbi Arthur Hertzberg, Gaynor Jacobson, Herbert Katzki, Isaiah Kenen, Gustave Levy, Rabbi Theodore Lewis, Isador Lubin, Sidney Marks, James Marshall, Samuel Merlin, Ernest Michel, Charles Mintz, Irving Moscovitz, Emanuel Neumann, Rabbi Herbert Parzen, Bernard Postal, William Riegelman, Daniel Rosenberg, Edmund Rosenthal, William Rosenwald, Joseph Schwartz, Ze'er Sher, Sanford Sollender, Rudolph Sonneborn, Leroy Sugarman, Marc Tabatchnik, Rabbi Isaac Touben, Edward M. M. Warburg, Irving Warner, Joseph Willen, Abraham Zeitz, and Charles Zibbell.

My debt is also great to individuals with whom I corresponded. Rabbi Leon Feuer answered questions about Rabbi Abba Hillel Silver; Irmgaard Gleavecke wrote me about her uncle, Captain Adolf Ernst Schroeder of the S. S. *St. Louis*; Jacob Rader Marcus confirmed that it was possible for a colonial Jew to accumulate £60,000 in 1720; Manfred Minzer noted his UJA and Israel bond adventures; Henry Montor clarified aspects of Ben-Gurion's July 1945 meeting in Rudolph Sonneborn's apartment; and Terence Smith answered questions about Israeli society.

For library and archival research, I am indebted to Harry Alderman, of the American Jewish Committee's Blaustein Library; Rose Klepfisz, of the American Jewish Joint Distribution Committee archives; Anne Blatt, Linda Morgese, and Jacqueline Tynes, of the Greenburgh Public Library in Westchester; William Stewart, of the Franklin D. Roosevelt Library; Zosa Szajkowski, who suggested sources at the YIVO Institute for Jewish Research; and Sylvia Landress and Rebecca Zapinski, of the Zionist Archives and Library.

Public relations officers and staff at various agencies arranged interviews, provided brochures, described their agency's history, and permitted me to use files. Morton Yarmon, of the American Jewish Committee; Edith Pitashnick, of the Council of Jewish Federations and Welfare Funds; Robert Smith, of the Federation of Jewish Philanthropies of New York; Hannelore Koehler, of the German Information Center; Meyer Steinglass, of State of Israel Bonds; and Leon Aaron, of the United Jewish Appeal, were especially helpful.

The kind assistance of the following people is also appreciated. Carla Jenkins in Rep. Peter Peyser's office found out how much Phantom and Skyhawk fighters cost; Howard Katz at Federation of Jewish Philanthropies of New York talked at length about an active campaign leadership; Bea Raskin of Sen. Jacob Javits's staff found out about United States grants and loans to Israel; and Rabbi Ronald Sobel of Temple Emanu-El shared with me his catalogue of the *American Hebrew*.

For yeomanlike labors as typists and secretaries, I am grateful to Barbara Behar, Joan Evans, and Janice Levin, and for reading and commenting on sections of the manuscript, I thank Bernard Postal, Edmund Rosenthal, and James Marshall. I am solely responsible, of course, for points of view and accuracy.

As in all my work, my wife, Aranka Nemcek Goldin, exercised patience and considerable editorial talents pointing out unclear wording and inconsistencies. My debt to her is incalculable.

Introduction

THIS BOOK HAD its origin in my experiences during the mid-1960s as a fund raiser at a Jewish hospital. Orthodox doctrines informed its founders; and *kashruth* (dietary laws) informed its physicians and nurses, its administrators and clerks, its patients and staff. Elsewhere, the faithful might be hanging on by their fingernails; near Eastern Parkway, in Brooklyn, they reigned secure and supreme.

I often spoke with colleagues who have also worked for both Jewish and nonsectarian organizations. Again and again we agreed that goals are higher, solicitors more diligent, and volunteers more aggressive in Jewish institutions. Refusal to give is an affront, not only to the solicitor, but to the divine order of things. Where else does one find "card calling" luncheons, published lists of donors (with gifts carefully noted), and meetings, meetings, meetings? Where else are brochures largely unnecessary because contributors will give in any case? Where else does generation after generation of a family devote hours and dollars to a cause long after anyone can remember its original purpose?

Yes, the complex brew of welfare, religion, meetings, social climbing, and exquisite political infighting stirs something deep within countless American Jewish breasts. I searched for a book that would tell me why

Jewish philanthropy developed in the United States the way it did. I was particularly interested in the people who really made it all possible, the big givers of the Jewish establishment. Who are they? Where did they come from? How did they earn their money? What were their politics? Which agencies and institutions did they favor? How did non-Jews react to their wealth and to their contributions? How did they react to anti-Semitism? And above all, why did they give? Failing to find a single, comprehensive book in which these questions were considered, I decided to write this one.

MILTON GOLDIN

March 1976

PART I

Portraits of Three Migrations

1
Sephardim

IN THE LATE summer of 1654, twenty-three men, women, and children, forerunners of the largest, richest, most powerful Jewish community in history, arrived in New Amsterdam,* the tiny Dutch colony at the tip of green Manhattan island. The travelers were Sephardim, descendants of Jews expelled from the Iberian peninsula by Ferdinand and Isabella in 1492. They were fleeing from the Portuguese, who were among the leading anti-Semites of the period. They came from Recife, a prosperous Brazilian colony seized from Portugal by the Dutch in 1633 and retaken by the Portuguese after a bloody battle in January 1654. They had traveled to New Amsterdam via Martinique, Jamaica, and Cape St. Anthony in Cuba.

Their arrival was a sad and subdued affair. The Jews had left Recife with very little money and could pay Captain de la Mothe, master of the *Ste. Catherine*, only a third of their collective fares. The captain and his crew, which shared in proceeds, asked a Dutch court to intervene. After

* But there is evidence that they were not the first Jews in the town. Jacob Barsimson and Salomon Pietersen, merchants, arrived earlier that summer from Holland, possibly to arrange for Jewish immigration.

an auction of the passengers' possessions, there was still a balance due, and two passengers were imprisoned while the rest were ordered to pay the full amount. This was impossible, but it was not until late October that authorities released the hostages, the *Ste. Catherine* sailed away, and the Dutch agreed the refugees could write brethren in Amsterdam for help.*

This less-than-warm welcome was typical of New Amsterdam, a town run by and for the Dutch West India Company, which had been granted a trade monopoly in North America by the States-General of the Netherlands. West India Company directors were interested in beaver, marten, and otter pelts, not in the motley collection of clerks, soldiers, merchants, trappers, slaves, and freebooters who populated the place and were constantly in court with each other over personal and business disputes.

Although West India Company directors cared little about what happened to settlers, the town obviously needed a strong boss. In May 1647, it got Peter Stuyvesant, a stocky, hawk-nosed, fifty-five-year-old former West India Company soldier who had lost his right leg in a Dutch attack on the Portuguese island of St. Martin. Stuyvesant told town elders that he would govern the people "as a father his children" and threatened that "if any one, during my administration, shall appeal [to Amsterdam], I will make him a foot shorter, and send the pieces to Holland, and let him appeal that way."

The governor wanted no Jews in his colony. While the court was deciding what to do about the unpaid fares, he wrote the company's Honorable Lords, its directors, that Jews had arrived and would "nearly all like to remain here." He suggested they be expelled. His letter continued, "The people having the most affection for you" (meaning himself) found them repugnant. Stuyvesant slyly added that "owing to their present indigence they might become a charge in the coming winter," leaving the impression that their poverty would be immediately burdensome to a poor colony and ultimately burdensome to the thrifty officials of the company.

The Dutch were not unkind, and a seventeenth-century British ambassador, Sir William Temple, found that "Charity seems to be very national among them." Charity was a lesser priority abroad, where the idea was to make money, not to spend it. Among its 167 stockholders, however, the West India Company included seven Jews with large invest-

* Financial assistance was evidently provided, because the matter was never again brought up in a Dutch court.

ments. Amsterdam Sephardim were stretched to the limit caring for penniless refugees from Brazil. With New Amsterdam closed to Jewish immigrants, there would be one place less for brethren in an unfriendly world. Dismayed when the West India Company decided not to issue passports to Jews following receipt of Stuyvesant's letter, they asked the Honorable Lords to reconsider:

The merchants of the Portuguese Nation residing in this City respectfully remonstrate to your Honors that it has come to their knowledge that your Honors raise obstacles to the giving of permits or passports to the Portuguese Jews to travel and to go to reside in New Netherland, which if persisted in will result to the great disadvantage of the Jewish nation. It also can be of no advantage to the general Company but rather damaging.

Amsterdam Jewish worthies proceeded to argue that spacious Dutch possessions could accommodate refugees. "The more of loyal people that go to live there, the better it is in regard to the population of the country as in regard to the payment of various excises and taxes, . . ." wrote Sephardic stockholders. Other countries had set a precedent: the French permitted Jews to live in Martinique and the British were similarly liberal in Barbados.

It was shrewd of the petitioners to dwell on the connection between the Jewish settlers and income for the company. People who could foster international trade were assets in a period of emergent capitalism, and the Honorable Lords of the West India Company were never reluctant to help anybody if they could help themselves at the same time.

Jews were repugnant and new territories should not "be allowed to be infected" by them, directors admitted in a letter to Stuyvesant. Yet there were moral reasons why they should be permitted to remain, among them that "the consciences of men" ought to be free. The Jews could stay but were not to be given licenses to run businesses or keep stores. And they were not to be allowed to worship publicly. They were also to be warned "that the indigent among them shall not become a burden on the Company or the public, but shall be maintained at the expense of the Jewish nation."

As Stuyvesant predicted, one thing the Jews could not do was care for themselves. During the bitter winter of 1654–55, when waters around New Amsterdam froze so hard that people walked across the East River from Long Island, Sephardim appealed for help to the Reverend Johannes

Megapolensis, head of the Dutch Reformed Church in the colony. Like Stuyvesant, he was an anti-Semite. "It would have been proper that these had been supported by their own nation," Megapolensis grumbled to the Classis, the governing body of the Dutch Reformed Church in Amsterdam, "but they have been at our charge, so that we have had to spend several hundred guilders for their support." Megapolensis appealed to his superiors for help to expel the Jews, who had "no other God than the Mammon of unrighteousness and no other aim than to get possession of Christian property." He was no more successful than the governor; the Classis would not help.

Stuyvesant and Megapolensis still hoped to undermine the Jews and force them to leave, using their poverty as a lever. The Jews of New Amsterdam could not open stores or trade with Indians; nor could they serve in the militia, vote, or hold office. Enough of these restrictions, thought the governor and the cleric, and Jews would not only be unable to care for one another, but would leave of their own accord.

Sephardim refused to cooperate in Stuyvesant's plan. Somehow they managed to accumulate goods for improvised shops and secretly traded for furs with Indians. They constantly tested Dutch tolerance and Stuyvesant's power. In August 1655, Stuyvesant ruled out Jewish membership in the militia owing "to the disgust and unwillingness of the mass of Citizens to be fellow soldiers with the aforesaid nation, and to be on guard with the same at the guard house."

Under a Stuyvesant decree, every male Jew between sixteen and sixty was assessed at a tax of sixty-five stivers. But two Jewish settlers, Asser Levy and Jacob Barsimson, petitioned the astonished town council to be permitted to stand guard like other settlers, claiming they were too poor to pay the tax in lieu of service. Stuyvesant and the council took a very dim view of the petition: If Levy and Barsimson did not like New Amsterdam's rules and regulations, they should consider moving elsewhere. On the other hand, what good would it do to antagonize stockholders in Amsterdam? reasoned Stuyvesant. Levy and Barsimson were permitted to stand "watch and ward."

This was just another episode in a tug of war between Stuyvesant and the Jews, who were careful not to burden Amsterdam with their welfare but kept needling local officials for improvements in their status. In November 1655, three Sephardim, Salvador Dandrada, Abraham de

Lucena, and Jacob Henriques, requested permission to trade along the Delaware River and in Fort Orange (now Albany). The following month Dandrada purchased a house. Stuyvesant would not tolerate Jews trading with Indians, nor would he tolerate Dandrada's action; Jews were not permitted to own houses.

Stuyvesant and the Jews again sent missives to Amsterdam requesting clarification. The letters arrived while Rabbi Manasseh ben Israel, representing Sephardim in the Dutch capital, was trying to convince Oliver Cromwell in London to permit Jews to reenter England. The rabbi argued that Dutch Sephardim were very prominent in West India Company operations and could benefit the English economy. The description of their prominence was an exaggeration; nonetheless, it was true that the Dutch had no desire for rich Sephardim to leave Amsterdam, taking their wealth away to rivals. With some annoyance, the Honorable Lords wrote Stuyvesant that Jews could be allowed to trade and to purchase real estate, but should not be permitted "to establish themselves as mechanics . . . or allowed to have open retail shops."

Whittling away at Stuyvesant's restrictions, Asser Levy led the protest against bans on Jewish trade. When the town council announced that burgher rights—licenses to run a business or keep a store—were necessary to practice certain trades, he went to court and asked to be admitted as a burgher so that he could become a butcher.

At this point four other Sephardim—Dandrada, Henriques, de Lucena, and Joseph d'Acosta—took up the battle, arguing that since the West India Company had already granted them the same rights "as other inhabitants of New Netherland" and they had assumed the responsibilities of citizens, they should be given burgher rights, too. Worn down by altercations and legalisms, authorities finally admitted the petitioners to burgherships.

Six years after Sephardim arrived, New Amsterdam's population of Jews and Christians reached 1500. Thanks to inept management, the Dutch West India Company suffered business reverses throughout the world and, in 1661, the colony went bankrupt. Four years later, Stuyvesant heard rumors that a fleet and soldiers were leaving Portsmouth, England, to attack the town. Britain had not declared war on the Netherlands, but Stuyvesant prepared for an onslaught and wrote home for instructions. The West India Company told him not to worry, the ships were really headed for Boston. Everyone relaxed; Stuyvesant headed upstate with a military expedition to fight Indians.

This was one time Stuyvesant was right and the company was wrong. An English squadron of four frigates and 450 soldiers entered the Narrows, anchoring off Coney Island. Stuyvesant rushed back, but only 200 militiamen and 160 regulars could be mustered. Levy turned up at Stuyvesant's side and was assessed 100 guilders for a defense fund. As the British closed in, the governor tore up a surrender demand from the English commander and prepared to fight. His secretary picked up the pieces, pasted them together, and handed the letter to the town burgomasters. Some ninety people, including one of the governor's sons, petitioned Stuyvesant not to provoke a slaughter that would reduce New Amsterdam to ashes. The governor finally decided to give up; a few minutes later a white flag flew above Dutch headquarters in the Battery.

Stuyvesant took defeat hard. Fellow citizens went on with no backward glances. There were few major differences between British and Dutch rule and one important similarity: like West India Company directors, Englishmen could not see much point to an empire that didn't pay. Pursuit of trade was the outstanding fact of London's colonial policy. Religious dissenters could become residents if they obeyed the laws, helped the economy, and contributed to the support of the Anglican Church, which dominated the lives of all settlers and set approved styles of thought and behavior.

There were mixed feelings about Jews. By 1664, Jews were permitted to live in London and were no longer considered aliens. With this precedent set, their right to live in New York was unquestioned. Trade was to be expanded no matter who did the trading, and, under the terms of surrender, freemen had religious liberty. Yet Old World mores also had to be honored, and in Europe Jews had been excluded for centuries from all commercial activities except peddling, petty trades, and moneylending.

How then to fit them into an expansionist, pragmatic system that valued talent and money as much as prejudice? As befit seventeenth-century rationalists, the English opted to make Jews second-class citizens who could worship only in private and would care for their own poor, but could sell or buy from anyone in public, be he Jew or Christian. Jews discovered that authorities overlooked the sorts of inroads about which Stuyvesant complained to Amsterdam.

Nothing ventured, nothing gained, thought New York's Jews, who maintained the only Jewish community on the continent until 1720. The best opportunities were in commerce, and most stayed in the lower middle class selling dry goods, wet goods, hardware, and liquor. A few leaped upward to riches: New York had sixty-seven prominent merchants in 1705; five of them were elite Jewish tidewater merchant shippers who utilized the services of relatives and friends in Europe, the West Indies, South America, and other British North American colonies to establish large-scale import and export operations. All the relatives of a merchant were key participants in the family business. Levys in New York and Levys in London served as agents and partners for each other's transactions on both sides of the Atlantic. The Gomezes, the most influential Jewish family in New York in the 1700s, exported salmon, liquor, and flour; imported chintz, silk, calico, and taffeta; dealt in real estate; and traded with Indians. Abraham de Lucena imported Madeira wine; exported grain, bacon, and flour; and married his daughter Rebecca to Mordecai Gomez, effecting closer relations between two energetic merchant clans.

Of all religious groups in New York, only the Episcopal Church and the Dutch Reformed Church were granted charters. Without a charter, Jews could not jointly own land for a cemetery or a synagogue. This worked to their advantage as well as to their disadvantage. In eighteenth-century Europe, the right of any individual Jew to live in any particular place was dependent on local restrictions on Jews as a group. Since New York's Jews were not members of a legally recognized group, no restrictions could be codified. Assimilation was possible, and this, in turn, led to intermarriage, necessitated by the discouragingly few marital choices within the Jewish community.

Without a charter, the officers of colonial New York's single congregation, Shearith Israel (Remnant of Israel), could not levy taxes on the Jewish community by statute. Discipline had to be tempered with discretion lest part of the congregation drift away. Shearith Israel, on the edge of the wilderness, had to protect the young from intermarriage and also had to be made attractive to pioneers who flouted ancient rituals and dietary laws in the quest for riches. Jews contributed to inspire other Jews to stay Jewish. Coreligionists had to be circumcised, educated, married, and buried in consecrated ground, cared for by their own people from cradle to grave, according to the Law or what passed for the Law among the untutored.

No ordained rabbi would come to a town of so little consequence as New York. Religious development was necessarily haphazard. In the breach, the rich functioned as leaders in both religious and secular spheres, establishing a pattern of lay control that would ever afterwards characterize American Jewry. Both the synagogue and the Jewish community were under the firm hand of the *parnas*, president of the congregation, acknowledged head and "ruler" of New York's Jews, "Minister of the Jewish Nation" to the *goyim* (gentiles), empowered with his board to set schedules of services, assign seats, keep financial records, give out honors, collect fines for offenses to the righteous, engage communal employees, settle quarrels among congregants, and raise communal funds.

Far from great centers of Jewish learning, New York's Sephardim were heavily influenced by their neighbors' Protestant ethics. Communal organization, like commerce, reflected stability, good order, and reciprocal obligations that were neatly spelled out. Man was created in God's image, and every event bore the imprint of His higher design, inscrutable as that might be. One reason for the existence of the rich was to help Him keep things going.

Only a few merchants had the wealth, time, or administrative ability to serve as *parnassim*. Candidates who willfully tried to evade their responsibilities to serve as *parnassim* were fined. But aristocratic eminences such as Lewis Gomez made loyalty to Shearith Israel a family tradition. Jacob Franks, probably the leading Jewish merchant in New York at mid-century, was a *parnas* seven times between 1730 and 1764.

There were only 225 Jews among 8000 New Yorkers as late as the 1730s, but in that decade Shearith Israel offered congregants a wide variety of services, including a school in which secular as well as religious subjects were taught, a ritual bath, ritual slaughterers, and medicines, nursing care, and physicians for the sick and the dying. In 1746–47, an elderly woman was "allowed a doctor," a congregant fallen on hard times was given back all the money he had previously contributed, and other needy applicants were provided with pensions, loans, wood for their fires, and sheets. "Deeds of loving-kindness" were religious imperatives, and the Jews, who had cared for their poor through the ages, would not now send them to public almshouses.

Parnassim spent much time on charity matters, and it was their responsibility to investigate applicants and actually dole out the help. "The poor of this congregation who need Sedeca [sic]* are to be assisted with as much as the Parnas and his assistants shall think fitt," says the synagogue's 1728 constitution. Charity arrangements were kept simple. Orphans boarded with relatives, and if relatives lacked cash they received it from the congregation. The old and the sick remained in their homes, at synagogal expense if necessary. Nobody was penalized for being poor.

There were so few Jews in the New World that vagrants were not as much of a problem for Shearith Israel as for Christian denominations, but New York was frequently visited by transients requesting help to get to some other Jewish community. They came from Europe and Palestine, the West Indies and South America, and they put a heavy strain on synagogal resources because they had to be provided not only with fares but with ample stores of kosher food for long voyages.

Some transients were *shaddarim*, "messengers" from the holy cities of Palestine, Hebron, Jerusalem, Tiberias, and Safed, dispatched to collect funds for the support of scholars and the poor. For centuries, *shaddarim* had traveled to Europe to locate prospects for the best fund-raising possibilities. In New York, they appointed "treasurers" such as Hayman Levy and Daniel Gomez, who were authorized to raise funds for specific purposes in the Holy Land.

These financial responsibilities put a heavy burden on Shearith Israel's elders. *Parnassim* appealed to wealthy brethren to help get large bills paid. In 1728, when the congregation built a synagogue, Lewis Gomez wrote sister congregations in the West Indies and in Europe that "We have already purchased an appropriate site for the edifice and another for [an additional] cemetery, but for want of sufficient means the *Yehudim* [Jews] here being but few, we have not been able to carry out our intention, and until our hopes are realized we must continue for the present to congregate in a synagogue rented from a *goy* [gentile]."

* The Jews of Biblical Palestine tried to combine charity and religion, religion and social justice, and social justice and charity. Their language, Hebrew, reflects how close these concepts were in their outlook. The word *zedekah* connotes the three concepts of charity, social justice, and righteousness.

In reply, £22 came from Barbados, £7 from Jamaica, a munificent £136 from Curaçao, and 300 florins from Jews in the jungles of Surinam. In London, Abraham Moccata, "considering the few Days a man hath to live and that every man hath an obligation to assist an other and more particularly in such good works, . . ." sent £150. In September 1729, Lewis Gomez told the congregation that four foundation stones were for sale, and, as befitted a *parnas*, he bought one himself.

Yet Shearith Israel never found it easy to meet the urgent needs of its congregants. Offerings could not support all its good works, nor could donations, charity boxes affixed to the walls of the synagogue, subscription campaigns for fuel, or legacies. "The Parnas with his assistants shall tax the mens Seats in the Sinagog [sic], as they are now seated," resolved the elders in 1728, and fines were devised to punish the wicked and to increase the treasury. There were assessments for eating *traef* (ritually unclean food), for breaking the Sabbath, for not offering up blessings for the health of the *parnas*, and for not attending services. An obstreperous member could be fined "for the disturbance he raised." In the countryside, "every family or private person . . . that is in circumstances" had to contribute or forego *mitsvoth* (religious privileges). Delinquent assessment payers were "excluded of being a member of this congregation," and *parnassim* took a very dim view of affluent congregants whose gifts were minimal.

There were still those who would not step forward voluntarily. Near the end of the century, exasperated elders decided that direct taxation was the only solution. Any Jewish resident who received congregational benefits and did not "contribute twenty shillings per annum towards its support . . . if in a situation to do so" could not be buried in the cemetery.

In the end, it was the rich who carried the major burden of philanthropy just as they carried responsibility for overall operations in the Jewish community. Though big givers were rare, the few available at once established a pattern in American Jewish life. Anyone called to read a portion of Holy Scripture at a service made a donation (which could be credited against seat charges), and fund-raising committees tirelessly visited prospective givers.

Parnassim and their peers furnished the synagogue and provided it with pentateuchal scrolls. They received admiration from coreligionists, blessings at services, and listings in Shearith Israel minute books in order of the amount of their gifts. They vied with each other for synagogal honors and became upset if their respective scrolls were not taken out and used during services. It was not ordinary gifts that elevated them; annual contributions well over assessments were necessary for special honors. In 1737, Shearith Israel's elders resolved that "honors or privileges" would be restricted to those who donated more than forty shillings.

By the end of the seventeenth century, Ashkenazim* were joining Sephardim in New York. In 1730 they may well have outnumbered descendants of the founding fathers in Shearith Israel. There was little dissension between Ashkenazim and Sephardim. Immigrants arrived singly or in small groups, causing little inconvenience to established Jewish residents.

This was a sharp departure from Sephardic-Ashkenazic relationships elsewhere. In France, Germany, and England, rich Sephardic merchants and moneylenders disdained pious Ashkenazim who lived from hand-to-mouth in ghettos. Ashkenazim, in turn, resented haughty Sephardim who paid scant attention to the exactness of Judaic ritual, concentrating on trading and making money. In London, Sephardim and Ashkenazim had particularly troublesome problems with each other, complicated by the fact that many of the city's 6000 Jews in 1730 were impoverished immigrants from the continent. The Jewish poor were totally dependent on wealthy Sephardim who were just beginning to move out to estates in the London suburbs and who had enough problems of their own dealing with status, Christian friends, and Sephardic poor.

Although Jews could live in England, Judaism was not a recognized religion in the British capital. Waging a struggle to upgrade their own status, British Sephardim welcomed any opportunity to keep poor Jews, especially Yiddish-speaking Ashkenazim, off synagogal relief rolls. This was not easy in a city where poverty was widespread and lives held so cheaply that hangings were a Sunday amusement.

George II, unmoved by sufferings around him, noticed the poor as seldom as possible. A few aristocrats and clerics were deeply concerned; Bishop George Berkley wanted to build a college in the "sea girt Bermuda Islands" where the poor could be educated. Col. James Edward Oglethorpe investigated prisons with his friend John Perceval, later the

* Jews from central and eastern Europe.

Earl of Egmont, and roused the House of Commons with a report on harsh and inhuman conditions. Oglethorpe wanted to found a colony for debtors that could also serve as a buffer state between Florida, a Spanish possession, and the British colonies. He got control of various endowments including half a £20,000 government grant given to Bishop Berkley.

These did not provide enough capital, but the 1730s were great years in London for colonization investment schemes. Oglethorpe and Perceval convinced vicars, viscounts, and lords to take subscriptions. Anthony Da Costa, Francis Salvador, and Alvaro Lopez Suasso, members of the Sephardic congregation in London's Bevis Marks section, volunteered to be fund raisers. The trio was directed by the synagogue's board to intercede "with those who have permission to arrange settlement in the English colony north [sic] of Carolina. . . ." Rich Sephardim hoped large-scale emigration to distant shores could solve local problems with the Jewish poor.

The colony's trustees debated the question of Jewish settlers and in mid-January 1733 decided they would be unwelcome. "The report of our sending Jews has prevented several [businessmen] from subscribing to us," they said in a letter asking Da Costa, Salvador, and Suasso to return their commissions. The three Sephardim requested permission to delay until Oglethorpe returned from a trip to Georgia.

Oglethorpe had left Gravesend in November 1732 with over 100 British and German settlers. Four days after the new town of Savannah was laid out into streets and wards in July 1733, the colonel and his pioneers were unexpectedly joined by forty-two Jews who arrived from London on the *William and Sarah*, the largest single group of Jews to arrive in any North American port during the colonial period.

Their debarkation precipitated great confusion. Obviously they were not supposed to be in Georgia. But could they be arbitrarily sent away? Oglethorpe consulted lawyers in Charleston, South Carolina, and found that Jews could not be legally barred because they were not papists. Yet when news reached London, trustees were adamant that the Jews had to go.

More Sephardim and Ashkenazim arrived, and at the end of the year there were seventy Jewish men, women, and children in a colony that was not supposed to have any. In December, trustees again demanded Da Costa, Salvador, and Suasso return their commissions and account for funds raised, threatening to "advertise the world of the demand" if they refused. The trio acknowledged the demand, but declined to return commissions or money, offering trustees a "civil, but trifling excuse for sending some of their nation to Georgia without our knowledge." The trustees now developed a very hard outlook. Jews were ordered "removed from the Colony of Georgia." This provided a necessary incentive, and, one year after the corporation asked for the return of commissions, the three solicitors handed them over.

For trustees this was a step in the right direction, although it did not solve the problem of what to do with Jews already in Georgia. Oglethorpe began a correspondence with London in the style of Stuyvesant's exchange with the Amsterdam Chamber—with the difference that Oglethorpe, who was angry at first, wanted the Jews to stay. Why Oglethorpe changed his mind has never been fully explained; one reason offered by historians is that he was a Mason influenced by Jewish members of the order.

In July, a contagious disease broke out in Savannah. One of the Jews, a physician named Dr. Samuel Nunez, "entirely put a stop to it, so that not one died afterwards." Trustees were not placated and wrote Oglethorpe that the doctor was not to be given land. By this time Oglethorpe had assigned the standard colonist's allotment of fifty acres—five for a town plot and forty-five for a farm—to several Jewish settlers. Immigrants also opened export-import businesses in Savannah with corresponding agents in New York and London. By January 1736, the corporation owed Abraham Minis and Collman Salomons £215, and Minis was trading with Jacob Franks in New York.

The integration of Jews into the colony's business life was ruining some fine chances for conversion to Christianity, thought Reverend John Martin Bolzius, the Germans' pastor. A good many Sephardim and Ashkenazim, however, were worried that integration was having the opposite effect. There had already been name-changing—Collman Salomons became Solomon Coleman and Daniel Nunez Ribiero was sometimes known as Daniel Nunez Rivers—and Jews associated freely with John Wesley, founder of Methodism, when he visited the colony in 1735.

It was partly fear of Christian evangelists that led to the organization of a congregation, Mikve Israel (Hope of Israel), in 1735. Here, antagonisms between Sephardim and Ashkenazim were immediately renewed. Reverend Bolzius heard overwrought Ashkenazim declare that Sephardim "persecuted" Ashkenazim worse than Christians persecuted Jews. Equally bad, Sephardim insisted on running the congregation.

Factious though Jewish colonists were, Mikve Israel showed signs of life. The Jews arrived equipped only with a Torah scroll, an ark to house the scroll, and a circumcision kit. Benjamin Da Costa of London sent a Torah, a Chanukah lamp, and some prayer books to enable the colonists to remain Jewish. By 1738, a ritual bath was built for women, and Oglethorpe allotted a plot on the commons for a Jewish cemetery.

In the end there was no hope for the Hope of Israel. The Jews split into two warring factions so antagonistic that a synagogue could not be built. Perhaps even this handicap might have been overcome if there had not been a precipitous decline in the colony's fortunes. Corrupt officials, a bane in colonial life, became increasingly blatant in their thievery; laws banning slave-holding and real estate transactions put Georgia's settlers at an economic disadvantage compared to settlers elsewhere.

The Georgia colony was disintegrating in 1739 when war broke out between England and Spain. Spaniards considered all non-Catholics heretics, and both Protestants and Jews were unnerved by the prospect of capture and torture by enemy troops from Florida. Morale was not helped when Oglethorpe, outfitted with guns and equipment by Jacob Franks in New York, led an unsuccessful attack on St. Augustine. Settlers began to abandon Savannah and nearby plantations for Charleston, New York, and the Caribbean islands. In 1741, Oglethorpe wrote trustees that "all the Jews except one have left the colony," and Mikve Israel's sacred items were sent to Shearith Israel for safekeeping.

The Bevis Marks congregation still needed a place to send poor Jews, however, and during the mid-1730s and 1740s other colonies were sought. South Carolina was one possibility, but when the British Lords of Trade were asked for a tract of land they refused, saying that a Jewish settlement would involve England in problems with Spain and France. Just how a few poor Jews could involve three great nations in confrontations with each other is not quite clear. What probably motivated the lords was fear that Jews would not assimilate with Protestant settlers.

This did not stop Bevis Marks from further colonization attempts. In 1747, James Peyn, a London merchant, proposed to settle Jews and Germans on 500,000 acres along the South Carolina-Georgia border. There they could establish a naval station and produce potash, pitch, and turpentine. It later developed that the real mover behind this scheme was an entrepreneur named John Hamilton, who had many Sephardic friends and cut the request to 200,000 acres. The Lords of Trade asked how much could be put up to finance this colony and were offered £2000, with more later if necessary. This was evidently less than the board wanted, and the idea was dropped.

The following year, Bevis Marks offered grants to Jews who would go to Nova Scotia, but there were few applicants for travel to that northern place. Two years after that, an impecunious Scottish nobleman, Sir Alexander Cuming, proposed that 300,000 Jewish families be settled in the "Cherokee mountains" in the backlands of Georgia. Cuming, himself in a London debtors' prison, planned to establish a bank in Georgia, the profits from which would pay off part of the £80 million British national debt. Indians also were to be farmers and tradesmen, and ultimately Jews and Indians would convert to Christianity. Nothing came of this fantastic plan—for one thing, there were probably fewer than 300,000 Jewish families in all of Europe—and no further large-scale Jewish emigration attempts were made.

Of all the colonial towns, Newport, Rhode Island, was dominated most by the international trade Sephardim everywhere favored. New York's Jewish merchants were doing business in Rhode Island during the seventeenth century, and in 1658, fifteen Sephardic families are said to have arrived in the town.* Blocked from use of their most valuable commercial resource—contacts with coreligionists in Holland and the Dutch West Indies—the Sephardim departed.†

Sometime in the mid-1670s, another group of Jews came to Newport, but Maj. William Dyre, Roger Williams's successor, was not very tolerant of them, and looked for ways to drive them out. Jewish traders continued to drift into Newport from New York early in the eighteenth century, but the town's Jewish population hardly grew at all until the late 1740s and 1750s

* A dearth of documentary evidence leads some historians to question whether Jews were, in fact, in Newport at this time.

† The British Navigation Act of 1681 provided that no goods could be imported or exported from any English colony except on British-built or British-owned vessels; in 1663, another Navigation Act prohibited goods imported from anywhere but the British Isles.

when an economic boom was stimulated by King George's War and the French and Indian Wars. Sensing commercial opportunities, Moses Lopez and Jacob Rivera brought their families from New York; Aaron Lopez and his family came directly from Portugal.

Newport's Jewish population still did not grow by leaps and bounds, but by 1760, sixty Jews were prominent in Newport's booming commercial life. The Riveras opened the first factory in Newport to produce candles made out of spermaceti, a whale oil solid. This became one of Newport's most important industries, and in 1761, a syndicate of spermaceti chandlers (about half of them Jews) was established to fix minimum prices and thus to control the market. Jews also began to manufacture soap, became workers in brass and iron, and opened a "Scotch Snuff Manufactory."

Seventeen Jewish taxpayers paid more than 4 percent of the town's taxes. In 1759, nine of them took a step marking them as Jewish men of substance and formed a core group to raise funds for building a synagogue. Yeshuat Israel (Salvation of Israel), the local congregation, had engaged Isaac Touro as its *hazzan* (cantor) on the recommendation of Amsterdam's Portuguese congregation two years before. Four men, Naphtali Hart, Jacob Rivera, Aaron Lopez, and Moses Lopez, alternated in the post of *parnas*, but Newport's ten to fifteen Jewish families were too few to purchase land and finance construction of the grandest synagogue to be built in the colonies. In the time-honored tradition, letters appealing for funds were duly sent to London, Jamaica, Curaçao, Surinam, Barbados, and Shearith Israel. "The pious intentions of a congregation yet in its infancy . . . may plead a sufficient excuse for this address," Rivera wrote New York in 1759.

Rivera, a former Shearith Israel member, described a group of Jews "almost totally uninstructed in our most Holy and Divine Law," devoted to the assistance of the "Distressed." Despite their own wealth, Newporters frankly thought New Yorkers duty bound to help and could "entertain no doubt of your Zeal, to promote the good work." In response, Shearith Israel sent £149 and a letter acknowledging that the "pious design was a sufficient inducement to promote the success of your request." Elsewhere, the building campaign fared less well. From London, Newporters got best wishes and prayers, but no cash.

Construction of a synagogue under the supervision of Naphtali Hart had scarcely begun when the French and Indian Wars ended, bringing on a business depression. In New York, Samuel Judah contributed a perpetual lamp, Samuel Hart gave candlesticks, and Hayim Myers sent 100 pounds of wax. Yet in 1763, the building campaign had fallen on such bad days that the *parnas*, Aaron Lopez, wrote the Curaçao congregation that Newporters could barely manage to collect enough to pay the 8 percent interest on a mortgage. Things got worse; by the third annual due date, interest could not be paid. Lopez desperately wrote sister congregations that "we flatter ourselves that since the practice of *mitsvoth* is so deeply ingrained in your spirit, you will unanimously agree to come to the aid of this effort." Unfortunately, the collapse of the economy left congregations everywhere bereft of means to support themselves, let alone a new congregation in Rhode Island.

Undaunted Newporters dedicated a beautiful, debt-ridden, Georgian synagogue on the first day of Chanukah 1763, after four years of construction. Congregational leaders carried pentateuchal scrolls in a procession that dazzled Jews and Christian visitors, including a local minister named Ezra Stiles, later to become president of Yale. Festivities did nothing to reduce the debt, however, and as late as 1768, Lopez, who paid for a cornerstone, offered two guineas to help complete the building campaign.

Happily, better economic times enabled Yeshuat Israel not only to survive, but to prosper during the early 1770s, Newport's golden age. A school, an oven to bake *matzoh*, and a mortuary chapel were built, thanks to gifts from congregants now well able to support communal activities.

Aaron Lopez, whole or part owner of twenty-seven vessels carrying goods from North America to Europe, Africa, and the West Indies, became Newport's biggest taxpayer and probably the richest Jew in the colonies. Handsome, small, large-nosed, and wiry, Lopez referred to himself as a "Portuguese gentleman" and joined his cousin Jacob Rivera in the spermaceti candle business. He also shipped liquor, rice, candles, sugar, and rum to Canada; bought cocoa in Providence; sold English dry goods, apparel, and china in Boston; took on naval stores, lumber, and provisions in North Carolina; and sent livestock, poultry, and pickled oysters to the West Indies. Whale oil, furs, and fish were traded in Spain for salt, wines, and fruits. Pig iron, indigo, and potash were exchanged in Britain for Irish indentured servants, English textiles, and coal. Kosher cheese and beef went to Jews in Jamaica. In Newport, the entrepreneur built houses, rigged and overhauled vessels, operated a farm, and sold lottery tickets. Business, he declared, was the "real happiness."

Lopez was an eighteenth-century prototype of a twentieth-century wheeler-dealer and big giver who repaid creditors slowly and could not resist the sharp practices that ornamented many a colonial magnate's dealings. He smuggled tea into Rhode Island in molasses barrels to avoid tariff payments and urged employees to reduce expenses whenever possible by bribing public officials. In a particularly spectacular display of *chutzpah* (sheer gall) during the early days of the Revolution, he convinced the British to permit his whaling fleet to leave Newport because of his loyalty to the Crown and persuaded rebels to allow it to depart because of his complete devotion to the American cause.

Holding together a commercial empire took time and energy, but Lopez, who played the violin, did not neglect social pleasantries or communal responsibilities. He was a frequent guest on the *Rose*, a British naval vessel assigned to ferreting out smugglers, and he made offerings as many as ten times during a service. He purchased a candelabrum for the synagogue, contributed or gave candles at cost to the congregation, and was unfailingly generous to Palestinian visitors. A traveler from the Holy Land, Rabbi Haim Isaac Carigal, spent three months in Newport in 1773 and compared Lopez's largesse to the favors God bestowed on Jacob; Tobiah ben Yehudah Lev, a rabbi from Poland, asked blessings on the merchant for kindnesses to Torah students.

Lopez's reputation for good works made the rounds in the colonies. The merchant was beseeched for help by Christian and Jew, employee and peer. Robert Mathews, in prison for a four-dollar debt, implored Lopez to advance the sum so that he could be released. Nicholas and Joseph Brown solicited help for six-year-old Rhode Island College (later Brown University), and Lopez sent 5000 feet of lumber worth £400. Moses Calonemos got passage money for a voyage from Newport to Charleston from Lopez and Rivera, and seventy-year-old Hannah Louzada in New York wrote to say that she had heard of his *buenafama*, or good reputation, and wondered whether he couldn't help her out, too.

But Newport's golden age and Lopez's period of grandeur were all too brief. The Revolutionary War was a disaster from which neither the town nor Lopez recovered. During the British occupation, twenty-seven members of the Rivera and Lopez families fled to Providence. Lopez sent a donation to Norwalk, Connecticut, and kept in close touch with "the Callamities and Insults the wretched inhabitants of Newport were enduring."

In 1782, a year before the end of the war, Lopez started back to Newport. Near Providence he stopped to water his horse. The animal suddenly bolted forward into deep water, pulling along a sulky with Lopez in it. A servant rushed to help, but Lopez drowned before he could be reached. In Newport, Reverend Stiles, who was none too fond of Jews, wrote in his diary that Lopez's problem was that he was Jewish and had not "perceived the Truth as it is in Jesus Christ." A ray of sunshine pierced the gloom of Stiles's depression: perhaps the heavenly hosts would forgive this stubborn adherence and admit the merchant anyway.

Newport, occupied by 8000 British and Hessian forces, was almost totally destroyed. Loyalist sentiment had run strong, and Isaac Touro, cantor of the synagogue, was one Jewish Tory who steadfastly refused to join the revolutionary cause. Remaining throughout the occupation, he and his family left when the British abandoned Newport. In British-occupied New York, he officiated at Shearith Israel, emptied of Jews supporting the American cause. When continentals retook New York, Touro and his family fled to Kingston, Jamaica, where he died in 1783.

The widow Touro took her family to her wealthy brother, Moses Michael Hays, in Boston. Judah, her oldest son, became an apprentice in Hays's counting house and in 1798 was a supercargo aboard a ship bound for Mediterranean ports. The vessel was attacked by a French privateer, and Touro displayed unusual courage defending it. This brought warm thanks when he returned to Boston, but not the hand of Moses Hays's daughter Catherine. According to one story, Touro "formed a romantic attachment" for her that did not lead to nuptials because her father did not approve marriage between close relatives.

Little is known about Touro's youth; whether it was because of Moses Hays or some other reason, he left Boston in 1801 for New Orleans, a small, disease-ridden port strategically located at the mouth of the Mississippi River. There he became an agent for New England merchants. He was not the most brilliant businessman in New Orleans, and he was not fated to be the most respected Jewish businessman. He saved everything he could get his hands on and his strict economies verged on the bizarre. Touro would not give credit, opened and closed the shop himself, and rarely employed more than one clerk. When he died in 1854 his estate was valued at $928,774.

In his personal life as in his business life, Touro was a solitary, close-mouthed introvert who never married and lived a frugal existence in cheap rooming houses. The one deep attachment of his life was to Rezin Shepherd, a fellow merchant who saved his life during the War of 1812. On a dangerous mission for American forces during the Battle of New Orleans, Touro was hit by a twelve-pound shot, and he was left for dead on the battlefield. Rezin Shepherd refused to abandon him and carried Touro back to New Orleans. Shepherd was made Touro's principal legatee.

After the war, Touro had little interest in Jewish matters, refusing fund-raising appeals from congregations in New York, Cincinnati, and Savannah. Nor was he particularly charitable to nonsectarian causes, ignoring victims of cholera epidemics, revolutions, and fires. The *hazzan's* son leaned to Christian churches favored by Rezin Shepherd. Touro purchased a pew in Episcopal Christ Church, where Shepherd was a warden, paid $20,000 to buy the First Presbyterian Church when its Session was unable to meet mortgage payments, and for twenty-eight years did not charge the congregation rent. Similarly generous to Catholics, Touro bought 10 percent of the bonds sold to construct St. Louis Cathedral in 1851.

If his life had ended at this point, Judah Touro's break with Judaism would have been complete. When New Orleans's first Hebrew congregation was organized between 1827 and 1828, he did not become a member. Another Hebrew congregation, Nefutzoh Yehudah (Dispersed of Judah) was later founded. The choice of name possibly alluded to the fate of Newport's scattered Jews. At first, Touro did not join this congregation either, but he was persuaded—possibly by Shepherd—to trade some land for the Christ Church building and to remodel the Christ Church building into a synagogue.

The opening of Nefutzoh Yehudah marked a sudden turning point in Touro's life. He began attending services, paid for a schoolhouse next to the synagogue, and helped choose a rabbi. He offered an annual prize for the student at the University of Louisiana who excelled in Hebrew, and in his will he provided more largesse to more Jewish institutions than any previous American Jew: Nefutzoh Yehudah got $48,000; $40,000 went to build a Jewish hospital in New Orleans; and the Jews of Palestine got $60,000 for almshouses. Hospitals, religious schools, and benevolent societies in seventeen American cities from Boston to St. Louis shared $143,000.

These institutions were chosen scant weeks before his death in 1854. To the end, the philanthropist was ambivalent about bequests for Jewish organizations. "I am thankful to God that . . . I got the most of what I wanted for Israel," wrote one of Touro's friends. "Arguments, changes and counter-changes in the sums for Institutions, till my heart sickened. I appeared calm, but indeed was almost crazy, ever dreading that nothing would be achieved in the end. The list of Jewish institutions I made up as well as I could."

Perhaps it was the introduction of a new form of Judaism to New Orleans that inspired the change; the 1840s and 1850s saw the arrival of Reformist German Jews. At Nefutzoh Yehudah, Touro could acknowledge Jewishness and simultaneously justify a lifelong dislike for Orthodox ritual. Or perhaps it was pathological self-hatred and fear of anti-Semitism engendered by Isaac Touro's Toryism that motivated the son's lifelong ambivalence. We shall never know the motivation, because he ordered all his private papers, files, and accounts destroyed after his death.

The supreme irony of Judah Touro's life was that his will made him the first American Jewish philanthropic folk hero. Some ingrates complained because the bulk of his estate went to Shepherd, but coreligionists were as pleased as non-Jews by the munificent bequests. Touro was an example of the new breed, a self-made man who did not turn his back on Jewry. To Jews in Europe, this was a sharp contrast to the emerging portrait of American Jews as rough and crass. Here was proof positive that it was possible to be both Jewish and American, a full-fledged member of a democratic order. Assimilation along American lines had something to recommend it. Judah Touro proved that.

2
Yahudim

ON THE EVE of the American Revolution, there were 2500 Jews in North America. Possibly 50,000 lived in France, where philosophes provided rationales for the ascendancy of the insurgent middle class, arguing that not only could man master his environment, he could achieve perfection in economics, science, the arts, and government.

Few philosophes were Jewish, although Jews would one day be among leading exponents of the new beliefs. Jewish intellectuals studied Torah and Talmud, wrote commentaries on the wisdom of ancient rabbinical authorities, and taught new generations of Talmudic scholars. A tiny minority were bankers and moneylenders. The overwhelming majority, barred from almost all handicrafts, professions, and farming, practiced "traditional" Jewish occupations: trading, selling old clothes, and peddling.

For most of seven centuries, ever since the ghetto era began in the German town of Speyer during the eleventh century, it had been this way in Europe. Mutual help was essential to survival, and over the centuries the Jews of Europe not only prayed together and developed close-knit family ties, but contributed to communal societies known as *hevrath* to help coreligionists.

Communal organization flowered as Jews were forcibly isolated. By the mid-eighteenth century, when one of every three Jews was impoverished, welfare practices had long been institutionalized and societies were financed through taxes, fines, honors auctioned off in synagogues, special assessments, and contributions.

France was a microcosm of Europe in transition and a focal point for Jewish life during the second half of the eighteenth century. It had two distinct Jewish communities, one Sephardi in Paris and Southeastern France, the other Ashkenazi in Alsace. Great Sephardim were not only traders but had close connections with aristocrats. Ashkenazim and Sephardim viewed each other with mutual distaste, and both were heavily taxed by royal governments in Paris, which levied lump-sum assessments on Jewish communal councils.

While the status quo was maintained in ghettos, the gentile avant-garde busily prepared the way for revolution and incidentally for Jewish emancipation. "In short, we find in [the Jews] only an ignorant and barbarous people, who have long united the most sordid avarice with the most detestable superstition and the most invincible hatred for every people by whom they are tolerated and enriched," wrote Voltaire in the *Dictionnaire philosophique*. Alsatian deputies meeting in Paris to help draft the "Declaration of the Rights of Man" voted unanimously to oppose Jewish emancipation. Yet the contradictions of a revolution against privilege and status that declared all men except one group born free and equal were distasteful to men who prided themselves on their rationality. Jews were emancipated because nobody could think of any real alternatives.

News of the emancipation decree traveled like wildfire and inspired enthusiasm among the newly freed. But in Alsace, Christians, unable to pay debts to Jewish moneylenders, continued to ask the government to solve their problems by exiling the Jews, just as they had asked royal governments to do in the past. In 1806, Napoleon got a similar request. Instead of exiling Jews, he called for an "Assembly of Jewish Notables," who cheered the Emperor, pledged support, and told him what he wanted to hear, that the secular "prince" was the ultimate authority in political and civil matters.

Pleased by the results, Napoleon convoked a "Great Sanhedrin," another assembly of seventy-one notables modeled after the Jewish ruling senates of ancient times. Its purpose was to ratify decisions at the earlier meeting and to convert them to doctrinal laws binding on "all" Jews. The Sanhedrin declared the religious laws of Israel "absolute and independent of circumstance and time"; Judaism's political precepts were declared invalid because there was no Jewish nation.

The Jews were deliriously happy. Their isolation was officially ended. No longer were they a humiliated nation within a nation. The impact of the Sanhedrin and its decrees was felt throughout the world. In Russia, the czarist government feared that its Jews might rally to Napoleon's cause and halted forced evacuation of Jewish villages.

By far, the largest concentration of Jews in western Europe was found in the German states and Austria-Hungary. Authorities divided Jews into three categories: common, foreign, and court. Simply put, distinctions were between a few individuals who could supply kings and nobles with that indispensable ingredient of the good life, money, and a vast majority of poor Jews living in the countryside and ghettos.

Thanks to several expensive wars, Prussian kings were among the most persuasive German rulers to encourage "court" Jews to settle in their territories. Prejudices were cast aside in favor of commercial development. Napoleon's troops entered Berlin in 1806 to find that there was no ghetto. Moreover, the rise of a Jewish bourgeoisie had led to the rise of Jewish intelligentsia. This, in turn, led to close social contacts between youthful Christians and youthful Jews, who shaved their beards, wore periwigs, and paid less and less attention to the exhortations of rabbis.

Despite newly found fellowship, even converted Jews were not fully accepted into Christian society. And, although individual Jews might be free, there was no great enthusiasm to emancipate the "Jewish nation." Traces of pre-Napoleonic anti-Semitism lingered. The French occupation, liberal ideas, and Jews were linked together in the minds of Germans. Money could not erase suspicions. The word *judenschmerz* was coined to denote the intense mental anguish suffered by one born Jewish and subsequently denied complete social acceptance.

The era of good feelings came to a sudden and dramatic end with Napoleon's downfall in 1814 and a nationalistic reaction to the French. "The rights already conceded [Jews] in the several federated states [of Germany] will be continued," said one resolution at the congress, but Jews were again barred from trades and professions. Having taken emancipation seriously, they were staggered. The great surge of progress that began in 1789 slowed to a crawl and even went into reverse in several places. Messianic expectations were brought to earth. Hundreds emigrated to America in flight from a new and even more vicious anti-Semitism.

In 1848, massive revolutions again swept Europe. In Bavaria, anti-Semites outdid each other assaulting Jews; local legislators cried, "Banish the Jews to America!"

Now thousands of Jews were unwilling to remain in central Europe. Leopold Kompert, a Bohemian novelist, characterized anti-Semites as "servile hordes and sordid-minded people," and decried traditionally passive patterns of Jewish behavior, as well as reliance on deliverance by Christians. Kompert exhorted Jews: "Let us go to America! The Jews do possess the qualities and virtues so indispensable for reconstruction [sic] in that country; foresight, sobriety, economy, discipline and loyalty."

Provisional Jewish emigration committees sprang up in Vienna, Budapest, Prague, and Lwow; meanwhile, German and Austrian authorities discovered that good taxpayers were departing and devised new levies to meet the emergency. No matter, wealthy Jews were expected to contribute more for fares than the poor, and everyone could make payments in kind—silk or wool, for example, in lieu of money.

Nor was political freedom the only motivation for the exodus. By 1848, after sixty years of on and off emancipation, probably 70 percent of Europe's Jews were still overwhelmingly poor. Economic opportunities in the New World were limitless: during the 1840s, 17 million Americans had more merchant ships and more railroad mileage than Great Britain, the richest country in the world. No task, material or spiritual, appeared too great for the men and women of the New World.

"Jewry has quickly taken root in the new country," said Dr. Max Lilienthal, a recent immigrant writing home to the *Allgemeine Zeitung des Judentums* in 1847. "There are many Jewish handicraftsmen in all areas; the inclination for farming has been awakened especially in Wisconsin. [Yet] during the last summer people arrived who had neither the inclination nor the ability to work. The congregations have sent them back at their expense with voluntary contributions. Jewish men who have families, a job or a position in Germany may stay there. America needs men with industry, courage, and patience."

How could immigrants who spoke no English and lacked skills find work? For tens of thousands, the solution was peddling. A five-dollar investment bought a newcomer straw hats, shawls, leather goods, thimbles, pocket knives, playing cards, and silk ribbons. He then started walking toward the frontier, seeking customers for his wares.

As railroads pushed west to the Pacific, peddlers established trading posts throughout the Rockies and the Southwest. Some became nattily-dressed traveling salesmen representing wholesalers; others became merchants and opened general stores in towns and cities. A typical sequence in the peddler rags-to-riches story was to walk door-to-door, then to acquire a horse and buggy, and finally to open a general store where goods were sold to other peddlers and to settlers. As proprietor, the former peddler served as his own clerk, looked to a small margin and a rapid turnover for profits, and was careful to give his customers value. An astounded Dr. Lilienthal wrote home to Germany that New York had Jewish retail merchants whose businesses amounted to $100,000 or $200,000. "And these people, upon their arrival six years ago, had not a penny in their pockets."

There was Adam Gimbel, who arrived in New Orleans in 1835 and opened a store in Vincennes, Indiana, where he sold a variety of goods and refunded the purchase price of any item with which a customer was dissatisfied. His seven sons were trained to carry on the business. In 1887, they extended it to Milwaukee; in 1894, to Philadelphia; and in 1919, to New York.

Joseph Seligman quit Bavaria for Pennsylvania in 1837. He then sent for his seven brothers, for whom he had an almost paternal devotion. The brothers pooled their money and began peddling in the South, where Joseph opened a small dry-goods store. In 1857, the brothers were reunited in a New York clothing and importing firm, and in 1862, they branched out into banking. During the Civil War, the Seligmans supplied uniforms to Union armies and sold $200,000,000 in Union bonds on the Frankfurt exchange.

Abraham Kuhn began as a peddler, became a storekeeper, and then opened a factory making men's and boys' pants in Cincinnati. He hired Solomon Loeb, a highly emotional immigrant from Worms to help at the factory and to open a New York outlet. After several years commuting between the two cities, Loeb married Kuhn's sister. An accommodating sort, Kuhn married Loeb's sister, the firm was renamed Kuhn, Loeb & Co., and both men and their families moved to New York where they opened banking offices.

An immigrant prospector named Levi Strauss went to California with a roll of tent canvas from his brother's New York store. "Pants don't hold up worth a hoot in the diggings," complained a disconsolate forty-niner. Strauss began manufacturing canvas pants, the pockets of which were reinforced with copper rivets. Under the trademark "Levi's," they became a staple of Western clothing.

And then there were the Guggenheims, Swiss Jews who left Europe in 1848. Simon peddled on city streets while Meyer, his dark-haired, good-looking son, peddled in the anthracite regions of Pennsylvania. On Sundays, the two men separated for the week's work; on Friday evenings, they met for the Sabbath meal. Within four years after his arrival in the United States, Meyer Guggenheim was well established in business. Before he died, eight Guggenheims—Meyer and his seven ambitious sons—would comprise the richest Jewish family in the United States, spending Friday nights listening to Meyer's thoughts on business strategy rather than on religion.

The success of the Gimbels, the Seligmans, the Guggenheims, Strauss, and Kuhn and Loeb testifies not only to the rewards of hard work, clean living, perseverance, and inner fortitude, but to the unquestioned adherence of Yahudim to American mores. Tight-lipped and thrifty, Yahudim were staunch believers in free enterprise and Jewish dispersal throughout the nation. Some 3000 Jewish soldiers served in the Confederate Army, 7000 served in the Union Army, seven won Medals of Honor, and one became the Confederate secretary of state.

An enterprising group destined for great things, Yahudim felt a lack in the ancient laws, commentaries, rituals, traditions, and beliefs that make up Orthodox Judaism. In a burst of energy beginning in the 1840s, they came forth with an American version of Reform Judaism, a religion that would dominate American Jewry until the turn of the century, a religion filled with the optimism of the open frontier and liberal social and political ideas.

Isaac Mayer Wise, the fourth ordained rabbi to arrive in the United

States, was the Moses of the new Judaism. In 1854, he went to Cincinnati, a stronghold of Reform with the second largest number of Jews in any city in America. There he served the largest Jewish congregation in the country, built a seminary (Hebrew Union College), organized rabbis (the Central Conference of American Rabbis), organized congregations (the Union of American Hebrew Congregations), and wrote a prayer book, the *Minhag America.*

Thanks to Wise's organizational genius and prodigious energy, the number of Reform congregations kept pace with the influx of Yahudim, leaping from four or five in 1849 to 128 by 1883. Reform's most important stronghold was not in Cincinnati, however, but in New York's Temple Emanu-El, destined to be the wealthiest, most powerful, most influential, and most fashionable Jewish congregation in the country. Its members included several merchants and bankers who had moved to New York from the interior, some after humble beginnings as peddlers. Among them were Adam Gimbel, Joseph and Jesse Seligman, and those leaders of Jewish society, the Guggenheims.

It was these men and their families who referred to themselves as "Our Crowd"—aloof, secretive, clannish, and deeply imbued with Wise's "American outlook." They stood at the very peak of Jewish wealth in America, linked through marriage to rich Yahudim in other cities. Their power stemmed from a tightly-knit social network created from mutual religious, business, and philanthropic interests.

But great Yahudim were often deeply troubled by uncertainties. Social mobility was what America was about, and Jewish immigrants perhaps more than any others were eager and willing to pay any price for acceptance. Yet during the Civil War there were frightening eruptions of anti-Semitism when the *Boston Transcript* and *Harper's Weekly* singled out Jews as traitors, shylocks, and secessionists, and New York's *Commercial Advertiser* singled out Jewish officers in the Union Army as dishonest. In 1862, General Ulysses S. Grant issued his notorious Order No. 11, expelling Jews from Mississippi, Kentucky, and Tennessee, which was withdrawn only at Lincoln's insistence.

After the conflict, property values fell on fashionable Boston streets when German Jews bought homes there. In 1877, no less a personage than Joseph Seligman was refused his customary accommodations at a

Saratoga Springs resort. Were rich, assimilated, Republican, Reform Jews *really* Americans?

Sephardim of the 1830s, elegant, aristocratic, and well on their way to full assimilation through intermarriage, found Yahudi newcomers aggressive, ill-mannered, and crude. The poverty-stricken wretches had all the wrong characteristics, which called attention to "Jewish" features better left unnoticed by Christians: large noses, outlandish clothing, and conversations in Yiddish, an "abominable garble of German and Hebrew." To differentiate themselves from a Central European rabble that needed to bathe, Sephardim called themselves "Hebrews"; the Germans were "Jews."

On their part, Yahudim resented Sephardic attitudes of superiority and missed the kinship and Jewish communal solidarity they knew in Europe. Aloof Sephardic synagogue officials provided little in the way of companionship. Lonely Yahudim found that fraternal orders offered a respite from daily toil and a welcome substitute for the shared intimacies of family gatherings. They practiced secret rites with Masons and Odd Fellows and spoke in German at *Pioneerverein* meetings. Yet there were gnawing thoughts that they would be happier in Jewish fraternal organizations, and gnawing fears that even Americans and liberal German-Americans would attempt to convert them.

So great was the need for companionship, mutual benefit, and an end to Sephardic dominance, that a Jewish fraternal order, B'nai B'rith (Sons of the Covenant), was organized. Twelve Yahudi founders met in a Manhattan restaurant in 1843 to dedicate themselves "to uniting Israelites in the work of promoting their highest interests and those of humanity. . . ." The purest principles of philanthropy, honor, and patriotism were also to be inculcated.

By the end of the Civil War, B'nai B'rith had 5831 members in sixty-six lodges from coast to coast and $267,341 in its treasury. Strict neutrality were the watchwords in theology; and, by 1868, the organization was concentrating on philanthropy. After the 1880s, few causes would be immune from its interests. Jewish farmers in the Dakotas received gifts and Johnstown flood victims heard from lodges throughout the country. Orphanages became lodge projects, a school for technical instruction was begun in San Francisco, a Junior B'nai B'rith Lodge was founded in Vicksburg, members were assessed ten cents a year to build a hospital in Hot Springs, and in 1899, the Jewish National Hospital was opened in Denver. B'nai B'rith organized new lodges in Germany, Bulgaria, and Egypt, established cooperative relations with foreign Jewish agencies, and during the 1890s, founded a colony of Jewish settlers in Palestine.

Americanized and assimilationist in outlook, B'nai B'rith members looked to Jewish good citizenship and passivity to promote religious tolerance at home. Members were confident that influence in the "right quarters" would stifle anti-Semitism. Yet a seminal discovery of the 1850s was that the only cause that could really unite Jews was fear of anti-Semitic eruptions. These seemed to occur more and more frequently in the Near East and Europe. In 1840, a medieval belief that Jews kill Christians to use their blood for ritualistic purposes was revived in Damascus. Eight years later, a Russian *ukase* forced Jews to move to the interior of that country. The rising tide of anti-Semitism climaxed in 1858 when a Jewish child named Edgardo Mortara was secretly baptized by his Catholic nurse in Bologna and spirited to Rome by papal police. In New York, two thousand Jews and Christians asked President Buchanan to protest to the Pope.

Nothing much came of the protest. Mortara received a Catholic education, was ordained a priest by special dispensation, and eventually visited England and America. His mission was to convert Jews. But the Damascus Affair and the Mortara Case shook Jews in western Europe and America into an awareness of the trials of coreligionists in less enlightened places. In France the Alliance Israélite Universelle was established, and in London the Board of Deputies of British Jews (founded in 1790) was put on a permanent basis to aid Jews in "backward" countries.

Reflecting on the Mortara Case, Rabbi Samuel Isaac of New York thought Washington should have been prodded by a united American Jewry. His Orthodox congregation sponsored a national meeting at which representatives from twenty-four congregations, thirteen of them outside New York, met at the Cooper Institute and subsequently formed the Board of Delegates of American Israelites, the first organization of American Jews dealing with problems of overseas Jewry.

At once, suspicious Reformers saw the board as a subtle maneuver by traditionalists to retake control of American Jewry. New York's Temple

Emanu-El declared it a "mistake for Jews to act together for social and political purposes for thus they [will] become an *imperium in imperio* in America, and others [will] believe that the Jews [feel] they [are] in exile." It also insisted that "congregations themselves could dispense charity without the help of the Board."

In a frank bid for friends in all camps, the board announced that its role would be mainly to keep a watchful eye on events at home and abroad. Yet letters poured in citing domestic and foreign problems with which it tried to cope. During the Civil War, the board helped convince Congress to authorize Jewish chaplains in the armed forces and opposed efforts to make Christianity the official religion of the United States. It was especially alert to persecutions of Jews and, in 1866, persuaded Washington to intervene with the Swiss government in an effort to secure equal rights for Swiss Jews. It could not convince Washington to act on behalf of Russian Jews, but it raised $20,000 for the relief of Moroccan Jewish refugees, one third of the total amount raised throughout the world; it also helped raise $15,000 for the victims of a cholera epidemic in Palestine. Before it merged with the Union of American Hebrew Congregations in 1878 and passed out of existence, the board also contributed lesser amounts to refugees in Tunis, Galicia, and East Prussia.

So determined were prosperous Yahudim to keep up the good work of assimilation that, by the mid-1860s, 150,000 American Jews could read five monthly American Jewish magazines and think about joining five national American Jewish organizations and an unofficial B'nai B'rith ladies' auxiliary. "Our people (as everywhere in this great Republic) have thrived beyond measure," Benjamin Franklin Peixotto, president of the Supreme Lodge of the Order of B'nai B'rith, reported enthusiastically after an official visit to Milwaukee. "On every side, witnesses of their wealth and prosperity appear."

In Cincinnati and Boston, there were periods when no Jews needed to receive relief from coreligionists. But in New York, where one third of the nation's Jews lived, poverty and despair were widespread. In 1837, the first major national depression wreaked havoc among newcomers who had quit central Europe hurriedly, without friends or family in the New World. Three New York congregations and four philanthropic societies provided assistance. Nine years later the Jewish population of New York reached 60,000; twenty-seven congregations and ten independent associations clothed, fed, and sheltered the Jewish poor.

The fact that benevolent societies were now helping the poor illustrates a basic change wrought by Yahudim during the 1840s and 1850s. Synagogues were unable to respond effectively to newcomers because of conflicts between traditionalists and Reformers and because they did not have adequate financial resources. This precluded them from remaining the dominant force in Jewish life. The subsequent rise of secular societies would be the hinge on which American Jewish philanthropy turned, and it followed the lead of emancipated western European outlooks.

This coincided with two other important sociological changes, one outside, the other within the Jewish community. During the first third of the century there was a trend toward social stratification along class-ethnic lines. Protestant charitable agencies were bellwethers of status, organized on a national basis, offering contributors the ultimate in social recognition. Prior to the 1830s, Jewish *nouveaux riches* with requisite credentials were welcomed as contributors and participants; afterwards, their entry was blocked.

Furthermore, traditionalist Yahudim could not take positions in Shearith Israel commensurate with their new wealth and authority. A hierarchy of Sephardim and "English" Jews attempted to make congregational membership (as opposed to attendance at services) a privilege dependent on approval by trustees, thereby deflecting Yahudi thrusts for power. Denied congregational leadership, required to bid for seats against the establishment, and unhappy over the system of offerings, angry Yahudim departed to form a new congregation, taking the Hebrew Benevolent Society along with them.

Meanwhile, epidemics ravaged New York; immigrants worn out after years of back-breaking toil went to city almshouses to die. In 1849, the worst cholera outbreak in New York's history was recorded, while starving people ate garbage on the Lower East Side. By August, 5000 people were dead and public schools were used as hospitals. Adding to Jewish woes, Christian clergymen were unusually aggressive in seeking last-minute conversions.

A Jewish hospital was deemed a necessity, not least because it would eliminate the only charity of consequence provided by non-Jews for Jews.

President Mordecai Manuel Noah of the Hebrew Benevolent Society, a playwright, businessman, and politician, called for meetings in 1851 with the Assistance and Education Society, the German Hebrew Benevolent Society, and the Young Men's Hebrew Benevolent Association. His hope was to raise $25,000 for an "Asylum for the Aged and Sick of the Hebrew Persuasion" and then apply to the state legislature for grants and land. Founding societies would contribute sums ranging from $500 to $1000 a year.

Unfortunately, interorganizational disputes prevented further progress. The following year, Sampson Simson, a long-haired, seventy-two-year-old bachelor, announced a plan to establish "Jews' Hospital," ignoring a request for information from the Hebrew Benevolent Society. Simson, the first Jewish graduate of Columbia College, planned a hospital financed without synagogal help or Yahudi representation, reflecting the new outlook in charity and the old outlook in power structures. For five dollars a year, members would join an association; in addition, a young men's group pledged to raise $1000. Simson would donate land.

The early 1850s were not propitious times to raise money. Besides epidemics, unemployment had come to New York, and in 1854, there were riots after a crop failure and wild speculation sent prices soaring. Nearly 200,000 men, women, and children were in dire need, and at mass meetings radicals called for the seizure of private property. Despite harrowing business and social conditions, Simson forged ahead. Congregations abroad were solicited for gifts; a circular was sent to local prospects.

Directors themselves contributed promptly, and on Thanksgiving Day, 1853, ground was formally broken in the city's outskirts on Twenty-eighth Street. Two months later a "very large and respectable company, composed of Israelites and our fellow citizens of other Denominations," met Simson, heard speeches, and danced the quadrille, polka, schottische, and waltz at a fund-raising dinner. Soon after, news arrived that Judah Touro had willed the hospital $20,000, and two additional lots were purchased for expansion.

Jews' Hospital was dedicated in May 1855 and opened to twenty-eight Jewish patients. The hospital became nonsectarian in 1865 and also treated outpatients, "if the sick are able to come and present themselves once or twice weekly." By 1857, one resident physician, one salaried surgeon, and nine nonmedical staff members shared $1684 in salaries. Total operating expenses were $9700, up from $5473 in 1855–56.

Keeping pace with growing financial needs taxed the resources of founders. "Funds being exhausted" in October 1858, the rich were summoned to yet another banquet so that the hospital's "mission of charity and benevolence [might] be continued." The event overshadowed other social events (including the Hebrew Benevolent Society's) and raised $13,000, the largest sum yet raised at a function in the city. Nonetheless, a basic problem was seen to be exclusion of Yahudim—potentially the biggest givers of all—from membership in the elite group. There were no German Jews on the board of Jews' Hospital.

In the end, the press of finances forced reconsideration by hard-pressed Sephardi trustees. A change in establishment views was encouraged by N. K. Rosenfeld's gift of $1000, the largest single contribution to Jews' Hospital or to any other Jewish institution in New York in 1858. The rise of German Jews to leadership positions in the nation's largest Jewish community was symbolized at the Jews' Hospital dinner in 1859, when the president of the German Hebrew Benevolent Society sat at the head table with the Hebrew Benevolent Society's president and Shearith Israel's *parnas*. Acceptance was complete when Joseph Seligman became the first "German" member of the board.

Jewish philanthropic unity made a great impression on Christians, but big givers resented editorials in Anglo-Jewish papers, particularly the *Occident* and the *Asmonean,* calling on Jews' Hospital to remove wall tablets inscribed with names of philanthropists. The hospital board "paid no attention . . . [continuing] publicly to exhibit the names of benefactors," setting precedent for other Jewish institutions to display similar honorific plaques.

By the late 1860s, Jews' Hospital, now Mount Sinai Hospital, needed to expand, and a building with twice the bed capacity was planned further uptown between Sixty-sixth and Sixty-seventh streets. Benjamin Nathan, president of the Mount Sinai board and a Shearith Israel member, spoke at cornerstone ceremonies in 1870, and Joseph Fatman, a Yahudi businessman, contributed $10,000, matching the largest gift to the hospital from a Shearith Israel member. Seven years later, Temple

Emanu-El's Hyman Blum became president, and the ascendancy of Yahudim was complete.

The new building, made of the "best Philadelphia brick," was spacious and modern, but could not accommodate sufferers from chronic diseases, such as tuberculosis, a scourge steadily worsening in a city with no overall supervision of water supply or sanitation until 1867. They were to be treated in a second great institution founded by New York's Yahudim, Montefiore Home for Chronic Invalids, destined to be the largest Jewish hospital in the world in 1912 and named for a leading British Jew of the period.

Montefiore's first home in 1884 was a tiny, box-like house rented for thirty dollars a month. Like Mount Sinai's, Montefiore's patients were initially Jewish. And like Mount Sinai, it, too, quickly became non-sectarian. Four years after it was opened, 1700 people of all faiths gathered at dedication ceremonies for a larger Montefiore further uptown. Mayor Abram Hewitt said that "if the Hebrews [are] unjustly sneered at in some quarters for their talent in money-getting they might claim the reputation of knowing how to spend wealth when they acquired it." Located in the green and houseless outskirts of the city, the new hospital could care for 140 patients in three four-story buildings, and in 1894, bed capacity was increased to 270. The following year, Jacob Schiff, Montefiore's second president, observed "there [is] too much pulmonary trouble [here] under one roof" and contributed $25,000 toward a Montefiore country sanatorium for which Lyman Bloomingdale, the merchant, had previously pledged $25,000.

A 136-acre farm was purchased in Bedford Hills, forty miles from New York City, and in 1900, Schiff, Bloomingdale, and a large crowd heard Col. Theodore Roosevelt, the next president of the United States, declare, "I have come to express to you the debt of obligation that the people of the United States are under to you, not only for the deed itself but for the example of the deed. There is an appropriate lesson to be learned in the citizenship which limits only the source from which it draws and leaves unlimited that to which it gives."

Such praise was manna to Yahudim. What better proof that Jews, being good citizens, were no longer the downtrodden of society, the castoffs of civilization? In America, Jewish bankers were not "court" Jews to be used and then discarded. In America, they were equal members of a great society.

Affluent and influential, great Yahudim were acclaimed for supporting Jewish poor with Jewish funds and were integrated in the lives of their communities, winning acclaim from Christians for sensible, charitable, assimilated ways. Jewish hospitals served people of all faiths in Cincinnati, Philadelphia, and Chicago, as well as in New York.

Yahudim tried hard to prove that they were like other respectable Americans, but many *goyim* could not get that through their heads, and they banned intermarriage as determinedly as did Orthodox Jews. During the 1840s, New York's Knickerbocker gentry was also frightened off by the first Yahudi immigrant to scale the heights of society life. A dapper, short, thickset dynamo, greedy in business and disinterested in religion, a connoisseur of *objets d'art*, horses and dogs, a voluptuary who could no more be ignored than a loud brass band, August Belmont came to Wall Street via Germany and Cuba in 1837. He opened the banking firm of August Belmont & Company with Rothschild backing. He joined the exclusive Grace Church congregation and soon caused a lot of talk by alternately making money and making merry, both on a grand scale.

Gotham's elders were pained that a Jewish upstart could so quickly push himself to the pinnacle of social and financial power. Belmont couldn't even do business like a respectable banker. He ignored old pre-Revolutionary War families and dealt with similarly gregarious *nouveaux riches*. Obviously, this rascal had to be ostracized. But could a wealthy, sophisticated, aggressive, brilliant loudmouth be ignored?

More arrivistes like Belmont would have caused both Yahudim and gentry to suffer collective cardiac arrest. Fortunately, American *shtadlanim*, representatives with substance and propriety, "court" Jews with democratic outlooks, stepped forward. These *shtadlanim* had made their way up the ladder of success inspired not solely by gross ambition, but by solid middle-class ideals. They stood foursquare for sobriety, thrift, charity, industriousness, and monogamy. Their probity and conservatism were every bit as spotless as any upper-class WASP's.

No American Jew came closer to the ideal *shtadlan* than Jacob Henry Schiff, Solomon Loeb's short, round-shouldered, neat, bearded, aristocratic, aloof, utterly determined, and austere son-in-law, the possessor of an authentic killer instinct in the world of high finance. During a period in which the stock market went on one wild spree after another, Schiff made millions for Kuhn, Loeb by financing major railroads and a Pennsylvania Railroad tunnel under mid-Manhattan. In 1897, he backed Edward Harriman in complicated but successful maneuvers to take control of the Union Pacific Railroad and, through it, the Southern Pacific Railroad. In 1901, Schiff and Harriman seized control of the Great Northern Pacific from James J. Hill, precipitating a stock market panic. Schiff escaped unmarked from a subsequent federal investigation, but his Northern Securities Company was dissolved under anti-trust laws.

The *shtadlan* was also a director of the Equitable Life Assurance Society of the United States, a firm investigated by a state commission after it was revealed that Kuhn, Loeb sold it more than $49 million in stocks. New York State insurance laws prohibited such transactions. Schiff came through committee hearings "unscathed in reputation," which was more than could be said for other directors. From both railroads and insurance he emerged with a fortune and prestige that set him apart in the business community; after J. P. Morgan & Co., Kuhn, Loeb was the most important private investment banking house in the country.

Born in Frankfurt, Schiff had come to New York in 1865 as a bank clerk. Two years later he went into partnership with two other young men in the brokerage business, but returned to Europe, first going to London and then Frankfurt, where he met Abraham Kuhn in 1874. Kuhn invited him to join Kuhn, Loeb. Schiff was an energetic, brilliant, prompt, aggressive, and loyal employee, always at his desk working and thinking about stocks and bonds. That, but mostly his marriage to Therese Loeb, Solomon's daughter, made him head of the firm when Loeb retired in 1885.

Second only to riches in Schiff's *shtadlanimdom* was his stature as a patriarchal figure in the Jewish community. "Nothing Jewish [is] alien to his heart," Yahudim proudly told each other as they read news of his benefactions, and none dared commence major communal activities without first consulting him. Schiff would not travel on the Sabbath, said prayers every morning, and kissed portraits of his father and mother. Yet he did not practice the Orthodox Judaism of his fathers. "He was attracted to [Reform Judaism] . . . by a number of circumstances," wrote his biographer, Cyrus Adler. "But the one he mentioned most frequently was that it satisfied the religious cravings of those who could no longer adhere to the ancient rabbinical religion *and thus averted 'conversion' to Christianity.*" [Italics added.]

Adler, a dutiful scholar paid to write the biography, either did not realize the implications of the observation or did not dare offer further comment. But Schiff's habits, carefully described by Adler and other admirers, reflect a tight control always necessary lest dimly perceived wishes break loose. He was a tyrant so devoted to religion, to liberalism, and to his family that he lectured his father-in-law about Judaism and intercepted and answered letters written to his daughter Frieda by her future husband, Felix Warburg. He argued against income and inheritance taxes, but contributed generously to dozens of causes and wrote that the "surplus wealth we have gained, to some extent, at least, belongs to our fellow beings; we are only the temporary custodians of our fortunes. . . ."

Schiff was firmly committed to the tenet that all Jews must tithe 10 percent of their income to charity; gifts above this figure he considered philanthropy. His own interests were broad, ranging from hospitals to agencies and institutions, including Columbia, Harvard, the Salvation Army, and the International Congress of Gregorian Chant, which sent him a letter by accident but received a contribution anyway. Schiff was one giver who needed little recognition for altruism, and the size of most Schiff contributions would be closely-guarded secrets. Like Andrew Carnegie, the biggest big giver of the time, he believed in making gifts during his lifetime when he could keep a close check on developments, rather than allowing posterity to manage his money.

Schiff's philanthropies began in 1878 with contributions for the relief of Jews in the Ottoman Empire. He was almost immediately available for synagogue construction gifts in smaller communities. His involvement with Montefiore, which dated from its founding, was his longest affiliation. Montefiore was the only cause for which he would ordinarily solicit contributions; he personally acknowledged gifts from his desk at Kuhn, Loeb. Initial financing to begin the hospital came largely from two sources: a bazaar for which Schiff was chairman and his own checkbook. Schiff arranged excursions for patients, listened to complaints from employees, and paid for their vacations. He went through wards on Sundays, greeting each patient by name. Schiff could not understand a lesser devotion to the chronically ill than his own and berated board members after he and two other directors were the sole attendees at a meeting that took place during a snowstorm.

Slender, bearded, gentle Oscar Solomon Straus was the second in a trio of *shtadlanim* that dominated American Yahudim during the last decades of the nineteenth century and the beginning of the twentieth. While Schiff exerted influence from a base at Kuhn, Loeb, Straus went to the very bastions of power. In 1887, he was appointed by President Grover Cleveland envoy extraordinary and minister plenipotentiary to Turkey. Thereafter, he served every president through Harding. Straus was a member of the Permanent Court of Arbitration at The Hague and Secretary of Commerce and Labor (the first Jew to serve in a cabinet position) under Theodore Roosevelt.

Public service had long been a Straus family tradition. The *shtadlan's* great-grandfather was one of Napoleon's Jewish Notables. Oscar's father, Lazarus, arrived in Talbottom, Georgia, in 1852, and began his business career in the Yahudi manner by peddling. He proudly taught Hebrew to visiting Christian clergymen, and his sons Isidor, Nathan, and Oscar had a strong identity with Jews, although early attendance at Baptist and Methodist Sunday Schools also created an affinity with rural Protestants. Oscar would later see nothing odd in a Jew leading delegates in a rendition of "Onward Christian Soldiers" at a Bull Moose convention.

After the Civil War, Lazarus and his family went north to New York, where they opened a crockery shop in 1866. Nathan persuaded a customer named R. H. Macy to allow him to sell glassware and china in Macy's store, and in 1883, the Strauses and Macy became partners. The Strauses also joined another merchant in a new department store called Abraham and Straus.

Oscar, who stayed out of the crockery business, had little to do with the Strauses' upward climb to riches. He was graduated from Columbia Law School in 1871. In 1882, he married; with that practical bent characteristic of Yahudim, he thereupon abandoned the law and joined the family firm. His contributions to business life were minimal, consisting mainly of the L. Straus & Sons Employees Mutual Benefit Association, one of the first such groups in the nation.

Nor was Oscar noted for financial contributions on the scale made by his brothers Isidor and Nathan. Oscar Straus's major contributions—as viewed by Yahudim and politicians—were his total loyalty to Republican progressivism and his role as a Jewish spokesman. Sober, softspoken, and courtly, Oscar Straus was a scholar and gentleman who believed in the sanctity of the home, morality in politics, and keeping differences between Jews and Christians to a minimum. He was a *shtadlan* who did not decry materialist values, but emphasized spiritual ones. He favored Jewish ethical traditions and fought radicals.

Louis Marshall, the third of the trio of great *shtadlanim*, was the only one born in the United States. His fame did not come from commercial achievement—Marshall was never wealthy in the Schiff or Straus family sense—but from his great reputation as a specialist in constitutional and corporate law. Nor did Marshall, whose parents were Orthodox, leave Syracuse for New York City until he was nearly forty, when he joined the new firm of Guggenheimer, Untermeyer, and Marshall. His great dream, appointment to the Supreme Court, was never fulfilled.

Marshall's articulateness made him a prime choice for the top group of *shtadlanim*. Though he wrote poetry and was an ardent conservationist, his real avocation was the defense of "the rights of Jews wherever these rights [are] assailed." Marshall overawed Jews and Christians alike with his phenomenal memory and forensic abilities; there was no "Jewish" position on which he would not expound at length to Jew or non-Jew. "He was chosen by God Almighty to lead the children of Israel," thought admiring Yahudim.

Marshall was a teetotaler, read the Bible as often as he could, never took a cab when he could board a streetcar, and rejected the grosser aspects of philanthropy. Contributions to Emanu-El were refused because he feared additional plaques "would turn [it] into a mausoleum." Charity was "self-fulfillment," not a matter for public recognition. Though seldom a major contributor himself, he encouraged Schiff, Nathan and Isidor Straus, and other men of greater wealth to make substantial gifts to causes he favored. An untiring correspondent, Marshall also elucidated the problems of Jews for senators, congressmen, *shtadlanim*, Henry Ford, and others who wrote to him.

In 1900, Schiff, Straus, and Marshall "represented" 1 million American Jews to 75 million American Christians. They turned for advice to a group of *shtadlanim* of slightly less magnitude that included Mayer Sulzberger, Hebrew scholar and judge of the Court of Common Pleas of

Philadelphia; Sulzberger's cousin Cyrus, a prominent New York merchant; and Jesse Seligman; as well as Guggenheims, Lewisohns, Lehmans, and Adolph Ochs, a *shtadlan* who published the New York *Times*, married Isaac Mayer Wise's daughter Effie Miriam, and did not want Jews to open "Jewish" colleges in America. There was also Felix Warburg, Schiff's meticulous, compulsive son-in-law, destined to succeed him as the head of American Jewry.

This self-appointed group spoke for all Jews independently of any referendum and looked forward to full integration of Jews in American life. They were willing to use money, power, and influence unstintingly to achieve their goal. Unanimity of purpose would be their most striking characteristic; *shtadlanim* were remarkably free of the backbiting, distrust, and struggles over power that common efforts usually engender.

The weakness in this noblesse oblige was detachment from the masses they represented. *Shtadlanim* sought no public approval and were not much interested in conferring with social inferiors about the issues that faced Jews. Unity, like charity, was established from the top down by men of quality. All right-minded people knew this.

3

Yidn

IN 1880, monumental degradation and strict Orthodoxy distinguished 5 million Jews in Imperial Russia, two-thirds of all the Jews in the world, from prosperous and emancipated coreligionists in western Europe and America. Yidn (east European Jews) were penned in the "Pale of Settlement," a gigantic, 386,000-square-mile ghetto wedged between Austria-Hungary, Germany, and Russia. The Pale was the creation of Catherine the Great, who annexed vast Polish territories with large Jewish populations during the latter part of the eighteenth century. Russian officials promptly ousted Jews from village occupations, claiming that they exploited peasants and caused discontent. Jews were further isolated by reason of religion, customs, and their language, Yiddish, which they shared with no neighboring people.

Following the medieval patterns of life in Russia, Jews were ruled through *kahals*, quasi-governmental assemblies that collected taxes and kept Russian officials, who earned the modern equivalent of ten dollars a month, supplied with bribes. Meetings lacked discipline of any kind, and delegates customarily argued cases by shouting insults. Yet *kahals* were responsive to the people they governed and provided Jews with a rallying point in a hostile world, helping them withstand wars, plagues, pogroms, taxes, and each other.

Convinced that they were His Chosen People, the vast majority of Russian Jews were politically passive during most of the nineteenth century and obeyed a hierarchy of the rich and learned. They looked forward to emancipation by the same forces that enslaved them, praying for each monarch's well-being (including that of the anti-Semitic ones). They were told by their leaders that czars were really benevolent fathers at heart; it was the local officials and their bureaucratic superiors in St. Petersburg who caused problems. Changes for the better would occur when a czar no longer listened to "evil" advisors. Meanwhile, patience and strict religious adherence were essential.

If there was any consistent imperial policy it was to keep Jews fearful, docile, and poor. There are always some individuals who make their way despite all handicaps, and a few families, such as the Poliakovs, the Gunzburgs, and the Brodskis, became rich through dealings in railroads, banks, and oil refineries. For the masses, however, dozens of trades and professions were barred, and, given the huge number of unskilled workers in Russia, few employers felt any compulsion to hire Jews. Thousands turned to garment manufacture, which called for a relatively small capital investment in materials. Peddling was another prime occupation. Jews practiced a variety of professions, many of which became so overcrowded that people fought each other with maniacal savagery for pittances.

By the middle of the nineteenth century, millions of people were pauperized. During the enlightened reign of Alexander II, possibly 20 to 25 percent of all Jews in the Pale lived on charity. In Odessa, the city with the largest Jewish population in the Ukraine, 63 percent of the Jewish dead were to receive paupers' funerals by the end of the century. In Vilna, a great center of Jewish learning, a writer found that "fully 80 percent of the Jewish population . . . [does] not know in the evening where [it] will obtain food the next morning."

Yet among Russian Jewry's most striking characteristics were its humor and its indestructible optimism. "Let's drop these dismal subjects and talk of cheerful things," writes Sholom Aleichem in a story set in that mythical town, Kareilevsky. "Tell me, what's the latest about the cholera in Odessa?" Nihilism and black despair were simply not in the Jewish tradition. The fact of survival since time immemorial was proof enough Jews would always survive. No calamity was final, and every calamity had one positive value, serving as a subject for gossip.

Yiddishkeit (Jewishness) and *menschlichkeit* (humanity) were part of every activity whether in *shul*, home, or market, and the sun around which all revolved was Orthodox Judaism. Religious practice *was* Jewish life; *shtetls* (Jewish towns) lived by the Jewish calendar. Ancient sages listed 613 proscriptions—248 do's and 365 don'ts—and these served as guidelines for the pious of all ranks. The Lord's righteousness and will were beyond question. Rabbis were final authorities in all matters, temporal as well as spiritual. There was a law for everything, and everything came under some law. A deed was either permitted or forbidden. All differences were referred to rabbinical courts.

The prime *mitsvah* was sacred learning. Second only to sacred learning was charity, interpreted in the broadest possible sense to include construction of ritual baths; relationships between landlords and tenants; attendance at funerals, weddings, and bar mitzvahs; and Passover meals for the poor. To be a *balebatischer mensch*, a man of respectability and social position, demanded constant demonstration of enlightened largesse. Only those who had money could give it away, but merely possessing it was no guarantee of respect. A rich man had to know the proper way to be generous or he was not, ipso facto, of the upper class. Generous contributors earned *koved*, or honorific recognition, and possibly *yhkus*, a state of grace which could only be earned through an accrual of *mitsvoth*.

Attempting to impose some order on a disorderly world governed by madmen in St. Petersburg, Yidn preferred organized approaches to philanthropy. Societies devoted to specific social problems were formed. The Hakhnosses Kaleh provided brides with dowries; the Beys Yessoymim subsidized orphanages; and Talmud Torahs offered schooling for orphans as well as for other children. The Bikkur Khoylim provided medical treatment; the Hakhnosses Orkhim subsidized indigent strangers; and the Moyshev Zkeynim, or Home for the Aged, offered shelter and care for the old. The Gmilus Kheysed advanced funds for short-term business loans, and a Chevreh Kadisha served as a burial society for rich and poor alike.

Despite their overwhelming poverty, Jews in the Pale were intensely proud and independent and disliked taking charity. The poor dropped pennies into collection boxes to support rabbis in the Holy Land. The rich, called to read a section of the Torah during services, contributed to the synagogue—the longer the section, the larger the gift. Two respected officers from each society went from house to house demanding, cajoling, pleading, urging, threatening inhabitants who jockeyed for advantages while obligations were being settled. It was unheard of to refuse point-blank to contribute when asked; the cost would be ostracism.

Schnorers, professional beggars, were licensed by *kahals* to station themselves at strategic points around a *shtetl.* "The Jewish pauper does not ask for alms, as does his Christian counterpart standing before the door or near the window and bending down to the ground," found a Russian investigator. "But he brazenly enters the room and demands a gift as if it were his due. If he is refused, he becomes abusive and curses." Nonetheless, schnorers were held in contempt, not because they asked publicly for donations, but because contributions earned minor credit toward *koved*, which demanded something more of givers than merely handing over money.

The warmth of Jewish life in the Pale is much more apparent to audiences of *Fiddler on the Roof* than it was to those who actually lived there, and for the young the increasing congestion, poverty, and lack of opportunity were maddening. There were almost as many solutions as there were dissidents. Could ancient beliefs be retained or was secularization the only way out? The rich called for assimilation, assorted radicals called for revolution, the Orthodox called for greater piety, and some idealists called for a mass return to the Holy Land.

Torn by the questioning of the young and by antagonism between Orthodox and "enlightened" theologians, *shtetl* hegemony began to crack. Jewish birth rates were nearly double Christian birth rates in the 1880s, and the large number of people with no work and little hope brought life to the very edge of disaster. Rivalries, hatreds, and quarrels simmered at family gatherings, *kahal* meetings, and in synagogues. People could not decide whether to abandon one another and make their own way or to hold on for dear life.

On March 1, 1881, Alexander II was assassinated in St. Petersburg by a bomb-throwing member of Narodnaya Volya, a terrorist band that included a few Jews. The assassin died in the act, and by mid-April, six conspirators were apprehended, tried, and executed. Surviving Narodnaya

Volya members expected uprisings throughout the country, but there were only desultory disturbances. The following Easter, newspapers accused Jews of being pro-Western proponents of rational thought and congenitally opposed to the "nature" of Russia and its institutions. Russian patriots could not bear such outrages.

Sensing official approval, hooligans began robbing, murdering, and raping Jews in 160 towns and cities. The Russians described these savage acts as popular reactions to Jewish exploitation. The only people who believed them were anti-Semites. Protest meetings were held in Paris, in London, and in New York. Yet no radical or humanitarian leader in Russia—not even Tolstoy—protested the bloody atrocities. On the contrary, revolutionaries claimed Jews were czarist tools and some applauded pogroms, saying peasants were working up the proper fervor to overthrow the Romanov dynasty.

Encouraged by these events, Alexander III proclaimed "temporary rules" or "May Laws." A half million Jews living outside *shtetlach* were forced to return to the enclosures. In places where Jews made up 30 to 80 percent of the population, their enrollment in secondary schools and universities was cut to 10 percent of the student population. Jewish merchants were forbidden to open their stores on Christian as well as Jewish holidays.

The pogroms profoundly affected the Jews, who, theretofore, had been passive. Hundreds, then thousands, and then hundreds of thousands would, to use Lenin's phrase, "vote with their feet." Repression was one thing, violence another. Masses of Yidn suddenly grasped a fact that had escaped both assimilated intelligentsia and revolutionaries: It was impossible to trust either a government that deliberately encouraged murder or terrorists willing to see Jews annihilated as part of a "historical process."

The assimilated Jewish establishment opposed flight. Poliakoff, the railroad magnate, Baron Horace Gunzburg, the banker, and thirty-eight other wealthy Russian Jews held a conference in April 1882 (just as news arrived of new and bloodier disorders) and declared organized emigration "subversive of the dignity of the Russian body politic and of the historic rights of the Jews to their present fatherland. . . ." Not far behind, Orthodox leaders opposed emigration on grounds that the faithful would neglect ritual and custom away from the great centers of Jewish learning.

Proste (common) Yidn were in no mood to heed the views of their religious and economic betters. Attacks on Jews were just beginning, predicted a prescient writer named Peretz Smolenskin in an essay, "Let us search our ways." "Jewish philanthropists in Russia," he asserted, were merely imitating German Jews in hopes of achieving success and honor in the non-Jewish community. Where to go, not how to stay, was the basic issue. Millions agreed and looked toward America, the land of opportunity.

Discussions waxed in markets and homes, synagogues and yeshivas. Schnorers, petty tradesmen, respectable Yidn, *proste* Yidn, rabbinical students, entire *shtetlach* began selling belongings and joining the stream to the *goldene medina*, the golden land of America, where there were ample territory, commercial opportunity, and wealthy coreligionists to hold out a welcoming hand.

Even to students of migrations, the exodus from eastern Europe between 1881 and 1920 presents an awesome spectacle. An immense, dynamic, leaderless mass of 2 million Jews moved inexorably across Europe and then boarded vessels for a 3000-mile ocean voyage. Its transportation was financed at first by the Alliance Israélite Universelle in Paris, but later travelers paid for their own food, shelter, and steerage tickets. Nothing like this had been seen since Irish emigrants fled their ancestral homes during the Great Famine; nothing quite like it would ever be seen again.

There were American Yahudim who preferred not to see it at all. In 1870, America's 200,000 Jews were happily readjusting to Jewish-Christian relationships reminiscent of the halcyon ante-bellum period. That year a few hundred impoverished Lithuanian Jews arrived in New York, forerunners of the thousands who would take flight in 1881. The Board of Delegates wrote the Alliance Israélite that immigrants would be assisted only if "groups of not more than one hundred able-bodied persons each were shipped, and provided they did not remain in New York City but moved to the West or South." The threat succeeded in limiting the number who entered the country.

With a heavy influx of east Europeans impending, Yahudim who lived on the Lower East Side of Manhattan, soon to become New York's ghetto, moved uptown, joining the well-to-do in Yorkville, Harlem, and along Central Park West. Shearith Israel went with them to Seventieth Street, across from Central Park. "Uptowners" could congratulate themselves that Temple Emanu-El was already safe on Fifth Avenue and Forty-third Street, as was Mount Sinai at Lexington Avenue and Sixty-seventh Street. Private clubs for Yahudim—the Freundschaft, the Fidelio, the Progress, and the ultra-elite Harmonie, where German was spoken almost exclusively until 1900—were founded in the new neighborhoods.

American Jews sympathized with Jewish problems thousands of miles away in Russia. But what man could predict the ultimate consequences of an invasion by a "mass of illiterate, uncouth, mainly superstitious foreigners"? True, Yidn were coreligionists; true, they had strong family ties. What other similarities were there between assimilated Yahudim and this hopeless rabble? The *Jewish Messenger* complained that "there is a lack of refinement and true spirituality despite the exactness with which they adhere to their traditional habits." In Cincinnati, Isaac Wise sneered at Yiddish as a jargon and worried about "semi-Asiatic Hasidim and medieval orthodoxy." In New York, United Hebrew Charities complained that its purpose was "to care for the needy of New York and not of the world." The Conference of Managers of Associated Hebrew Charities offered up a resolution against "the transportation of paupers into this country," stressing that "all such as are unable to maintain themselves should be forthwith returned whence they came."

German, French, and English Jewish establishments were equally at a loss. Refugees had to be helped because they were Jewish. In Paris, Berlin, Vienna, and London, relief committees were formed to help refugees go elsewhere, and it was hoped as far as possible from Paris, Berlin, Vienna, or London. By agreement of all committees, the Alliance Israélite took overall leadership and urged Yidn to stay in Russia. Barring that, it established way stations in central Europe and provided tickets for speedy trips to America.

A refugee assembly point was set up in Brody, a poverty-stricken Galician village in Austria just over the Russian border. By the winter of 1881, it held 10,000 Russian Jews and within months, 14,000 more refugees. From Brody, joyous, liberated throngs moved to Lemburg, Cracow, and Breslau, then on to Hamburg for ships to New York and Philadelphia, Boston and Baltimore, Liverpool and London. In the British capital, philanthropists worked desperately to repatriate refugees or to send them on to America, but half the Yidn arriving in England insisted on remaining in London or settling in the Midlands.

In New York, where the first ship filled with Jewish refugees docked in September 1881, Yahudim hastily organized a Russian Emigrant Relief Committee. At once it misjudged its task: The committee had expected 500 refugees and had raised $50,000 to feed, clothe, shelter, and send them "to points West and South." An official soon cried out that "over 1200 are here and they are but beginning to come."

In November, the *Jewish Messenger* reported that "Jewish leaders" proposed to "return to Europe all those who are paupers or likely to become [paupers]." Two hundred Yahudim met to form a permanent, incorporated relief committee. Judge Meyer Isaacs thought that the migration was a temporary phenomenon and Jacob Schiff opposed the establishment of any agency devoted exclusively to Jewish refugees as "smacking of sectarianism." But even while these views were being aired, something had to be done for refugees recently arrived or en route. A Hebrew Emigrant Aid Society was duly organized and opened a refuge on Ward's Island, helped by a $10,000 contribution from Schiff.

Swamped like the Russian Emigrant Aid Society before it by arriving refugees, the Hebrew Emigrant Aid Society dispatched Moritz Ellinger, who had lately been traveling around the country organizing relief committees, to Europe in January 1882. His assignment was to work out cooperative procedures with European committees. In reports home, Ellinger exaggerated local enthusiasm for his mission, writing that "there was not a hamlet in Germany, Austria and Hungary where collections were not taken up." Aid Society officials became suspicious that refugees were simply being dumped by Europeans in New York, judging by the increasing numbers of Yidn showing up daily, weekly, and monthly at the immigrant depot at Castle Garden. Overworked staff members quit regularly. In less than a year the Hebrew Emigrant Aid Society had three presidents and four secretaries.

Ellinger claimed that "Europe has been told" after an April 1882 International Jewish Conference, but Europeans demanded the right to supervise refugee operations. Ellinger also boasted that his persuasiveness led Baron Alphonse de Rothschild to contribute 200,000 francs to immigrant relief, but barely had the conference ended when another series of pogroms began in Russia and 20,000 more refugees, including the infirm, grandfathers, grandmothers, and entire families with young children, descended on Brody. In New York, the Hebrew Emigrant Aid Society launched a fund-raising drive threatening that "the pauper population would increase by at least 12,000 Jews" if contributions were not forthcoming. When 1300 refugees arrived in a single week, the staff said that it could no longer cope with "any Russian refugees or other Jewish immigrants who may arrive in this city." In June, London agreed that the United States had taken as many refugees as it could accommodate; in July, London said that no more refugees would be sent on to New York.

In mid-1882, pogroms seemed finally to be ending and 5000 refugees in Brody returned to Russia. In New York, the Hebrew Emigrant Aid Society prepared to disband and gave its remaining $10,000 to United Hebrew Charities. Another international meeting of aid committees was convened in Vienna in August. Edward Lauterbach, the American representative, said flatly that New York "would receive no more emigrants except in a few exceptional instances." Lauterbach observed that "immigration was not popular among our own people, and this unpopularity had, to some extent . . . been caused by the character . . . of emigrants themselves, and there was no prospect that the grade will be improved." August Levey, secretary of the Aid Society, agreed that "only disgrace and a lowering opinion in which Israelites are held . . . can result from the continued residence among us . . . of these wretches. . . ."

But what of those wretches already in New York, dozens of them daily visitors with their young to the Hebrew Emigrant Aid Society Office? Thousands of Christian New Yorkers were now coming into contact with Yidn for the first time, and results bore out deep-rooted Yahudi fears. Ragged, ill-kempt, hungry newcomers made a poor impression. "Their filthy condition," complained the *Tribune* in 1882, "has caused many of the people who are accustomed to go to [Battery] Park to seek a little recreation and fresh air to give up this practice. The immigrants also greatly annoy the persons who cross the park to take the boats to Coney Island, Staten Island and Brooklyn." Jewish-Christian relationships were not helped by the arrival of Mme. Zénaïde Alexeïevna Ragozin, a Russian matron who explained in *Century Magazine* that pogroms were caused by Jews goading peasants to violence by stealing their money, or by the arrival of Telemachus Timayenis, a Greek immigrant who devoted three volumes to portraying an illusory, age-old struggle between noble Aryan and scheming Jew.

Greater efforts would be made to disperse heavy concentrations of Yidn in New York, the city Henry James called a "Hebrew conquest." Dispersal efforts promised to be costly—the New York Central had stopped offering discount rates to Yidn bound westward—and thus it was fortuitous that in the mid-1880s, Baron Maurice de Hirsch announced himself interested in Jewish resettlement.

Baron de Hirsch was a German Jew who had inherited vast wealth and later earned much more. In 1890, when he retired from moneymaking, the baron's fortune was reputed to be $100 million; he was thought to be the richest Jew in the world. Thoroughly emancipated, Hirsch hobnobbed with royalty and believed assimilation the "salvation" of Jews. Nonetheless, he was alarmed by pogroms and gave the Alliance Israélite 1 million francs for refugees in Brody. In 1885, he offered the czarist government 50 million francs to build Jewish trade and agricultural schools in the Pale. The price was Jewish equality with Russians, a condition St. Petersburg would never accept; the Russians insisted that all funds had to be under their control, a condition Hirsch would not accept. The offer was dropped after Hirsch advanced 1 million francs, which was used by the Russians to train priests for the Russian Orthodox Church.

In contrast to Jewish assimilationists in Russia, Hirsch was convinced that mass emigration was essential if lives were to be saved. He feared the consequences of disorderly mass flight and emphasized the need for "beneficial and generous" assistance from the Imperial government. Hirsch made another offer: "Let a period of twenty years—let us say—be fixed: let it be agreed that every year a certain number of Jews will leave the country. . . . If the Czar will order a measure of this character to be adopted, those who are interested in the fate of the Russian Jews will do what is necessary to provide funds for conveying to their new country the number of emigrants ordered to leave yearly." The Russians were more amenable to this plan, and in 1892, a rescue committee was organized with czarist approval in the Russian capital.

In 1887, while Hirsch was thinking about the countries to which emigrating Russian Jews might go, he traveled to Constantinople to settle a claim against him by the Ottoman government. Oscar Straus, the American ambassador to Turkey, was asked by the Grand Vizier to serve as arbitrator in the dispute. Hirsch described his philanthropic and business problems to Straus, and the *shtadlan* asked him to consider Mesopotamia, a Turkish possession, as a resettlement location. Hirsch thought the Ottoman government too difficult to deal with and ruled out the Turkish dominion as "quite impracticable." Hirsch thought about the island of Rhodes, but finally rejected that, too, since it was under Turkish control and the Russians might oppose Jewish colonists going there.

Hirsch owned land in Argentina, and because of this, the sparse population, and the relative open-mindedness of its government, he leaned toward that country as a site for Jewish emigrants. Straus urged him to consider the United States. There, Jewish communal settlements had long been advocated by a handsome Polish immigrant named Michael Heilprin who wrote for the *Evening Post,* the *Nation*, and *Appleton's New American Cyclopedia.* Heilprin founded communal farms in Oregon, Kansas, the Dakotas, and New Jersey.

Straus asked Heilprin to write a proposal for Hirsch, requesting funds to make immigrants self-sufficient via the agricultural life or training in trade schools. What Hirsch thought of Heilprin's ideas we do not know, but in May 1889, Isidore Loeb, secretary of the Alliance Israélite, wrote that Hirsch wanted to establish a fund for Russian and Rumanian immigrants in the United States. Nine Americans "experienced in charitable matters," including Oscar Straus, Jacob Schiff, Jesse Seligman, and Leopold Lewisohn, were asked to help decide how to spend the baron's money. Eventually fourteen *shtadlanim*, including four from Philadelphia and Baltimore, devised a plan in which Hirsch would invest $2.4 million "in land or in any other sound real estate investment"; set aside $240,000 for the purchase of land for colonies; and use the income from investments (estimated at $120,000 per year) for industrial training, housing, colonies, and "temporary relief to be distributed through United Hebrew Charities." The baron was also willing to send an additional $10,000 a month for one year to cover transportation, purchases of tools, and loans to Yidn who wanted to open small businesses. The entire loan and the educational and training programs were to be under American direction.

Reaching agreement was not easy. The baron wrote Schiff that "the time has arrived when we men of property must stand by the breach," but he had reservations about the plan, arguing that he should have the right to back out of financing at will. Yahudim in Philadelphia and Baltimore opposed colonization, fearing concentrations of Yidn in New Jersey, their back yard. The great *shtadlanim* stood firm on American control, on the irrevocable nature of the trust, and on the necessity to move Yidn out of New York, where they continued to congregate. All were frightened by the scrutiny Jewish immigration now got in the press and feared the impression might spread that American Jews were deliberately inspiring immigration to increase their numbers in the country.*

Schiff met Hirsch in London and was encouraged to learn that charity was not foremost in the baron's mind. Only those immigrants who could be made "self-supporting" should get help, he insisted. "I contend most decidedly against the old system of alms-giving. [It] only makes so many more beggars."

While *shtadlanim* were thus mapping out an agreement with Hirsch and seeking homestead sites, rumors began circulating in Washington and London that the Russians were planning new and worse pogroms. Asked by President Benjamin Harrison to investigate, Ambassador Charles Emory Smith was assured in St. Petersburg that no anti-Jewish measures were contemplated. Secretary of State James Blaine passed on to Oscar Straus and Jesse Seligman the message that the situation had been exaggerated. But it was a czarist habit to say one thing and then do another, and in March 1891, a sudden *ukase* extended the May Laws of 1882. Jews previously permitted residence in Moscow were suddenly and forcibly expelled on the first day of Passover. Scenes of the early 1880s were then replayed throughout the world: pogroms in the Pale; rescue committees in France, Germany, Great Britain, and Austria; refugees in Brody; 35,000 Russian-Jewish refugees in New York by September and 60,000 by the end of the year.

Hirsch and Baron de Hirsch Fund trustees were shaken by the new disaster, aggravated by a devastating drought and famine in Russia. Schiff urged French, British, and German leaders "to induce persons not absolutely compelled to leave, to remain in Russia." Hirsch pressed the Imperial government to permit an orderly emigration. Jesse Seligman and Dr. Julius Goldman went to an international Jewish conference in Germany where Goldman complained that refugees were an intolerable burden on a relatively small community of Jews in the United States, even while the Berlin committee was speeding Yidn westward in a desperate attempt to prevent them from settling in central and western Europe. Europeans wanted financial help from America, but unless Yahudim in New York

* Lest this be misinterpreted, Louis Marshall, Schiff, and other leaders of the American Jewish community, to their credit, constantly fought for liberalization of immigration laws.

got more money from Europe, threatened Dr. Goldman, refugees might be returned. New York would take 18,000 refugees between November 1891 and November 1892, if Europeans provided $400,000.

Hirsch also thought about what Yidn could do after they emigrated, and in 1891 concluded that Jews should definitely be farmers. It was "quite possible to reawaken in the race this capacity and love" for farm life, he wrote in the *North American Review*. Hirsch founded the Jewish Colonization Association in Paris with a $10 million gift, its purpose "to assist and to promote the migration of Jews from any part of Europe and Asia . . . and to form and establish colonies in various parts of North and South America." Some showplace was needed to display the achievements of Jewish yeomen, and the de Hirsch Fund purchased 5300 acres for a town and collective farm in Woodbine, New Jersey, "The First Self-Governing Jewish Community Since the Fall of Jerusalem."

Few Yidn heeded its call. Ten years later, Woodbine still had a small number of Jewish farmers trying to grow something in "stingy soil." A $500,000 expenditure and widespread publicity had inspired no rush among east Europeans yearning for plows and harvesters.* The absence of *shtetl*-like religious institutions, fellow Jews, and, above all, of *Yiddishkeit* was unendurable.

Woodbine was not the only failure. Colonies as far away as Texas and Utah were rapidly deserted. With little success, Cyrus Sulzberger bid Rumanians go to Mexico, to Brazil, or to Hawaii. Rabbi Isaac Wise's Hebrew Union Agricultural Society in Cincinnati sponsored a settlement for fifty-nine Yidn in Beersheba, Kansas, on land made available under the Homestead Act. In the *American Israelite*, Rabbi Wise happily observed that newcomers obeyed the superintendent "as soldiers," but Beersheba failed like other colonies.

With Yidn continuing to join Yidn in New York, *shtadlanim* despaired of ever finding a solution. "It is difficult enough to deal on business principles with people who come almost naked and helpless," Schiff wrote Hirsch, "but even if it were feasible with a few individuals or with a small number, it is entirely impossible when it is a matter of ten thousand

* Eighty-six percent of American Jewish farmers were found by the Jewish Colonization Association to settle in the vicinity of cities where many made "quite a considerable income out of 'summer boarders' especially during the first years of their farm-life. All except the South Jersey farmers. In that section the mosquitoes that infest the salt meadows along the Atlantic shore are of unheard of ferocity."

per month." In April 1899, Schiff appealed to the Jewish Colonization Association for more help, suggesting the creation of a credit union to finance agricultural and industrial homesteads. Ten months later a "Jewish Agricultural and Industrial Aid Society" was founded and devoted its first year of operations to an "investigation of methods." A year later, investigating directors advised that "the policy of the Society for some time to come must be that of acquiring knowledge and possibilities."

To induce Yidn to move on became a categorical imperative. "Families who apply to the charitable institutions for assistance could be told that assistance will be furnished to them if they are willing to leave the city," suggested Dr. Goldman. Another answer, thought *shtadlanim*, might be to aim the message at individuals rather than at masses. In 1901, the Baron de Hirsch Fund opened an Industrial Removal Office designed to forward east Europeans to specific locations anywhere in the country. Agents were dispatched to plead with Yahudim in towns and villages to provide jobs for "removalites." A "sober and industrious class of mechanics who could be relied upon at all times" was promised. B'nai B'rith lodges were enlisted, but many interior communities were disinterested. Some objected to the rough characteristics of Yidn supplied, others were surprised to learn that they were not to get domestics, strikebreakers, or indentured servants.

The so-called Ellis Island Experiment was tried. Perhaps newcomers would leave for the interior if they were met fresh off steamers by Yidn and urged in Yiddish to quit New York. A rabbi stationed on Ellis Island delivered the message. Refugees listened patiently, then took the next ferry to Manhattan.

Schiff and the commissioner-general of immigration, Frank Pierce Sargent, conceived the Galveston Movement. Where Hirsch merely wanted refugees dispersed on farms after they landed in eastern ports, Schiff wanted them caught on the fly, as it were, and transported directly from the Pale to the American hinterlands via the hot, humid gulf port of Galveston, Texas. From Galveston, immigrants would fan out through Texas, Oklahoma, and the Southwest. This dispersal would be accomplished with help from Israel Zangwill, a forty-two-year-old English playwright and former Zionist who broke with Theodor Herzl in 1904 and thereupon founded the Jewish Territorial Organization, which sought territory for an autonomous Jewish state wherever it could be found.

Zangwill wanted money to finance an exodus "for Jews who cannot or will not remain in the lands in which they live at present"; Schiff needed an agency in the Pale. The two men met in London where Zangwill staggered Schiff with a suggestion that he buy part of the American Southwest and establish a Jewish National Home. "I have become more firmly convinced than ever that the more thoroughly our people become dispersed among the nations, the nearer the great Jewish problem will be brought to a satisfactory solution," Schiff wrote Zangwill. "What I have in mind is that the Jewish Territorial Organization should take up a project through which it shall become possible to direct the flow of emigration.... After immigrants have once been landed at New York, Boston, Philadelphia, or Baltimore, they generally prefer to remain there, and notwithstanding all the efforts of the established removal offices, only a comparatively small number leave these centers...."

Schiff was ready to contribute $500,000, provided a like amount was supplied by the Jewry of western Europe. He doubted that more could be raised from Yahudim in America. Control would have to rest with the Industrial Removal Office. "It would be fatal to use the Removal Office in connection with your new and statesmanlike scheme," countered Zangwill in December 1906. "The Jew has been accustomed to being 'moved on' by all the nations. He does not want to be 'moved on' by his own people."

Another complication arose. The Industrial Removal Office in New York insisted that emigrants work on the Sabbath. Zangwill, a debonair, nonobservant Jew, asserted that "If this is a condition under which Mr. Schiff's plan can be carried out, not only shall we reject it, but we shall use our influence against it." By December, the offensive clause was amended and differences were resolved; emigrants were simply advised that strict Sabbath observance would be difficult if not almost impossible.

By 1910, Yidn were shunning Galveston as determinedly as they had shunned Cotopaxi, Vineland, and Woodbine. Only 5000 people had passed through the Texas port despite Schiff, Zangwill, a network of Industrial Removal Offices, and Rabbi Henry Cohen, a British-born cleric who traveled from one end of Texas to the other pleading with resident Yahudim to import immigrants. Schiff was mortified. Zangwill's recruiting in Russia, "careless [in] the selection of properly qualified immigrants," was held to blame by the *shtadlan*, as were Yiddish papers in New York that "never looked with favor upon the efforts to deflect Russian Jewish immigrants. . . ."

Zangwill wrote Schiff that he would come to America and help mold public opinion. Schiff was aghast at the prospect: "Nothing could be more certain to create further prejudice in the eyes of the authorities than if the head of a foreign society would try to influence them." Yet the *shtadlan* was not discouraged. "Great and far-reaching movements like the one we have on hand can seldom be worked out without difficulties of some sort," wrote Schiff, "and I still feel that, with God's help, we shall overcome the obstacles which are now being placed in our way."

And still they poured into New York: Talmudic scholars, rabbis, tradesmen, tavern keepers, peddlers, dairymen, blacksmiths, tailors, musicians—followed by wives, children, brothers, sisters, uncles, aunts, *babas*, and *zaydas*. Relatives were summoned as soon as a newcomer was settled. Twelve years after the first refugees arrived, there were as many Jewish newcomers in America as there were Yahudim in the country in 1880. The Jewish population of New York soared from 4 percent in 1880 to 9 percent in 1890, and then to 29 percent by 1920.

Most Yidn could not be budged across the Hudson. The National Council of Jewish Charities estimated that 75 percent "never passed beyond [city] limits." By 1910, 542,061 east European Jews lived on the Lower East Side of Manhattan, concentrated between Brooklyn Bridge on the south, Fourteenth Street on the north, Broadway on the west, and the East River. Had the same density obtained throughout New York, the city's population would have been 150 million.

The Lower East Side was the sinkhole of the city, its denizens plying any trade they could find. A disheartening report issued by United Hebrew Charities in 1901 pointed to immigration statistics and despaired of ever alleviating chronic poverty. Jewish criminals, virtually unknown in the Pale, made appearances in the slums of New York. Family desertion, a rarity in the Pale, was not unusual. In 1903 and 1904, 10 percent of the relief applications to United Hebrew Charities came from deserted women.

Under the frenzied conditions of life in America, *shtetl* traditions began to crumble. The "finest Hebrew grammarian in New York" could earn only five dollars weekly. Daily religious observances were an early casualty, and prayer was abandoned even on the Sabbath and high holy days for work in sweatshops.

While the lure of sacred learning declined, Americanization became the major immigrant goal. Nothing was so distasteful as to be thought a greenhorn, an inexperienced novice among Americans. Immigrants who had arrived in July felt superior to immigrants who arrived in August. Possession of a watch and chain was the ultimate sign of familiarity with the sophisticated ways of WASPS. A stout girth was accounted a sure sign of success; Boris Thomashevsky in over-stuffed tights represented manliness on the Jewish stage.

Attendance at schools and libraries attested to a hunger for secular learning; English, not Yiddish, was spoken at home by children whose dream was to go to college, not to a yeshiva. During the 1880s and 1890s, newcomers were unlettered as well as poor. Beginning in the early 1900s, students and intellectuals began to arrive, better-educated members of socialist, anarchist, and Zionist groups. The Lower East Side became a hotbed of radical activity; some groups planned the overthrow of the czar, some the end of capitalism, some a return to the Holy Land, and some the establishment of socialism in America.

For all radicals, Yahudim were enemies.* They controlled the garment industry and took full advantage of immigrants, using them to replace higher-priced workers and as strikebreakers. Greed inevitably provoked violent reactions, although many Yidn could not easily understand the necessity for unionization. A series of strikes in the garment industry between 1909 and 1914 has since come to be known as the Great Revolt. *Shtadlanim*, fearful of the publicity, intervened openly to end the labor disputes. Marshall, Schiff, and a brilliant Boston attorney, Louis Brandeis, drafted a "protocol of peace" that sounded the death knell of the sweatshop in 1910.

Yidn still had little faith in Yahudim. Uptowners had behaved unbelievably callously. Yet what could be expected from Jews who practiced no dietary laws, spoke no Yiddish, and read no Hebrew? And what could decent, pious Yidn make of Reform Judaism, a religion in which bare-

* They were not alone in exploiting coreligionists. In 1905, Isaac Rubinow noted that "almost every Russian-Jewish tenement dweller must pay his rent to a Russian-Jewish landlord."

headed men sat with women in temples where services smacked of *goyim* and their inhibited religious attitudes?

Equally loathsome was the cold, insensitive outlook of Yahudim to charity, their complete lack of *Yiddishkeit* and *menschlichkeit*. Not content to isolate Yidn in southern New Jersey and Texas, United Hebrew Charities agents in New York pressed immigration officials to send individuals back to eastern Europe. Careful, painstaking investigation of applicants was especially despicable. *Menschlichkeit* implied philanthropy without lengthy questions, without record-and-account techniques that resulted in applicants refused as well as helped.

As if all this weren't enough, Yahudim were insulting in the process of being helpful and uplifting. Mrs. Minnie Louis, a Temple Emanu-El stalwart, passed out cookies on the Lower East Side and urged Yidn to stop speaking Yiddish. In addition to these social contributions, she advised east European girls to bathe and wear clean clothes. It became apparent that urging the girls to clean up was not going to get anyone anywhere, nor was it any solution to their real problems, which revolved around poor housing and poverty. In 1884, Mrs. Louis and coworkers shifted from cleanliness to vocational training in the Hebrew Technical School for Girls. Adolph Lewisohn gave $500,000 to the school, the only institution in New York for girls who wanted to learn technical and business skills.

Yahudi largesse poured into the five-story Educational Alliance on East Broadway, originally the downtown branch of the Young Men's Hebrew Association. Liberal arts courses, a class in necktie making, a library, and dancing lessons from Eleanor Roosevelt were offered. One of the alliance's major purposes was to crush pluralistic tendencies in the young; there were no classes in Yiddish, and mixed seating was encouraged in the synagogue. The Educational Alliance also developed a paternalistic tone: Marshall, a board member, pressed its Committee on Moral Work to investigate "the moral condition of the inhabitants of the East Side and of the existing evils there prevailing. . . ." Jewish and non-Jewish speakers preached on the dangers of socialism, unionization, cooperatives, and free love. Immigrants hungry for learning were treated to discussions of economic dangers in nationalization of railroads.

Yidn differentiated between Our Crowd (them) and Our Kind (us) and decided the less help from uptowners, the better. Anti-Yahudim sentiment was dramatized in Jacob Gordin's play, *The Benefactors of the East Side*, which noted cooking classes, model bathhouses, and instruction in boxing and in wrestling among major gifts from the rich. No, said the *Jüdische Gazetten*, "it is up to us, the Russian Jews, to help our poor countrymen and keep them from being insulted by our proud brethren to whom a Russian Jew is a schnorer, a tramp, a good-for-nothing. . . . In the philanthropic institutions of our aristocratic German Jews you see magnificent offices with decorated desks, but along with this, morose and angry faces. A poor man is questioned like a criminal. He trembles like a leaf, as if he were standing before a Russian official."

Yidn established their own agencies. Beth Israel Hospital was founded in dismal Birmingham Alley so that newcomers need not travel to Mount Sinai, where east Europeans were barred from the staff.* An Educational League was formed to counterbalance the Educational Alliance, offering courses on a variety of subjects. Near the turn of the century, the Kimpetoran Society was formed to care for indigent—and often unmarried—Jewish mothers. The society gave a scuttle of coal, a clean bedsheet, a few diapers, and five dollars to the *kimpetoran* (new mothers).

Except for a city institution on Welfare (then Blackwell's) Island, there was no place for the Jewish aged in New York. The Orthodox were afraid they would be placed in a facility where dietary laws and rituals were not observed. Mrs. Bertha Dworsky, a young mother plodding home from market one day in 1897, encountered a coughing, tottering old man. She offered to help him to his home. "I have no home. I have nowhere to go," he said. The young matron rented a room for him and then called on nine friends to help organize the "Daughters of Jacob" to aid the elderly. Each housewife paid three dollars a year in dues saved out of household money and cajoled food from peddlers.

The Hebrew Free Loan Society was founded by eleven men one December evening in 1892, with a capital investment of ninety-five dollars. Modeled after the Gmulius Kheysed in the Pale, it made 227 loans totaling $1205 during its first year, without requiring collateral or any investigation except endorsements from merchants in good standing. Borrowers

* On the other side of the ledger, Mount Sinai treated more patients at no charge than any other private institution in New York; in the 1880s, 90 percent of its admissions were free.

had ten months to repay. Similarly, the Hebrew Immigrant Aid Society (HIAS) came into existence at a meeting of the Rabbi Yochanan Lodge of the Independent Order B'rith Abraham, partly to provide a countermeasure to the overbearing United Hebrew Charities representative on Ellis Island. HIAS's founders interceded with immigration authorities to prevent them from deporting immigrants, secured employment for the unemployable, and communicated with relatives of immigrants in Europe.

Above all, there were *landsmanschaften*, fraternal mutual aid societies of men from the same town in the Pale. Anyone over thirteen could join providing he came from the right place and was not a strikebreaker, bartender, or married to a Christian woman. In 1897, there were 204 *landsmanschaften*, and by 1918, there would be 1000 *landsmanschaften* with 100,000 members. In some *landsmanschaften* the number of members in New York actually exceeded the number of Jews still living in the original *shtetl*. For their dues, *landsliet* received insurance benefits, burial plots, and assistance for relatives in Europe. Jobs were found for sons and sons-in-law, disputes between quarrelsome members were adjudicated, orphaned girls were given doweries, and synagogues were built. Doctors were also hired to climb four or five rickety flights in tenements to treat members and their families.

To support *landsmanschaften*, hospitals, old-age homes, loan societies, and dozens of other agencies without going to *Yahudim*, downtowners embarked on such a variety of fund-raising campaigns as befuddles the imagination. They paid dues, they bought tickets for annual dinners, and they gave donations to collectors in the street. Their wives saved pennies from household budgets for yeshivas, old-age homes, orphanages, overseas relief, and the Jewish National Fund, which bought land for colonies in Palestine. The *Jewish Daily Forward* cried out against accepting gifts from the rich, even if the rich were Christians who offered unsolicited gifts to strikers. Faith must be put in the people, it said, and the people were besieged by armies of solicitors. *Meshullach* (fund raisers) made collections and constantly sought out new prospects. Their pockets bulged with papers, notebooks, receipts, hard-boiled eggs, and *pushkas*, collection cans that came in all shapes, sizes, and colors.

Fund-raising techniques new to devoted givers from the Pale were devised. "The homes of the people are such that it is impossible for them to enjoy a social life," reported a social worker to the First National Conference of Jewish Charities in 1900. "On weekdays, the theaters are used for benefit performances of the societies of the neighborhoods." For $25, benevolent and charitable societies, lodges, and unions could buy $100 worth of tickets. For $300, they got the entire house. Since theaters had forty-week seasons, possibly $1 million a year was raised from benefits.

Yidn could walk from their homes directly to the theaters located near Second Avenue below Fourteenth Street. This was an intentional accommodation for the Orthodox, unable because of religious bans to ride or to carry money on Friday nights, theater night on Second Avenue. During performances, patrons hissed, applauded, greeted lodge brothers and relatives, exchanged insults with fellow customers, and took nourishment. The show in the audience was sometimes better than the one on the stage.

By 1900, the sheer number of agencies seeking contributors on the Lower East Side of New York was overwhelming the most avid candidates for *yhkus*. The 1901 American Jewish Year Book notes 593 charitable societies, 415 educational and fraternal organizations, and 22 national organizations serving 1 million American Jews. In 1915, New York's *Jewish Communal Register* listed 3637 institutions and agencies serving 1.5 million Jews. Immigrants could resist few temptations to ask each other for donations or to form additional agencies. Impecunious newcomers could not resist the opportunity to wander from office to office on Wall Street soliciting gifts from Yahudi executives.*

Few observers were more appalled by the confusion, duplications in services, and multiple appeals than *shtadlanim* beseeched for gifts, and, like Marshall, fearful that unless order were imposed, "the entire charitable system of New York City" might go bankrupt. Schiff, who started three funds of his own at United Hebrew Charities—a "Self-Support Fund," a "Self-Respect Fund," and a "Self-Help Fund"—doubled the Hebrew Free Loan's capital with a $100 gift in 1893, but was convinced by 1903 that some form of federation was essential "to bring out the full support of the community for all of the institutions." Jacob Gimbel similarly urged federation "so that *all* [italics added] our coreligionists, able to contribute can be properly reached. . . ." A lesser-known but nonetheless

* One Jewish weekly cautioned givers against Julius Scheuer, a schnorer who carried a list bearing signatures indicating ten-dollar gifts from Kuhn, Loeb & Co., Speyer & Co., Simon Borg & Co., and other firms.

important *shtadlan*, Professor Morris Loeb of New York University, told the First National Conference of Jewish Charities that, although it was "the boast of our race" to care for the needy from cradle to grave, "the attention given at board meetings . . . to questions of ways and means paralyzes the activity of the management proper."

As Loeb saw it, consolidation or federation of charitable agencies was imperative. His objection to consolidation was that directorates might become "somewhat autocratic, somewhat opinionated, somewhat self-satisfied." Yahudim looked to the republic as a model in such matters; Loeb counseled that "the example of our country should be followed." A federation with "sufficient elasticity" might unite seemingly hopelessly antagonistic groups.

This approach made a great deal of sense to Yahudim on Wall Street, particularly to Felix Warburg and to another Kuhn, Loeb partner named Louis Heinsheimer. In 1908, forty-five agency heads met to determine the feasibility of federation. The following year Heinsheimer died, leaving $14 million, one million of it for a federation. His will provided that six establishment institutions served as founding members. Bitterly competitive, the institutions (which included Mount Sinai Hospital) refused to unite because each feared the effects of federation on its autonomy as well as on its income. Instead, a loose alliance of twelve agencies came into existence, the Council of Communal Institutions.*

Meanwhile, there was occasional direct participation by Yahudim in downtown charities. Joseph Buttenwieser, a Shearith Israel member, was a vice-president of Beth Israel Hospital, and Daniel Wolf of Temple Emanu-El left bequests to Lebanon Hospital (founded by Yidn) and to a Talmud Torah. In 1901, the Hebrew Sheltering Guardian Society had fifty contributors and an annual budget of $500. After the active intercession of several Guggenheims, its annual contributions climbed to $100,723 and its contributors list to 1800. A building campaign for the same agency saw a $30,000 gift from Adolph Lewisohn; $10,000 from Jacob Schiff; and $1000-and-over gifts from fifteen other New York Yahudim.

The size and complexity of New York's Jewish community bewildered both Yidn and Yahudim in their efforts to find common ground. Doctrinal

* Heinsheimer's bequest reverted to his brother, who used it as a basis for the Heinsheimer Foundation, later known as the New York Foundation.

differences and competing interests were almost certain to doom long-range, large-scale planning unless it could be proved that there were specific financial and functional advantages to federation.

This same problem (albeit less intense) existed elsewhere in the country. Beginning with Boston in 1895, Jewish communities in ten cities had developed federations which usually consisted of a hospital, a relief organization, and two or three educational institutions. Among the benefits discovered was that recalcitrant contributors could no longer claim gift budgets exhausted by previous callers from individual agencies. Listings of gifts also served as social registers and thus stimulated greater generosity. "Where formerly [fund raising] was done by a handful," advised Louis Wolf, president of Philadelphia Jewish Charities, "it is now a part of the life of our community—it is everybody's business (of course, the officers of the Federation principally) to see that everybody else is as large a contributor to the Federation as his means will permit."

New York's Jewry had already attempted federation in the Kehillah, an experiment in communal organization begun in 1909. Its establishment followed in the wake of Police Commissioner Theodore Bingham's charge that 50 percent of New York's crimes were committed by Jews. The Kehillah sought (successfully) to refute the charge and (unsuccessfully) to unite Yidn and Yahudim. For nearly fourteen years, it provided educational and welfare services for the Lower East Side, occupying offices in a Yahudi stronghold, the Italian Renaissance building that headquartered the United Hebrew Charities. Among its six constituent bureaus was one for Philanthropic Research, which conducted a survey of day nurseries, investigated credit unions, and supplied information about Jewish agencies to potential donors. Each constituent financed its own operations. Decentralized fund raising, however, led to one financial crisis after another; finally it led to the dissolution of the Kehillah.

The ten federated cities proved that a *modus vivendi* between Yahudim and Yidn was possible, albeit difficult. In Baltimore and Chicago, antagonisms ran so deep that two federations, one for Yidn and the other for Yahudim, were established in each city. Elsewhere, philanthropic agencies were classified as Uptown (Yahudim) or Downtown (Yidn). Beneficiaries were overwhelmingly Yidn, but contributors had the option to earmark gifts for agencies. Yahudim generally controlled affairs, and federations raised more for constituent groups than the constituent groups had been able to raise individually.

In the end, the calm, ordered efficiency of the federal approach was irresistible to *shtadlanim* in New York. An ad hoc committee of inquiry visited federated and nonfederated communities in 1915 and recommended to Felix Warburg the organization of a New York federation. During 1916, philosophy and financing for the supraagency were hammered out at a series of meetings in Warburg's home. Leo Arnstein, a Mount Sinai trustee, inspired a change in the founding group's name from "Special Committee for the Organization of a Federation of the Contributors to the Jewish Philanthropic Societies in New York" to "Special Committee for the Organization of a Federation for the Support of Jewish Philanthropic Societies of New York City," lest there be any doubt that Federation was an assembly of institutions rather than an assembly of philanthropists. There were concessions to small givers: Warburg wanted downtowners represented in high councils to unify the community and to prevent, at all costs, the formation of a second federation of Yidn.

The overall plan finally developed by the organizing group called for "an increase [in 1917] of $200,000 over the amount contributed . . . in 1916 to the beneficiary societies . . . or $700,000 in excess of the sum contributed by such subscribers in membership dues alone." Each prospective constituent agency was guaranteed the amount it had raised during the previous year. Another inducement to join was the promise that the federation would "make of itself a clearing house for charitable contributions to all members and all societies."

Committee members next got down to a basic—techniques for fund raising. Warburg thought that givers would best be approached on the basis that federation was an accomplished fact lest conservatives withhold gifts while they gauged the success of the initial campaign. There was little question how difficult the job would be. Two million dollars was a lot of charity money in 1917, and this was an appeal exclusively to the Jewish community for Jewish communal purposes.

Not one to merely cite problems, Dr. Harry Friedman, chairman of the Subcommittee on Canvass, offered up a plan to assure a fund raising so smooth that few would have strength to resist the blandishments of solicitors. Thoroughness, a Yahudi characteristic, was its essential feature.

Theater benefits, a downtown staple, would be discarded on the theory that people gave more in donations if they did not have to buy tickets. Between five and six thousand merchants and executives were grouped by trade in fifty prospect categories. As gingerly put in an official history of the agency, "a body of approximately one thousand solicitors [was to] venture forth to solicit gifts of ten dollars or more from these prospects."

Feats of publicity and organization were accomplished to help them. Advertising space was taken in all surface transportation in Manhattan and the Bronx; 400 posters were displayed in Long Island Railroad stations; 700 showings of slides announcing the campaign were made in motion-picture houses throughout Manhattan and the Bronx*; and full-page newspaper advertisements were taken in the *Post*, the *Mail*, the *Tribune*, and other English and German language dailies.

Such was the dedication of leaders and cohorts that when the campaign ended, Warburg and the organization committee heard that over $2 million had been pledged, more than twice as much as the agencies had raised on their own the year before. Harry Sachs, federation treasurer pro tem, concluded that "the conditions set forth in the constitution of the establishment of a Federation have been fulfilled," and within three weeks the organization committee was voted out of existence. In its place appeared a board of trustees with Warburg as president.

The success of the campaign signalled a new order of things, and not only in finances. The upper social levels of the Jewish community began to include a downtown elite. High status at federation was possible despite origins in the Pale. Yet deep in the heart of the Lower East Side, away from the newfound camaraderie of the rich, *proste* Yidn remained suspicious of Yahudim at the head of a unified welfare effort. In February 1917, an editorial in a Yiddish daily complained that a bill before the state assembly calling for incorporation of the federation would give the supraagency "the power to prevent the formation of any new institution in the City, or to close up any existing agency." The writer took a dim view of a clause in the prospective charter noting the necessity to avoid "unnecessary and wasteful duplication of Philanthropic effort," and interpreted this as a sign the federation would declare any agency that

* But not in Brooklyn, which had a Federation of Jewish Charities of its own from 1909. The Brooklyn Federation did not become part of the Greater New York Federation until 1937, when joint fund-raising campaigns became imperative.

displeased it a duplication of another existing agency. A protest meeting was announced in a second Yiddish newspaper.

Judge Aaron Levy, a downtown sympathizer, conferred with Assemblyman Abram Ellenbogen, sponsor of the incorporation bill. There was serious opposition on the Lower East Side, said the judge, and a hearing was imperative. Ellenbogen sensed the possible disappearance of large numbers of Orthodox Jewish votes at crucial elections and decided that it might be wise to recommit the bill to the Judiciary Committee.

Yahudim learned of this, read other attacks in the press, and came to believe that some Yidn might not be motivated by a disinterested search for truth and efficiency in philanthropy. Nonetheless, a counterattack in the press was restrained, as befitted *shtadlanim*. "When the Federation was organized its founders realized well that at the beginning there was bound to be some opposition. This was practically axiomatic," one article noted discouragingly. "We felt certain, however, that this opposition would disappear in time because the idea, although new to New York, has proved its merit and has shown by experience in other cities that it is sure to be successful. . . . We, who stand for Federation in charity, do not propose at any time to control the administration of funds."

Having sounded the sweet voice of reason, I. Edwin Goldwasser, federation executive director, went to Albany and specifically to James A. Foley, Democratic leader of the State Senate. After carefully elucidating for the statesman the federation's success and potential services to New York, Goldwasser expressed the hope that legislators would not become involved in "party politics." Community betterment was the only criterion that would prevail, said Senator Foley, who knew the sources of power in the city. In April the bill was passed and signed by the governor.

PART II

A Tool for Survival

4

Relief, Reconstruction, and Ransom

ON MONDAY, April 6, and on Easter Sunday, April 19, 1903, the Imperial Russian government ushered in a new era in European anti-Semitism with bloody massacres in the Moldavian village of Kishinev. Censors withheld news for days. When details were learned, the world was shocked. This was, after all, the beginning of the twentieth century. Civilized governments did not deliberately encourage religious strife and mob violence. The explanation in Western capitals was that the czarist regime had arrived at this insanity through its inability to rule and its wish to divert attention from that fact, not through any basic hostility to Jews.

It was in accordance with this view that Tolstoy attributed Kishinev to a "propaganda of falsehood and violence." But Russian officials offered another reason: the popularity of Jew-hatred in eastern Europe. Millions believed Jews were willfully exploiting Russian peasants, growing rich in the process, and secretly planning world domination. This sort of thinking made absolutely no sense to enlightened Westerners; yet the ranks of Russian anti-Semites included radicals, aristocrats, peasants, well-to-do businessmen, and intellectuals, among them Feodor Mikhailovich Dostoevsky.

Kishinev inspired mass protests in Europe and America, although demonstrations made no difference in St. Petersburg. *Shtadlanim* urged President Theodore Roosevelt and Secretary of State John Hay to issue a protest, and B'nai B'rith prepared a draft. The Russian ambassador in Washington made it clear that the document would never be considered in the Russian capital. St. Petersburg confirmed this, adding that its foreign minister would not even look at a petition if one was presented to him. No country could tell Russia how to conduct its internal affairs or how to treat its people, a position with which Hay agreed.*

The Kishinev tragedy occurred on the eve of the 250th anniversary of the Sephardic arrival in New Amsterdam, and American Jews could not help compare their peaceful and prosperous lives with those of east European Jews, who appeared doomed unless drastic measures were taken.

But what drastic measures were possible? No one could force the Russians to stop their internal lawlessness. Relief appeared to be the only viable form of help. In June, the American branch of a Kishinev Central Aid Committee raised one-quarter of worldwide relief funds in the first major overseas relief campaign mounted by American Jewry.† At the end of the month, a conference of American and west European Jews trying to organize an exodus collapsed, with Yahudim worried about its cost and the effect on Christians of more Yidn in New York. It was feared that Washington might bar immigration completely if too many Jews suddenly sought entry.

One way the Russians might be brought to their senses would be to withhold money, hoped *shtadlanim.* Although czarist ministers were unwilling to hear complaints about their barbarism, they needed cash desperately and gladly talked with Jewish bankers. The French and British governments prodded financiers to provide loans, but Jacob Schiff urged bankers in both countries to turn down requests unless the Jewish situation in Russia improved. This was an unpleasant surprise for the Russians, who could not simply ignore it as they had public protests about pogroms. Through a Jewish underling, Constantinovich von Phleve, minister of the interior, intimated that if Schiff came to Russia some solu-

* Hay nonetheless made a personal contribution of $500 to the Kishinev Central Aid Committee and wrote Schiff, "I feel precisely as you do in regard to it. . . ."

† $50,000 came through William Randolph Hearst's newspapers in New York, Chicago, and San Francisco.

tion might be found, although it was offensive to Russian dignity to think that "conversations on financial arrangements" could be a basis for Jewish emancipation.

This was the wrong approach to take with Schiff. His brisk and concise response was not quite what Phleve had expected: "If his Excellency . . . really wants me to come he must not expect that I shall appear before him as a suppliant, and he must not say . . . that he is prepared to receive me; he must say that he wishes me to come—and the invitation must be addressed to me direct."

Phleve's invitation came at a low point in Russian fortunes. Schiff's influence had already been a decisive factor in attracting American financing of the Nipponese effort during the Russo-Japanese War. In August 1905, while peace was being negotiated between warring powers, in Portsmouth, New Hampshire, another pogrom occurred in Ekaterinoslav. At that same time, Schiff and a group of *shtadlanim* met Count Sergius de Witte, a Russian envoy. Witte had been Imperial minister of finance from 1892 to 1903 and was among the principal advocates of foreign investment in Russia and possible accommodation with Jewish bankers. Schiff agreed to the meeting with few expectations, "first, because I know it can do no good; secondly, because I do not wish to have it said that I want to discuss Russian finance. . . . There is one thing we can do: To give as hard knocks to Russia as we can. . . ."

At the meeting, Witte took a calm, cool view of Jewish misery, agreeing with the Americans that Russian Jews should be treated better. Unfortunately, they were "not sufficiently prepared for the exercise of full civil rights," and "the feeling" of the Russian people was such that Jews could not be placed on an equal footing "without causing serious internal disorders. . . ." Schiff "made a sharp retort," which Oscar Straus toned down, but Yahudim admitted that many Jews were revolutionaries.

The meeting ended indecisively, as expected. *Shtadlanim* were adamant, but Witte could promise nothing in the way of improvement.

Three months later, Nicholas II asked Witte to head the government, tottering in the aftermath of defeat by the Japanese and the hopeless incompetence of its bureaucracy. The country was reeling, in a state of near anarchy, with mutinies in the fleet, strikes in the civil service, and open revolt in the countryside. Political reform became imperative if bloodier confrontations were to be averted. Witte wrote a manifesto for Nicholas

II's signature "to grant the people their fundamental civil liberties," including parliamentary representation. Reforms calmed popular discontent, inspired hope in the Pale, and brought violent reactions from the far Right. Workers, radicals, students, and Jews were murdered or beaten wherever they could be found. In November 1905, the bloodiest pogroms anyone alive had ever seen swept the Pale in seemingly endless waves of death and destruction.

Compared to this, Kishinev was child's play. When order was restored, 1000 Jews had been slaughtered, 7000 to 8000 injured, and property losses in the millions of rubles were reported. Nicholas had no regrets. His foreign minister, Count Vladimir Nicholaevich Lamsdorf, was convinced that the disorders were actually the work of "World Jewry," especially the Alliance Israélite, which possessed "gigantic pecuniary means," a large membership, and support from a Masonic network. Lamsdorf proposed an alliance with the Kaiser and the Pope to fight the international Jewish menace.

In New York, more meetings were held and 125,000 Jews marched to Union Square in a protest demonstration. Yidn also met to raise money for arms. Schiff cabled Witte that the American people stood aghast at the atrocities and later wrote that the disorders were instigated by "the very authorities who in adequately governed and civilized states exist for the proper protection of life and property."* He received two cablegrams: The first expressed official dismay; the second assured Schiff that authorities would cooperate in relief efforts.

Another international relief effort was hastily organized. Schiff, Straus, and Cyrus Sulzberger sent more than a thousand telegrams soliciting contributions. Christians as well as Jews were deeply concerned, and an American National Committee for the Relief of Sufferers by Russian Massacres raised more than $1.25 million in ninety days. The succession of pogroms also led Cyrus Adler to call on Schiffs, Sulzbergers, Warburgs, Strauses, and Guggenheims, the *crème de la crème* of the Jewish establishment, to meet periodically and ponder national and international issues of concern to Jews. Out of their elite discussion group, the "Wanderers," would come

* Schiff urged President Theodore Roosevelt to intervene militarily, using the recent Cuban intervention as precedent. The United States would be faced by stronger forces than the Spanish navy, however, and the president advised that he would not "threaten aimlessly."

the leadership of the American Jewish Committee, a "religious and social body" that would function as a representative group for American Jews.

Whom, exactly, would it represent? Concerned about radical activity downtown as well as events in the Pale, Yahudim wanted the committee to represent mainly stable Yahudim, not socialists or Zionists. *Shtadlanim* also opted to move quickly lest charismatic leaders in downtown camps whip up support for rival assemblies. "Unless [a national] organization [consists] of the most prudent and discreet elements the standing of the Jews might be seriously affected for the worse," warned Adler. "In order to avoid mischief it [is] desirable that we should take the initiative," the Wanderers thought collectively.

At conferences in February and May 1906, a self-selected Yahudi leadership plunged into organizational work, holding close some earlier tenets of the faith: no funds for emigration and the "emigration of the destitute" strongly discouraged. Six months later, the committee's founders drafted a constitution that stated the object of their mission: "to prevent the infraction of the civil and religious rights of Jews" anywhere in the world. Founders conceived of an agency whose members would be elected by synagogues throughout the country, an idea that originated with Louis Marshall. But as Marshall notes in an early history of the committee, "the only suggestion upon which a majority of the confreres agreed was that a small committee be formed of persons, who, while representative of American Jewry, need not necessarily be formally accredited representatives of any agency or group, nor in a political sense of Jews as a whole."

The problem was the same as with welfare efforts: to find a basis for unified action by those whom the rest of the country insisted on seeing as a homogeneous group, but who, in reality, were bitterly divided among themselves along class, national, economic, and religious lines.

Yet the committee reached a pinnacle of prestige in the Jewish community five years later when it brought to a head efforts to force the Russians to honor passports of American Jews. A commercial treaty signed by the United States and Russia in 1832 bound the two countries to honor the civil rights of each other's citizens, but the Russians' unofficial policy was to refuse American Jews entry. The State Department complained; Russians typically ignored any complaint not backed by the threat of economic or military force. *Shtadlanim* thought that if the

United States abrogated the treaty, Russia's need for trade and especially for foreign capital would force it to admit foreign Jews and possibly even to emancipate its own Jews.

After Pres. William Howard Taft refused to act, Schiff contributed $25,000 for a nationwide campaign to stimulate congressional action. Some 30,000 copies of a speech by Marshall describing Russian violations of the treaty were sent to congressmen, newspaper editors, clergymen, and judges. In New York, a galaxy of business and Democratic political leaders, including Woodrow Wilson, William McAdoo, and William Randolph Hearst, urged repeal on grounds that at stake was the integrity of American citizenship. Congressmen throughout the country were swamped by letters from constituents demanding action. By the end of the year, fifteen state legislatures voted in favor of abrogation, and a House bill for repeal was passed 301 to 1. The Senate passed a similar measure unanimously. On December 17, 1911, Taft announced repeal would become effective on December 31, 1912.*

Downtowners were overjoyed by results of the campaign, but many Yidn continued to be implacable in their hostility to Yahudim. Willing to try anything in the quest for unity and assimilation, Marshall learned to read in Yiddish and published a Yiddish newspaper. Schiff regularly appeared on the streets of the Lower East Side. Immigrants alternately loved and hated Schiff and Marshall, but the American Jewish Committee was consistently attacked in the Yiddish press, as before. "We seek recognition for eight times a hundred thousand souls, for a hundred thousand voters, for thousands of doctors and lawyers and for tens of thousands of businessmen," said the *Tageblatt*, a Yiddish newspaper. A central authority like the committee might be necessary, but could be successful only if *shtadlanim* "worked with us and not over us."

It seemed impossible to form a command structure capable of tying uptowners led by *shtadlanim* to downtowners led, at first, by nobody. At least not until Judah Magnes fortuitously stepped forward. Twenty-nine years old in 1906, Judah Magnes was associate rabbi of Temple Emanu-El and Marshall's brother-in-law. He was born in San Francisco and was

* Taft sought some way to the last to continue relations with the Russians. In an effort to head off congressional action, he suggested a joint American-Russian statement that the old treaty was being terminated in hopes of speedily renegotiating an updated one. The Russians refused to go along with him.

educated in Heidelberg, Berlin, and at the citadel of American Reform Judaism, Cincinnati's Hebrew Union College. He had held a pulpit in Brooklyn. He was bursting with idealism, warmth, intelligence, and wit, and he had been enchanted by the *Yiddishkeit* he found on a trip to eastern Europe. Magnes returned sporting a beard and observing dietary laws.

It was Magnes who led Jews up Fifth Avenue in 1905 to protest massacres, and it was Magnes's name that headed a committee that sponsored an "Appeal to the Jewish organizations of New York City" calling for unity in 1908. Magnes wrote Marshall that he was proud "of the indignation of our Jews and of their readiness at their mass meetings . . . to resent insult. This is the way every healthy and manly people gives expression to its elemental emotions." For Magnes, the American Jewish Committee would create a united Jewry only when it was "alive to its great duty of leadership."

Magnes pleaded as hard downtown for Yahudim as he did uptown for Yidn. "Mr. Marshall represents, in some measure, that section of the community with leadership and wealth," he wrote the editor of the *Tageblatt*. "You . . . represent in some measure, that section of the community with our masses and our hopes. An army without leaders is almost as absurd as leaders without an army. The opportunity is now at hand for leaders and soldiers to recognize the need they have of each other and to join ranks."

Six years later, Magnes's metaphor of American Jewry as an army in which Yahudim were generals and Yidn were soldiers was realized in a way he never dreamed.

In July 1914, Germany's war plan called for an overpowering offensive on the Western Front with a holding action in the east. Russia's General Alexander Samsonov conceived a plan to encircle a German army, thus opening the way for an attack on Berlin. But in great battles at Tannenberg and the Masurian Lakes in August and September, German armies utterly demolished ill-equipped and incredibly badly led czarist forces. Millions of Russians were killed, wounded, or taken prisoner.

Defeats on this scale were rare in any country's history. Russian generals accepted the huge losses in manpower, but blows to military reputation were something else. Scapegoats were needed to shift attention elsewhere, and

Jews were accused of contributing to disasters by spying on behalf of the Germans. Men, women, and children were executed for treasonable offenses without a scrap of evidence or even the formality of trials.

Large-scale expulsion of Jews from their villages began in March 1915. Two months later, a mighty Austro-German offensive in Galicia and Bukovina swept everything before it, leaving additional thousands homeless and hungry. In Lemberg, a reporter saw "dens filled with masses of naked people; 50 percent of the population was literally dying from cold and hunger." A cholera epidemic in Poland was stamped out by the Germans for their own safety, but in Warsaw, Jews were decimated by recurrent typhoid epidemics. Vilna was flooded with refugees. The annual Jewish death rate, 20.4 per 1000 before 1914, rose to more than double that in December 1916, and reached 97.5 per 1000 in March 1917.

Russia was on the verge of total collapse when the Imperial government again approached American bankers for loans. *Shtadlanim* remained adamant in their opposition to financial transactions unless there were changes in the legal status of Jews. At Kuhn, Loeb, Otto Kahn and Mortimer Schiff leaned toward underwriting an Allied War Loan in which the Russians participated. Jacob Schiff would agree only if no money went to Russia. The matter was dropped.

Cataclysmic events in the Pale received wide coverage in the press, and soon after the outbreak of war, Yidn and Yahudim alike searched for some way to alleviate the terrible suffering. No American Jewish overseas relief agency existed—the American National Committee for the Relief of Sufferers by Russian Massacres had long since closed its doors—and in the void three distinct groups organized separate fund-raising campaigns. The Orthodox were first, in early October 1914, with a Central Committee for the Relief of Jewish War Sufferers. A few weeks later the American Jewish Committee came forth with an American Jewish Relief Committee headed by Louis Marshall, with Felix Warburg as treasurer. Ten months later, socialists and labor groups launched the People's Relief Committee.

This led to confusion on several levels, including definition of purpose. Yahudim and the Orthodox wanted funds used to help Yidn stay where they were, socialists felt Jews should be readied for the imminent collapse of capitalism, and Zionists wanted funds used to evacuate survivors to Palestine after the conflict.

Shtadlanim also worried about overseas fund-raising campaigns specifically geared to benefit Jews. How would this look to non-Jews? Warburg wrote Marshall that the American Red Cross might be given "an excuse for excluding the Jewish sufferers from help. . . ." Similar fears were voiced in Cincinnati by Rabbi David Philipson and in Chicago by Julius Rosenwald, president of Sears Roebuck. Schiff answered flatly that "a Jew would rather cut his hand off than apply for relief from non-Jewish sources." Marshall wondered who would help eastern European Jewry if not American Jewry. Could Yidn be abandoned to the mercies of the Russians or to the German High Command?

The prospects forced an immediate, albeit uneasy, unity on downtowners and uptowners. In November 1914, representatives from dozens of agencies attended a Temple Emanu-El meeting for discussions about forming a temporary agency to distribute relief funds in the Pale. That passion for exquisite detail which marked the philanthropic exercises of Yahudim in general and Felix Warburg in particular was soon evident. Forty organizations appointed a committee of five under Judah Magnes's chairmanship to head a federation, the Joint Distribution Committee of American Funds for the Relief of Jewish War Sufferers (JDC). Marshall was elected president and Warburg was elected treasurer. An uptowner, an Orthodox leader, a socialist, a Zionist, and a midwestern community leader who leaned toward Zionism comprised the committee of five. Orthodox and Yahudi relief committees joined JDC immediately; the People's Relief Committee joined soon after in the fall of 1915.

All this time, anxious Yidn on the Lower East Side sought ways to send private remittances into the Pale. Locating survivors appeared an insurmountable problem, but HIAS dispatched a representative named Isidore Herschfield to eastern Europe with instructions to organize committees "in every Polish and Russian city and town, which committees shall gather data regarding the people now living in those towns who wish to get into communication with their relatives in America."

This seemingly impossible assignment did not discourage Herschfield, an intrepid sort. In Poland, he found the German-Jewish agency, Hilfsverein der deutschen Juden, "splendidly equipped" to forward messages. Herschfield proceeded to enlist the cooperation of German and Austrian authorities in a gigantic mail campaign. Thousands of letters from refugees were sent through the Hilfsverein to the HIAS office in New York, at which point downtowners picked them up. By the end of the war, 250,000 messages had been processed. In addition, the *Forward* carried pages listing the names of individuals from whom it had received letters directly or via the European Yiddish press. JDC took responsibility for a system through which millions of dollars in private remittances were transferred.

On the other hand, fund raising lagged badly, moving at an agonizingly slow pace through 1914 and most of 1915. Jews might be "solemnly admonished" to contribute, but competitive drives by socialists, Zionists, and the Orthodox fragmented campaigns. Nor could Yahudim grasp the full dimensions of new international obligations suddenly thrust on American Jewry. "Our showing thus far is pitiable," Marshall wrote Schiff in December 1914; a year later, only $1.5 million had been raised.

Clearly, the bulk of contributions would have to come from the American Jewish Relief Committee. More specifically, Schiff, Warburg, Nathan Straus, and other *shtadlanim* would make the large gifts that spelled success. No one was completely blind to these realities, but after Straus proposed a startling $5 million JDC goal in 1915, even *shtadlanim* deemed it necessary to broaden the constituency of givers via mass appeals and to bring order and systematic canvassing to overseas relief campaigns.

Increasingly dire news from the Pale led to "democratization of philanthropy": publicizing the number of workers who contributed a day's wages as well as listing major gifts from the rich. A fund-raising apparatus that recognized class differences but stressed mass participation began to take shape. The People's Relief Committee concentrated on house-to-house collections, appeals in synagogues were the province of the Orthodox, and large gifts from Yahudim were channeled through the American Jewish Relief Committee.

Egalitarian fund raising worried Yahudim, who foresaw a Yiddish majority seeking control of overseas spending, perhaps even urging vast migrations to the United States. A bright side was found. Downtowners could be put under close supervision in a unified campaign, kept from roaming New York and soliciting any prospect they could get their hands on. Moreover, thought Schiff, everyone's help might be necessary.

The first mass fund-raising campaign in American Jewish history was launched at a December 1915 Carnegie Hall meeting. Magnes, the man everyone trusted, made the appeal. Basing his speech on the moral worth of charity—a message *shtetl*-bred Jews easily grasped—he was effective as perhaps no other man of the time could be. "As he spoke, women and then men wept and sobbed," said a New York *Times* reporter, "and then a dozen, and then hundreds, rushed forward to put their offerings at his feet." That night, $400,000 in cash and pledges was raised. After similar meetings around the country and mass canvassing by the Orthodox and socialists, more than $4.3 million was raised.

American Jews had never seen anything quite like this outpouring, and in the summer of 1916, Magnes traveled to eastern Europe to draft a report on the distribution of relief funds.* For four months the Germans allowed him to visit Warsaw, Vilna, Lodz, and Lüblin. The Russians would not permit him to travel in their territory. Horrified by the suffering and destruction he saw—of 1.76 million Jews, over 700,000 needed help urgently—Magnes could only wonder about conditions inside Russia. He returned to New York praising German-Jewish relief agencies and predicting that $10 million in relief funds would be needed in 1917.

Magnes's praise for German agencies led Yahudim to suspect that he was pro-German and Yidn to suspect that he was pro-assimilationist. Few believed American Jews could raise $10 million. As late as 1913, the most highly organized agency in America, the YMCA, had managed $4 million in New York only after considerable effort.

At another Carnegie Hall meeting chaired by Schiff in December 1916, Magnes again implored American Jews to help brethren in eastern Europe.† Contributions and pledges of $1 million were raised on the spot.‡ The "pace-setting" gift, designed to inspire contributors to dig deeper by challenging them to better things, was introduced to Jewish philanthropy. Julius Rosenwald offered to contribute 10 percent of all

* The trip was also an opportunity to clarify working relationships between American givers and the German-Jewish agencies actually distributing relief. There had been bitter complaints about JDC's "complicated schemes" and "numberless instructions." In Berlin, Max Warburg warned that it would become "simply impossible for us to carry on our relief work in occupied territories, . . ." unless less rigorous procedures were adopted. During his trip, Magnes insisted wide publicity be given the fact that relief funds came from America.

† "I bring you greetings, Jews of America," said Magnes, "from the Jews of Poland, of Lithuania, of Galicia. I bring you greetings from the Jewish people almost about to die."

‡ There were four "anonymous" pledges of $100,000 each from Schiff, Julius Rosenwald, Nathan Straus, and the Guggenheim brothers. In Chicago, Albert Lasker said he would raise $500,000.

funds raised, up to an astounding $1 million, if others raised the remaining $9 million. Rosenwald, like most Yahudim, had previously been an inhibited giver for overseas relief. In 1914, he had made an anonymous donation of $10,000, increasing his gift by only $5000 the following year.

The offer had an electrifying effect on prospective contributors. In Omaha, Morris Levy, a local businessman, said he would give $100 for every $1000 raised in that city. In fifty-nine other communities, Jewish communal leaders said they also wanted to become Julius Rosenwalds and contribute ten percent of local goals. Workers said they would contribute one dollar out of twenty they earned. Reporting to social workers at the 1918 convention of the National Conference of Jewish Charities, Jacob Billikopf, who had directed the drive and asked Rosenwald for the million dollars, said that "there is not a city in America where there is a single Jewish inhabitant in which at one time or another, we have not made an appeal."*

Half the funds were raised in New York. Here some 150,000 prospects were solicited by forty-two teams of volunteers spurred on by speakers who, "after the fashion of liberty-loan orators, whipped up enthusiasm." Team receipts, printed weekly in the *American Hebrew*, were followed as closely as baseball scores. Basic findings in prospect psychology were put to immediate use. Guilt was found to be one essential ingredient in Jewish fund raising—who could face his fellow Jews if he wasn't generous?—and *koved* was discovered to be another. "If a large number of individuals with good ratings† were approached and *asked to become chairmen* [italics added] of the Jewish War Relief Committee in their own towns, the amounts obtained in excess of previous years would be substantial," Billikopf told admiring listeners.

Contributing on a per capita basis between two-and-a-half and three times as much as non-Jews to overseas relief, Jews also continued to give generously to local federations. When the 1917 War Relief campaign was concluded, Felix Warburg and his New York Federation cohorts

* For this achievement, Billikopf had the model of Red Cross campaigns in 1917 and 1918, which marked the beginning of mass charity drives in America. Big-business techniques of quotas and tight organization were introduced with results that startled organizers and givers. In 1904, the Red Cross had $1702 in a bank account; in 1917 and 1918, it raised $273.2 million.

† Evaluations of a prospect's capacity to make gifts.

launched an equally successful appeal for local agencies. Warburg told the 1919 National Conference of Jewish Charities that philanthropy had now "wiped out" class antagonisms among Jews and predicted that increased Jewish giving would "have as great effect on American life as upon Jewish life." Privately he envisioned the American Jewish Relief Committee as a "parent organization for all Jewish activities, relief and patriotic, with offices in every town to cover education, Y.M.C.A. [sic], welfare, here and abroad. . . ." The "main thing" was to keep people interested and to make sure that "cliques" were not running things.

But Jewish success in raising money had a depressing effect on Yahudim. Secretary of War Newton Baker disapproved of separate Jewish relief campaigns and asked why Jews couldn't simply work through the Red Cross,* a question certain to unsettle nervous big givers. Marshall forthrightly responded that the Red Cross was not equipped to distribute relief funds in eastern Europe. Moreover, it had no Jew in a position of authority. He continued, "The Red Cross does not understand that, in the distribution of funds for the Jewish war sufferers in Poland and Rumania for instance, it would be utterly impossible for any help to reach the Jews unless the money were distributed under Jewish auspices." In Poland, an economic boycott against Jews initiated in 1912 was still in force, "more virulent than ever"; neither the president of the Polish National Committee nor the Polish premier was willing to call it off. "It should also be remembered," continued Marshall, "that, with great difficulty, we have organized distribution committees which are well calculated to accomplish the best results with the least possible expense and friction. The Red Cross would not be able to duplicate them."

Despite pride, acclaim, efficient distribution committees, and a $30,-158,588 income between 1914 and 1919, JDC remained an uneasy alliance of Yidn and Yahudim. Marshall insisted JDC was not a fund-raising agency and scrupulously ordered an American Jewish Relief Committee field man to stay out of synagogue campaigns for overseas relief funds. Downtowners attacked JDC's efficiency as a distribution agency and were apt to doubt the motives of the rich at the head of things, always making speeches, announcing gifts, toasting each other at banquets, and trying to

* In fairness to Baker, he sought to include all Catholic and Protestant agencies as well.

ignore the masses. *Landsmanschaften* raised $1 million a year for overseas relief and trusted no one but themselves to spend it. In May 1920, Yiddish dailies reported that sixty-two delegates from fraternal agencies were en route to Europe, the envoy to Pinsk armed with $175,000.

"The Jewish public [is] fast losing confidence," reported Magnes, head of JDC's executive committee. "It is ready to believe anything derogatory, however fantastic and impossible the report might in fact be." Yidn thought malfeasance, not currency exchange problems, caused recipients of private remittances in Poland to get less than exact sums sent through JDC. By the end of 1920, JDC lost $1 million on such transactions; Marshall angrily considered discontinuing the remittance program because of the "unreasonable attitudes" of downtowners. Finally the program was terminated, only to arouse cries of betrayal from the same people who had complained about it.

The Lower East Side also detected a Yahudi plot in efforts to quiet Yiddish critics of American immigration policies. As the doors in Washington slammed shut on further mass departures from eastern Europe during the early 1920s, *shtadlanim* privately sent protests to Washington. Publicly they admonished Yidn not to protest too loudly, offering as a reason the need to avoid focusing attention on Jews.*

On their part, big givers of the American Jewish Relief Committee were weary of noisy downtowners and constant pleas for money. A massive loan to east Europeans was considered, then dropped. Some Yahudim thought JDC itself should be dissolved. In March 1920, Magnes was certain that the time for "popular drives" had passed; savants such as Jacob Billikopf racked their brains seeking new methods "to separate folk from their money." Warburg threatened to resign as chairman, and young Herbert Lehman vowed to follow him out of the agency rather than be elected chairman. After Schiff's death in October 1920 there was no supreme patriarch to fortify the rich in moments of doubt and confusion. Yahudim looked to French and British Jews to shoulder more of the burden. In Versailles to attend peace talks in 1919, Louis Marshall

* "The American Jewish Committee . . . has devoted itself to this subject, and yet every little lodge and society deems it necessary to send its representatives to Washington," Marshall wrote Abraham Cahan of the *Forward*. "The result [is] that the Jews are frequently placed in a most inconsistent and ridiculous position."

told Baron Edmond de Rothschild that $25 million would be needed to restore the Jewries of eastern Europe and a third of this amount would have to come from European coreligionists.

Whatever else the Versailles talks brought, peace in eastern Europe was not among the benefits. Postwar years were marked by famine and destruction that have yet to find a chronicler. Communist, White Russian, and nationalist armies fought savagely over parts of the czarist empire while populations scavenged in the ruins for crusts of bread and rags. The Ukraine became the Flanders of the east, a battleground in which armies degenerated into rival bands of pillagers and cutthroats preying on a citizenry that now included Jews emancipated by the Bolsheviks in 1917.

What this catastrophe cost in Jewish lives during two black years, 1919 and 1920, we shall never know. Estimates are 200,000 killed in the Ukraine; 300,000 children orphaned; and 700,000 people left homeless. Families were scattered as far away as the Ural Mountains and Siberia. Tens of thousands fled to the cities of central Russia, in the largest mass movement since the exodus to America.

The Alliance Israélite appealed to the newly-formed League of Nations: "From Odessa to Vilna a multitude of people, maddened by their sufferings, are appealing for help, and in despair, are preparing to abandon their homes. The countries on the other side of the Atlantic are watching with alarm the arrival of the first batches of emigrants. The problem is fundamentally an international one. . . . Only the League of Nations can undertake this formidable task and all the problems it involves." The league, simultaneously importuned for help by the newly-founded states of Poland, Hungary, Czechoslovakia, Lithuania, Latvia, and Estonia, did not see Jews as an isolated, vulnerable people. Aid would be distributed through national governments. It was useless to point out that several of these governments had already demonstrated anti-Semitism. Meetings between league officials and Jewish leaders were followed by little more than expressions of sympathy.

Six months later, the Jewish Colonization Association invited major organizations to a conference in Brussels. Delegates read appeals from Yidn willing to go anywhere rather than stay in eastern Europe. Representatives of the great American, British, French, and German relief agencies agreed that only those individuals "fit" for overseas life should be encouraged to leave. No central emigration council was created. East Europeans were to remain where they were, lest they "schnor their way through Europe."

In September 1921, Zionist groups and other Jewish agencies held a similar conference in Prague, shunned by the Jewish Colonization Association, the Alliance Israélite, the Anglo-Jewish Association, and JDC. Yahudim refused to participate in any discussions likely to stimulate emigration. Yet one result of the Prague conference was EMIGDIRECT, a coordinating body with committees in sixteen countries seeking outlets in South America and Canada for east European Jews.

By mid-1921, the scope of the tragedy in eastern Europe impressed Washington with the need for immediate and massive relief if millions were not to die of starvation. Although the United States had no liking for the communist state whose economic policies helped bring on famines, it was unwilling to see Russia and Poland reduced to the level of central Europe after the Thirty Years' War. An American Relief Administration founded by Herbert Hoover to feed Belgians was given $100 million by Congress to distribute food and medical supplies in eastern Europe. Hoover could not see that Jews needed preferential treatment: They were now emancipated citizens of democracies. Moreover, Washington did not want private American relief agencies operating in Poland, which was preparing for a war with Russia.

Like Secretary of War Baker, Hoover wanted JDC to turn over its funds to the Red Cross. In August 1921, Felix Warburg finally convinced him that Jews were not being accorded the same rights as other eastern European peoples and might not receive any aid at all if distribution was entrusted to the new governments. A separate Jewish relief effort was then permitted—after a JDC contribution of $3.3 million to the Relief Administration, half to be used for a Polish Relief Committee.

In 1920, thousands of JDC solicitors asked prospects, "Suppose you were starving?" and the response was another great spurt of contributions that totaled $20.6 million between 1921 and 1924. Canvassing reached new heights. New York's motor vehicle bureau was carefully watched; as names of Jewish automobile purchasers were listed, each was approached "for a fitting contribution." The city was assigned a $7.5 million goal, in recognition of the many Yidn who had earned large sums during the war. Downtowners entered the upper reaches of the Jewish establishment as their contributions to overseas relief equaled those of Yahudim.

In this "last phase" of JDC operations, during which requests for help totaled $250 million, a fateful decision was made to concentrate on a vast "reconstruction" of Jewish life in eastern Europe. Relief might demoralize recipients, and mass emigration had to be discouraged. Bernhard Kahn, formerly of the Hilfsverein and now of JDC, feared that Polish Jews would "become accustomed to throwing all burdens upon their American brethren, just as before the war they placed them upon their European and American brethren. . . ." Therefore, credit unions, vocational schools, orphanages, old-age homes, hospitals, and tuberculosis sanitariums would replace the destroyed institutions of *shtetl* life, enabling Yidn to begin anew. To this end, in 1924, JDC and the Jewish Colonization Association established the American Joint Reconstruction Foundation.

The crown of reconstruction operations was "Agro-Joint," a combined JDC-Soviet effort begun in 1924, in large part the creation of Dr. Joseph Rosen, an American-trained JDC agronomist who was born in the Pale. Rosen returned to Russia in 1921 to find thousands of Jews wandering aimlessly; he believed they could be successfully settled on the land, not in the cities to which they were gravitating. In January 1925, the communist leadership of KOMZET (Committee for the Settlement of Jewish Workers on the Land) developed a plan to settle 500,000 Jews in the Ukraine and Crimea by December 1926. Some 40,000 families applied immediately, but the Russians were woefully short of money to finance transportation and to purchase farm equipment. Many of KOMZET's leaders were Jewish, and they sought funding in the traditional manner by appealing for help to Jewries in western Europe and America, no matter what their political leanings.

For once, radicals and Yahudim agreed on something: keeping Yidn in Russia. Soviet leaders denied that Jews were a separate nation within a nation, urged rapid assimilation, and presented an alternative to Zionist arguments for a mass exodus from eastern Europe to the Holy Land. KOMZET also stressed agriculture over commerce and self-help over perpetual charity. In an agreement with the Russians, $8 million in 5 percent Soviet bonds, about one third of the total cost of the program, were placed on the American market. Julius Rosenwald, whose personal worth was estimated between $200 and $300 million, bought $5 million worth of the securities. Felix Warburg took $1 million worth, and John D. Rockefeller, Jr., bought $500,000.

Between 1924 and 1928, 100,000 Jews were settled on 1 million acres of Jewish collective farms in the Crimea and in other Ukrainian provinces. Ten years later, 300,000 Jews were living on 3 million acres, far more Jews and acreage than Zionists could claim in Palestine. Soviet leaders used this success to prove that their agricultural technology was highly advanced and that a Jewish existence was possible in Russia. A self-reliant Jewish yeomanry, no longer living by barter or bargain, was unwilling to emigrate. Furthermore, colonies approached self-sufficiency and needed less American aid; settlers raised their own funds to finance construction and operations. By 1938, collectives were completely self-supporting, and JDC handed over full control to Jewish agriculturalists and to the Russians.*

With east European Jews relatively well anchored, the great Yahudi relief agencies of Europe and America breathed a sigh of relief: a period of crisis had passed with no great exodus.

Yidn, too, appeared content. Relief activities could be safely unified; in 1927, the Hebrew Immigrant Aid Society, the Jewish Colonization Association, and EMIGDIRECT formed HICEM (an acrostic of agency names) and jointly established an office in Berlin, capital of the country with the most highly-assimilated Jewry in Europe.

Perhaps philanthropy could divert attention not only from Zionists but from Jewish radicals at home, hoped Yahudim in the 1920s. In 1919, Attorney General A. Mitchell Palmer estimated that there were 5 million communists, socialists, and assorted left-wingers, many of them Jewish, exhorting the American masses to strife. Flappers, avant-garde social thinkers, and Jews were denounced in the Dearborn (Michigan) *Independent*, a newspaper into which Henry Ford, the automobile tycoon, poured millions of dollars. "Lately, I have been made aware of my Jewishness," said a writer in the *Nation* after a year of Ford anti-Semitism

* The communists then eased Jews out of positions of authority. Three years later, the Germans invaded Russia and put to death the Jews in the colonies; of 300,000 people, no survivors were found.

in which Yahudim were lumped with Yidn as sinister enemies of western, or at least American, civilization. Opening fire on Ford in June 1920, Louis Marshall telegraphed the magnate that two recent articles in the *Independent* were a "libel upon an entire people" and three million "deeply wounded" Jews were awaiting an "answer."

Thus began a seven-and-a-half-year contest in which Ford paid for publication of ninety-one anti-Semitic articles in the *Independent*, as well as reprints and translations into foreign languages. Yahudim responded with letters from Marshall and a protest against anti-Semitism issued by the Federal Council of the Churches of Christ signed by Woodrow Wilson, William Howard Taft, Newton Baker, and Clarence Darrow. In January 1928, Ford suddenly reversed himself, appeared in Marshall's office, and declared his anti-Jewish publications a "great mistake and blunder." "Henry wanted me to see his new car and asked me to select any of his products that I might desire," wrote Marshall to his son, James, but the *shtadlan* settled for a recantation and apology in writing to the Jews of America.

Why did Ford change course? Economics was probably the major reason. A Jewish boycott of Ford products and a $1-million suit brought by a Jewish lawyer in Detroit undoubtedly helped. But to Marshall and other Yahudim, his recantation was owing to solid arguments against anti-Semitism, Jewish stoicism in the face of insults, and the basic good sense of the American people.* The American Jewish Committee continued to loose floods of educational materials and hold private meetings between influential Jewish and Christian business and government leaders. The Anti-Defamation League of B'nai B'rith, created in 1913, kept careful track of slurs, held publicity on anti-Semitic incidents to a minimum, and sought court action against the prejudiced only as a last resort.

Much the same attitude characterized the leaders of German Jewry. Adolf Hitler's early anti-Semitic speeches were not minimized, but few people thought Nazism a social disease education could not cure. The Centralverein deutscher Staatsbürger jüdischen Glaubens, a German equivalent of the American Jewish Committee and the Anti-Defamation

* If not Ford's good sense. He later required suppliers serving the Ford Motor Company to contribute to Gerald L. K. Smith's violently anti-Semitic Christian Nationalist Crusade.

League, told Yahudim in New York that its members were "thoroughly able to hold our own and to fight successfully against the attacks made by Mr. Hitler and his followers." To be on the safe side, materials listing Jewish contributions to the economic and cultural life of Germany and expounding rational arguments against fascism were widely distributed. It was assumed this information would make a deep impression on a literate, intelligent public.

In 1928, the Centralverein appealed to the American Jewish Committee for $175,000 to pay publication costs. It wanted no advice on how to fight the menace. Marshall was disinterested, asking why rich German Jews couldn't pay the bills themselves. Anyway, Marshall felt the best policy was to ignore the whole thing: "we laughed this nonsense [the *Protocols*, Ford, and the Ku Klux Klan] out of court and succeeded in enlisting the sympathy of intelligent American opinion," Marshall wrote David Waldman, executive secretary of the American Jewish Committee.

At the outset of anti-Jewish persecution, Nazi policy was to encourage speedy emigration anywhere Jews could find a haven. Zionists and the Reich Ministry of Economics negotiated a large-scale exodus to the Holy Land in August 1933.* Some 50,000 Jews emigrated to Palestine during the next six years, but a large number returned, convinced that Nazism was a temporary aberration. Furthermore, Zionism was never a popular ideology in central Europe, and many Jews still thought that religious conversion or the economic value of their professions would buy safety.

Parallel to this relatively benign early Nazi persecution, however, was a growing consensus in Germany that Jews should be eliminated from national life. The atmosphere grew increasingly threatening and unreal. Nazi policy was accepted as beneficial by large sections of the public. "For years we told the people 'You can settle accounts with traitors, . . .' " said Hermann Goering, president of the Reichstag and prime minister of Prussia. "We stand by our word. Accounts are being settled." Recognizing the signal, the professional association of German physicians promptly

* Before leaving Germany, Jews paid their liquid assets into a "Palestine Trust Company for the Assistance of German Jews," which in turn financed Haavara, a company managing the transfer to Jewish capital. Funds were used to pay for emigration and for German products exported to Palestine.

declared that "no Jew should be permitted to undertake the medical care of German citizens."

At an American Jewish Committee Special Conference the rich met to urge solid, rational arguments at home and abroad as a first line of defense. "The first essential will be to analyze the misconceptions," said William Lieberman. Taking the idea a Napoleonic step further, Leo Wolfson suggested a "solemn conclave of the Jews of the world," which would prepare materials and "answer before the world every accusation that has been leveled against us." Conditions couldn't be all that bad, thought Ludwig Vogelstein: "Anybody who has lived in Germany in former times . . . will feel that there is no immediate danger." Rabbi David Philipson of Cincinnati counseled "that these outbreaks are not the expression of the German people or the German government." Buttenwiesers and Strauses formulated ideas for radio shows, religious booklets, and interfaith tolerance programs. Columbia's Professor Allan Nevins was recruited to keep a sharp eye out for anti-Semitic statements in history textbooks, and Cyrus Adler called on Secretary of State Cordell Hull to intercede on behalf of German Jews.

The American Jewish Committee and B'nai B'rith countered anti-Semitism with reason, radio, and the printed word, but labor unions and Zionists opted for a boycott of German goods, sponsored by the American Jewish Congress in August 1933. Yahudim fought the boycott, fearing Jew-baiters would claim it was proof positive of an international Jewish economic conspiracy. Several major New York department stores, some owned by Jews, refused to participate. Thus handicapped,* the boycott failed to make a serious dent in German exports to the United States, and no product, with the exception of cotton gloves, declined in sales by more than $1 million. Imports of chemicals, machinery, cameras, and vegetable products increased.

Confusion was further compounded by the Depression, a house collapsing on 100 million people, a nightmare of unemployment, despair, and destitution in which Jewish philanthropy was paralyzed and Jewish insecurity increased, with the likelihood that any search for scapegoats would begin and end with Jews.

* The boycott effort was also materially weakened when Zionists concluded the Haavara agreement with Nazis for the export of German goods to Palestine.

By 1931, overseas relief figured so low in the priorities of both Yahudim and Yidn that it took a personal plea from Albert Einstein to keep JDC alive. Income fell precipitously: in 1932, it dropped to $385,000. From 1930 to 1935, annual contributions for European relief and Palestine averaged thirty-seven cents per American Jew. Only 50,000 people out of New York City's 2.5 million Jewish residents contributed, and Felix Warburg declared, "there are no rich Jews left."*

But something had to be done for German Jewry, still largely unwilling to emigrate and yet despoiled on a greater scale each day. In 1935, a JDC staff member calculated that as much money would be needed for overseas relief and reconstruction in the next two years as had been raised since 1914—the impossible sum of $85 million. During an October international conference of Jewish leaders in London, the costs of transportation, reeducation, and resettlement of German Jewry were again calculated. Only American Jewry had the resources to bear the load, decided delegates, but the American representative, Lewis Strauss, responded that funds were simply not available in the midst of a depression.

In September 1933, the League of Nations created a High Commission for Refugees from Germany and put James McDonald, an American, in charge. The League was bending over backwards not to antagonize Germany, and the commission was powerless at birth, its purpose mainly to raise funds for relief and to find havens for refugees. McDonald refused to become a "Jewish High Commissioner" and tried to steer a middle course between Yahudim, who wanted meetings limited to big givers, and Zionists, who were pushing their own vision of the future. Adding to the discord, the Jewish Colonization Association, the only Jewish relief agency in the world with vast cash reserves, refused to spend anything for refugees unless resettlement projects were "constructive" and capital expenditures could be recovered.

Early in 1935, McDonald resigned, frustrated and bitter after two years and two months of seemingly useless activity. In Brussels, he found aristocratic Jews who needed education on their "basic oneness with German Jews"; in London, he found Jewish leaders unwilling "to face the realities." In New York, Yahudim complained to each other that German

* But he was able to give New York Federation $100,000 in 1932 and Hebrew University $100,000 in 1933. Fifty-four percent of JDC's income came from 1¼ percent of its givers.

Jews were not doing enough for themselves, and Warburg argued that there would be an increase in anti-Semitism if efforts to raise money were construed "as an effort by Jews for Jews from Jews."

McDonald's letter of resignation and appended documents filled twenty-seven printed pages; the basic point was that persecution within Germany must be stopped. Philanthropy alone could not solve the problem; a "terrible human calamity" was in the making unless political action was taken. Yet philanthropy was essential if lives were to be saved.

As if to underscore McDonald's words, conditions grew worse in Germany. "Out with [the Jews] from all the professions and into the ghettos with them," Hitler told his closest associates after the Nazi party rally in Nüremberg that produced the infamous "blood laws." "Fence them in somewhere where they can perish as they deserve while the German people look on, the way people stare at wild animals." For the "survival of the German race" marriage and sexual relations between Aryans and Jews were forbidden. Non-Aryans were stripped of citizenship.

In Berlin, *shtadlanim* were still unwilling to approve mass departures. The Centralverein announced "the solution of the Jewish problem" was within Germany and urged Jewish relief agencies to provide funds for "reconstruction," not for emigration. To depart was to admit tacitly that Nazis were right, there was no place for Jews in the new Reich. A broader coalition of German Jews including Zionists and workers, the Reichsvertretung der Deutschen Juden, protested the racial laws and called on Nazis to cease defaming Jews and boycotting their businesses. No one had any illusions that protests would change conditions, but something had to be done to lift morale: 8000 Jews had committed suicide by the end of 1935. The relief needs of a once rich and powerful Jewry were soaring. Professionals—doctors, lawyers, architects—could work only for the rapidly dwindling number of Jewish clients able to pay them. Merchants were equally at a loss, although many Christians continued to patronize their stores. Between 1933 and 1936, JDC appropriated more than $3 million for relief in Germany, and in 1937, it met one-third of total costs.

During the 1933–35 phase of Nazi rule, thousands of German Jews agreed with the Centralverein leadership that some solution within Germany was desirable. But by the end of 1935 it was clear that no solution was possible. Thousands clamored outside offices of foreign consulates and pleaded for visas to any place on earth that would provide asylum. No country would permit Jewish refugees to immigrate in large numbers. Up to 1935, the traditional haven of refugees, the United States, insisted on strict compliance with immigration laws.*

In January 1936, three prominent British Jews, Sir Herbert Samuel, Viscount Bearsted, and Simon Marks, came to New York to offer JDC a plan under which 20,000 to 25,000 German Jews between the ages of seventeen and thirty-five would emigrate each year to Palestine and to other countries. The plan called for a $15-million fund to be raised over a four-year period, one-third of it to be solicited in Europe and two-thirds in America. While no agreement was actually reached, discussions led to a concession by JDC that limited emigration, rather than reconstruction, might be the only real hope.†

Later in the year there was a sudden hiatus in violent German anti-Semitism. Many thought the radical era of Nazi rule had past. German officials said that 25,000 Jews would be permitted to leave annually after the payment of "flight" taxes. In July, McDonald announced the creation of a $10 million Refugee Economic Corporation; Warburg, who helped raise the money, hoped for a new and businesslike approach to relief.

But even if Nazis let them out, where would the Jews go? Countries throughout the world barred their doors to refugees. As the United States slid toward a worsening depression in 1937 with 10 million unemployed, American Jews became paranoid about anti-Semitism‡ sparked by refugees seeking jobs.

To a later generation, it is difficult to convey the utter despair that gripped most American Jews and their leaders. Zionists and non-Zionists took regular turns scoring each other. The American Jewish Year Book said there were too many Jewish doctors and lawyers. Of six Jewish congressmen in the New York area, four opposed changes in immigration laws; Rep. Sol Bloom sponsored a bill giving the president powers to exclude all aliens. A group of wealthy Yahudim called on President

* Zionists supported iron-fisted enforcement. At congressional hearings in April 1939, Rabbi Stephen Wise, firebrand leader of the American Jewish Congress, testified that no "sane person" would propose changes in immigration laws.

† "The plan means no mass exodus of the Jews of Germany, which it is impossible even to consider," said a JDC statement. "It does mean a hope for the future of those Jewish boys and girls whom we must first train adequately for industrial and cultural life and then enable to emigrate to all other countries that will accept them."

‡ According to Isador Lubin, a Roosevelt confidant, the president also feared widespread and perhaps violent anti-Semitism if the economic picture grew worse.

Roosevelt and begged him not to name Felix Frankfurter to the Supreme Court because the appointment was certain to stimulate Jew-hatred. The American Jewish Committee tried to tell indifferent Christians that Roosevelt's New Deal was not a "Jew" deal. The committee's educational program ran into competition with the Anti-Defamation League's Wider Scope effort. There were unseemly fights over money as both agencies solicited the same big givers for contributions; neither seemed particularly successful fighting intolerance.

In Berlin, the Hilfsverein office was besieged by an average 1000 callers a day who could neither find work nor emigrate. President Roosevelt called a world conference on refugees in Evian, France, in 1938. Thirty-three countries sent delegates, Jewish relief agencies sent representatives, and the Nazis permitted members of the Reichsvertretung and Hilfsverein to describe the situation of German Jewry. None of the participating nations was willing to take large numbers of refugees.

Evian's implications were not lost on the Nazis. After the Munich Conference in October, Hermann Goering demanded the Jewish "problem" be tackled "energetically and forthwith." An immediate expulsion of all Jews would make homes, shops, and businesses available for expropriation. With every conquest—the Rhineland in 1936, Austria in March 1938, and Czechoslovakia in September 1938—Jews were added to, instead of substracted from, Greater Germany's population. At this rate, central Europe would never be *judenrein*, free of Jews.

The Nazis were also on the lookout for pretexts to attempt more sweeping anti-Jewish action. On November 7, 1938, Ernst vom Rath, a German diplomat in Paris, was shot by a seventeen-year-old Jewish youth. Two days later, vom Rath died. On the anniversary of Hitler's abortive 1923 *putsch*, Goebbels made an inflammatory speech designed to incite a pogrom, using the murder as a pretext. It was followed by the *Krystallnacht*, the Night of Broken Glass, a destructive orgy during which teams of Nazi thugs dressed in civilian clothes set fire to thousands of synagogues and Jewish shops. At least ninety-one people were murdered while police looked on passively. Thirty thousand Jews were arrested "for their own protection" and sent to concentration camps. The thugs went free unless they committed "race pollution"—rape—or otherwise breached National Socialist discipline.

This night of horror was not an unqualified Nazi success. The party's moderate wing feared an adverse reaction abroad might encourage boycotts of German goods and wreck plans to finance rearmament. Worse, Reinhold Heydrich, SS Security Chief, told Goering that the teams had done their work all too well; Jewish businessmen would have to get restitution from Aryan insurance companies. Total losses in plate glass and consumer goods would run to hundreds of millions of marks, regardless of whether ruined buildings were owned by Christians or Jews. The fact was they were lost to the Reich.

This worried Goering. It was Nazi policy never to inconvenience the German populace, especially in the economic sphere. Moreover, Goering suspected Joseph Goebbels was upstaging him with Hitler as a Jew-baiter. In the emergency, however, Goebbels came up with a solution: Jews would foot the bill for property losses. Goering went on radio to announce a 1-billion-mark collective Jewish "atonement" fine "resulting from the people's resentment toward the agitation of international Jewry. . . ." Each Jew's share was 20 percent of the value of his registered property with an additional 5 percent tacked on later—in addition to the regular 25 percent "flight" tax on all property registered at more than 200,000 reichmarks should he leave the country. Whether or not to confine Jews in ghettos and to institute forced labor was discussed but left for a later decision.

As Heydrich pointed out after the *Krystallnacht*, this still left Greater Germany with 600,000 Jews, including those in Austria and the Sudetenland. These hostages presented Nazis with yet another opportunity to raise money for armaments. Hjalamar Schacht, head of the Reichbank, sensationally adept at forestalling payments on commercial debts and World War I reparations to the Allies, came up with an idea to extort money from every Jew in the world.

With Hitler's blessings, Schacht went to London in December 1938 with an emigration plan: 25 percent of the remaining assets of German Jewry, about 1.5 billion reichmarks, would be impounded in a trust fund to be administered by three persons, two of them chosen by Nazis. The trust fund would serve as collateral for a thirty-year bond issue financed by "International Jewry," which would enable 50,000 Jewish "wage earners" and their dependents to emigrate each year for three to five years. Bonds would be retired at a rate of 3 percent interest and 3 percent amortization each year, provided that German export revenues, which they were intended to bolster, increased.

Describing the plan to George Rublee, Director of the Intergovernmental Committee on Refugees (a by-product of the Evian Conference), Schacht stressed it provided a means by which poor as well as rich Jews could leave Germany. There were no negotiable conditions. The proposal was on a strictly take-it-or-leave-it basis, but concessions were possible: No property owned by American Jews in Germany would be confiscated and the bond idea might be dropped in favor of a plan under which Jews would set up a corporation to buy German goods for use in resettlement areas. The corporation would be capitalized at $50 million during its first year.

Nazis opted for Madagascar as a resettlement area, but tried to embarrass Washington by claiming America had "a moral duty" to admit refugees in view of its sponsorship of the Evian Conference. In the United States a pervasive dread of immigrants with "alien" ideologies afflicted the State Department. JDC constantly repeated that its job was to provide relief funds for refugees, not transportation to America. Joseph P. Kennedy, a Roosevelt spokesman, told Yahudim that appropriations by the federal government for refugee relief would only increase anti-Semitism.

Schacht's plan was rejected by Jewish agencies, amazed that even Schacht seriously believed in the existence of an "International Jewry" that would provide ransom funds. If a corporation financed by wealthy American, British, and French Jews were organized, it would play directly into the hands of German propagandists who would use it to prove the existence of an international Jewish financial organization. It would inspire anti-Semitic governments in Warsaw and Bucharest to issue calls on the same international Jewry to ransom their Jews, too. The plan became totally unpalatable when financial experts meeting in Paris concluded that there was no possibility of raising the sums Schacht wanted, especially after a 500-million-mark "service" charge was added.

British and American political leaders, among them Roosevelt and Hull, sought to continue negotiations. Jews sensed they would be forced to turn capital over to the Hitler regime as a sop. No one dreamed the Germans would resort to extermination. Lewis Strauss, asked to serve on a committee that would finance the corporation, was convinced "that the plan was an enormous hoax, a moneyed traffic in lives beyond any historic precedent."

In January 1939, Schacht quarreled bitterly with Hitler over the future of the German economy, staggering under huge arms expenditures, and was summarily dismissed. His place in ransom negotiations was taken by Helmut Wohltaht, a Goering subordinate. Wohltaht told Roosevelt's representative, Myron Taylor, that radicals around Hitler were urging "immediate liquidation" of the Jewish problem unless the Schacht agreement was implemented and "International Jewry" got busy supplying money.

In early February 1939, a statement of agreement was signed by a "Coordinating Foundation" set up by British Jews, American Jews, and Germans. Roosevelt liked a plan conceived by Herbert Hoover and Bernard Baruch, and endorsed by Albert Lasker and Julius Rosenwald, to resettle prospective refugees in a British colony; Jews worldwide would tithe $300 million to pay costs. The British suggested British Guiana in South America as a resettlement area and called for the two great democracies to match private funds with public funds, but Washington stressed that this ran counter to a resolution at the Evian Conference. An American foreign service officer, Robert Pell, added that most Americans and their congressional representatives had at best a "remote humanitarian interest" in the Jewish plight.

Nor was much money forthcoming from Jewish agencies. JDC said it would contribute a token $1 million, but would assume no responsibility for resettlement costs. Zionists opposed any scheme that did not include Palestine as the eventual destination of refugees. Rabbi Abba Hillel Silver, who headed the 1939 United Jewish Appeal Drive, categorically opposed any financial commitment to the Coordinating Foundation, declaring it was not a recognized Jewish agency.

Buffeted by Jews and without financial support from the French, British, and American governments, the plan for the Coordinating Foundation was discarded just before the beginning of World War II. Whether or not thousands of German, Austrian, and Czech Jewish lives might have been saved will forever be a moot point.

The failure of negotiations was used by Nazis as an excuse to strip Jews of remaining valuables. Goering demanded all jewelry, gold, silver, and platinum objects, including eating utensils. An additional assessment of up to 10 percent of the gross value of possessions was added to the tax levied after the *Krystallnacht*. The Gestapo seized Jews at random and told them that they must leave the country by some arbitrary date or face certain imprisonment in concentration camps. The terrorized victims paid $500 and $600 for visas and landing permits from Latin-American consuls encouraged to exploit them.

At this juncture, a voyage took place that was, in an almost mystical way, symbolic of German Jewry's fate. On May 13, 1939, the *St. Louis*, a Hamburg-American Liner, departed Hamburg for Havana. Nine hundred and thirty of its 936 passengers were Jews who had somehow managed to scrape together $262 each for passage plus $81 for return fare, in case it was needed. The ship was under the command of Capt. Gustave Schroeder, whose disgust with the Nazi regime was such that passengers were treated as honored guests. Seven hundred and thirty-seven held American quota numbers and would theoretically be eligible to enter the United States three months to three years after they were admitted to Cuba. The Cuban Director General of Immigration, Manuel Benitez Gonzalez, had issued landing permits at a cost of $160 each. Refugees were unaware that there was no official charge for these permits.

One day out from Havana, telegrams were received from Cuban authorities expressing doubt that landing permits would be acceptable. What this meant was unclear, but Captain Schroeder reassured his anxious passengers, promising that he would use his influence with the Cuban government when the vessel arrived in Havana. On May 27, only twenty-two refugees were permitted to debark. They had taken the precaution of paying an additional $500 each for a bond and received "visa authorizations" from the Cuban Departments of State, Treasury, and Labor. For the remaining 908 Jewish passengers, the Cuban government and President Frederico Laredo Brú were sorry, but landing permits had been improperly issued. Refugees would have to return to Germany. On June 2, the *St. Louis* was ordered out of the harbor.*

Brú had been influenced by Cuban labor leaders fearful that refugees

* The situation was the same for two other ships that arrived within twenty-four hours of the *St. Louis*. The S.S. *Orduna* was able to debark forty-eight refugees but steamed out with seventy-two who lacked "proper" visas and bonds. The S.S. *Flandre* debarked thirty-two but left with one hundred and thirty-two.

without funds would take jobs from native workers; Cuban and Spanish fascists also frightened businessmen with stories about Jewish agitators stirring up communist revolutions. On May 30, JDC rushed to Havana a representative authorized to post a bond up to $125,000 guaranteeing that *St. Louis* passengers would not seek employment in Cuba while awaiting entry to the United States. Another representative was detailed to make housing and subsistence arrangements for all passengers at JDC expense. Cuban authorities demanded a bond of nearly $1 million. Attempting to bargain with the Cubans, Lawrence Berenson, one of the represenatives, said it would take time to raise this amount; Brú responded that the *St. Louis* could always be recalled to Havana.

Aware of the talks, Captain Schroeder took as roundabout a route to Germany as possible, hugging the Florida coast in case the Cubans relented or the United States waived immigration regulations. On June 5, the *St. Louis* anchored off Miami for a few hours, and passengers could see the lights of the city. As the vessel steamed slowly northward, a United States Coast Guard cutter followed a short distance behind to insure that no refugees jumped overboard and succeeded in swimming ashore.

JDC desperately tried to negotiate with Brú. On June 5, he rekindled hopes: Refugees could land on the Isle of Pines if a $500 bond was posted for each person and a guarantee given that none would seek employment. But the next day, Cuban officials abruptly ended the talks. JDC deposited half a million dollars in a Havana bank to spur new discussions, but Cuban officials were disinterested. The *St. Louis* stopped cruising and made for Europe; its passengers formed a committee to prevent suicides. JDC appealed to South American and European countries to accept the refugees, and Captain Schroeder contemplated beaching his ship on the English coast rather than returning to Hamburg.

On June 12 and 13, Britain, Holland, France, and Belgium agreed to take *St. Louis* refugees—after JDC posted $500,000 to guarantee that they would not become public charges. On June 17, the *St. Louis* docked in Antwerp, where a Belgian Nazi group distributed handbills saying that it, too, wanted to help Jews: "If they call at our offices each will receive gratis a piece of rope and a strong nail." Two hundred and eighty-seven passengers accepted by the British were interned as enemy aliens. The 621 who found shelter on the continent came under German rule within a year.

While Hitler marched from conquest to conquest in the early 1940s, the Jewish civilization he hated and swore to destroy lay at his mercy in Poland, Russia, and in the cities and towns of his Axis partners, Hungary, Rumania, and Slovakia. Early in the war, Nazis were too busy digesting spoils to bother with Jews, although as early as September 1939 Heydrich considered an "ultimate goal." In this surreal atmosphere, JDC continued to help trade schools, orphaned children, and medical services in the German Government-General in Poland, which had the largest Jewish population in prewar Europe, 3 million. Artisans and workers who had lost belongings in the three-and-a-half-week September blitz got new tools and clothing. Soup kitchens were set up in Warsaw. Although nobody could have foreseen the result, humanitarian measures drew thousands from the countryside where they might have hidden, substantially easing the future work of extermination squads.

In Germany, 250,000 Jews contributed whatever they could scrape up for Jewish schools, hospitals, and old-age homes. About 250,000 of 500,000 had escaped; of those remaining, only a few thousand would survive the war. In France, the Vichy government recognized HICEM as the official Jewish agency coordinating emigration, and refugees departed from Marseilles after JDC paid incredible prices for tickets and ships. Eventually, the anti-Semitic zeal of Marshal Pétain's collaborationist government and the dedication of French police hunting Jews exceeded German expectations. Thousands tried to cross the Pyrenees into Spain and Portugal; for those who succeeded, JDC provided transportation elsewhere.

Nobody knows exactly when Hitler decided that the answer to the Jewish Question was extermination. He hinted at this development in a January 1939 speech, but most historians think the idea matured at the same time he planned to attack Russia, around March 1941. *Einsatzgruppen*, SS units of 500 to 1000 men, followed combat troops into Russia, shooting, clubbing, and gassing Jews to death in trucks disguised with Red Cross emblems.

In January 1942, this new Nazi policy—liquidation rather than forced emigration—was the subject of discussion at a luncheon meeting in the Berlin suburb of Wannsee. Presiding was Heydrich, now an SS Gruppenführer, or lieutenant general. Senior civil servants from various departments and SS Obersturmbannführer Adolf Eichmann, who took minutes, were also present. The participation of every man present was considered essential if an estimated 11 million Jews in Europe were to be killed. Heydrich brought cheer to the bureaucrats by remarking that Jewish banking houses abroad were helping the Nazi cause by not demanding payment in foreign currency for German bonds.

The Wannsee meeting lasted between an hour and an hour and a half, after which drinks and lunch were served. Eichmann felt honored to be present among personages making such high-level decisions. He was to be permanent administrator and arrange transports to death camps for Jews.* He had already discovered a way for German Jews to finance their own trips: victims "contributed" 25 percent of their remaining liquid assets. Where this was not possible, "the Jews with means had to finance the departure of the Jews without means. . . ."

On August 1, 1942, Dr. Gerhart Riegner, director of the Geneva office of the World Jewish Congress, heard with disbelief through underground sources the substance of the Wannsee meeting. A high-level German industrialist had risked his life to communicate the news. Riegner notified British and American consulates in Geneva and asked them to forward the information to Rabbi Stephen Wise, president of the American Jewish Congress, and to Sydney Silverman, chairman of the British section of the World Jewish Congress.

Wise asked Washington to check Riegner's information. Reports came back of mass deportations in France and Czechoslovakia. Riegner transmitted firsthand accounts of transports to death camps, but the State Department moved at an agonizingly slow pace, ostensibly because special efforts to save Jews might detract from the overall war effort.†

As week after week passed and nothing happened, Riegner became increasingly frantic. He pleaded for some measure to save lives. After a Riegner cable in January 1943 noting that 6000 Polish Jews were being murdered each day, the infamous State Department cable 354 was sent over Secretary of State Cordell Hull's name and Undersecretary Sumner

* Eichmann was a congenital liar. At his trial in Jerusalem he sought to prove that every office in Germany with the exception of his had a hand in killing Jews.

† This was the view of Assistant Secretary of State Breckinridge Long, responsible for refugee affairs. Long diligently prevented Jews from entering the United States and later lied about the numbers saved.

Welles's initials, telling the Bern legation to stop forwarding such reports "to private persons in the United States."*

Like the State Department, the Russians, the British, and the Vatican restrained their reactions to news about mass murders of Jews. Russians continued to charge duty on JDC relief packages sent via Iran to Jews in the Soviet Union. Neither Soviet, British, nor American air forces bombed concentration camp sites or rail lines leading to them.†

As the first crematoria came into operation in mid-March 1943, Washington and London began preparations for a conference on refugees to take place the following month. In lush Bermuda surroundings, Jewish organizations presented memoranda to an American delegation unwilling to change immigration laws and to a British delegation unwilling to lift the blockade of Europe for relief supplies. The Bermuda Conference, whose discussions revolved around the organization and financing of an Inter-Governmental Committee on Refugees, opened the same day SS troops armed with tanks, dive bombers, and flamethrowers launched their final assault on the ruins of the Warsaw Ghetto. Deliberations continued while mopping-up operations took place against Jews armed with a few pistols, rifles, and light machine guns.

As early as 1943, however, the attitude of Hitler's partners began to change with the prospect that the Third Reich might not last through the war, let alone the thousand-year period Hitler had envisioned. Fascists rushed to fill their pockets and establish clean reputations with Allied powers. In February 1943, Rumanian officials offered to release 70,000 Jews for fifty dollars each. The refugees could be sent to Palestine on Rumanian ships flying the Vatican flag. Ion Antonescu, the Rumanian dictator, bid the Central Organization of Rumanian Jews select people to be saved. Payments could be made in local currency by Rumanian Jewish merchants who would be reimbursed after the war in dollars or in Swiss francs by American Jewish organizations.

Both State and Treasury Department approvals were necessary to

* Four minor State Department employees were responsible for cable 354. There is little doubt that Long, however, was ultimately responsible for an attempt to conceal the situation of European Jewry from higher American officials.

† The official explanation was that final victory would do more for Jews than immediate raids. Thus the destruction of factories and German armed forces took precedence over efforts to halt, or at least to disorganize, the slaughter.

license disbursal of funds in enemy territories. Treasury was willing to move ahead, but State had reservations about complications.* The major complication was where refugees could go; the British, fearing that additional Jews in Palestine would bolster Zionist forces and offend Arabs, complained about difficulties relocating "any considerable number of Jews should they be rescued from enemy occupied territory." The issue was argued for eleven months, after which it was academic, since by then thousands of Rumanian Jews had been murdered.

The highest-placed Jew in the American government was Secretary of the Treasury Henry Morgenthau, Jr. "Let's call a spade a spade," Morgenthau told a staff meeting. "I am secretary of the Treasury for one hundred and thirty-five million people, see? That is the way I think of myself; I represent all of them. But if Mr. Hamilton Fish, Jr. [Republican congressman from New York] was to go after me, he goes after me because I am a Jew. Let's use plain, simple language. He doesn't go after me because I am Secretary; he goes after me because he thinks that I have done something for the Jews because I am a Jew."

Morgenthau was finally spurred to action. The World Jewish Congress was licensed by the Treasury Department to finance the evacuation of Jews from France to Spain and Switzerland. JDC was licensed to evacuate Jewish children from France and to support refugees in Switzerland. Morgenthau's staff prepared a bitter memorandum on State Department obscurantism for Roosevelt, and the president was visibly shaken by the report, read in Morgenthau's presence. Six days later, on January 22, 1944, Roosevelt created the War Refugee Board,† and a field representative, Ira Hirschmann, was sent to Ankara. There he arranged with the Rumanian ambassador to Turkey the rescue of surviving Rumanian Jews.

Various Nazis also indicated they were ready to enter the market for some big deals of their own. Early in the war, 50 Dutch Jews paid $10,000 each and were permitted to leave the Netherlands. Later, 30,000 Slovak Jews thought bribing the right people had bought them life, but

* There were no complications about sources for ransom money. American Jews, not the American government, would provide it.

† The board's major function was to display official American concern over the fate of Jews. Rescue techniques and relief funds continued to be supplied by JDC and HIAS. Many historians believe thousands more could have been saved had the board been set up earlier.

in fact the Germans were simply busy elsewhere. When they got around to Slovakia, transports carried the Jews to death camps despite bribes.

In 1944, Obersturmbannführer Herbert Kappler waited until Allied armies were 200 miles from Rome and then imposed a fifty kilogram gold ransom on the city's Jews, who were anxious to prove their willingness to cooperate and produced 160 percent of the amount asked. Kappler told his superiors that Roman Jews should live because they were "in contact with Jewish financial groups [sic] abroad* and one would be able to exploit these contacts for the intelligence services." Eichmann would have none of it. With the help of a list of names and addresses provided by the president of Rome's Jewish community, the roundup began and 7000 Roman Jews went to Auschwitz.

Kappler and Eichmann were pathological killers; they were also bureaucrats laboring to meet quotas, assemble accurate statistics, and get recognition in the Berlin home office. Heinrich Himmler, Reichsführer of the SS, was interested in bigger things. By 1944, he thought the war was lost, but was convinced he could whitewash himself by halting the murders. Perhaps, thought the Reichsführer, he could even become head of a new German government after Hitler's defeat if there should be a rift between the Western Allies and Russia.

The largest Jewish community left in Europe was in Hungary, the only country allied with Germany that enjoyed political independence early in 1944. Anti-Semites in the Hungarian government wanted to curry favor with the Nazis and "inherit" Jewish property after owners were killed. Thus far the government of Adm. Miklos von Horthy had kept things relatively quiet; 800,000 Jews and 150,000 converted Jews believed that at worst they would do forced service in labor camps. Meanwhile, they lived peaceably and even pleasantly while massacres went on in countries around them. Many still had large fortunes and none had to wear yellow stars. A fund-raising campaign in Budapest yielded $10,000 for the relief of inmates in the Theresienstadt concentration camp.

As the German retreat from Russia grew more rapid, Hungarian leaders sought a way to quit the Axis and sue for peace. The Germans got wind of this, and in March 1944, Hungarian independence suddenly ended

* This was true. Close contacts were maintained with HIAS and JDC via Switzerland and the Vatican.

when officials were hastily summoned to meetings with Hitler, from whom they learned their country would be occupied. At Himmler's behest, SS Obersturmbannführer Kurt Becher was dispatched to negotiate for major Jewish business firms, among them the Manfred Weiss Works, the largest industrial firm in Hungary. Unknown to Hungarian authorities, Becher offered freedom and $600,000 in American money* to the Weiss family for its holdings in the firm, 55 percent of the stock. Subsequently, forty-eight members of the family, including thirteen Christians, were permitted to leave for Portugal with cash, gold, and jewelry. Nine members stayed behind as hostages to insure that the others did not engage in anti-Nazi activities.†

SS dealings with rich Hungarian Jews enraged Eichmann; his negotiations with Hungarian authorities were hampered and a precept of his work violated. Jewish money was supposed to pay for transportation to death camps, not tickets to freedom. But for Himmler and high-ranking SS officers, Hungary heralded a fabulous new opportunity for big deals on an international level. For the Nazis, the wealth of American Jews, a bottomless fount, might be tapped for untold millions. The Berlin propaganda line was that Jews controlled American finance and Henry Morgenthau, Jr., controlled the Jews.

The Nazis may have been encouraged by news of sums Jews were raising for overseas relief. In the spring of 1942, Eli Ginzberg, professor of economics at Columbia University, published a *Report to American Jews on Overseas Relief, Palestine and Refugees in the United States.* About 40,000 Jewish families had a combined income of $1 billion in 1940–41, and the 10,000 wealthiest had an income of $500 million. Some $27 million was raised by the United Jewish Appeal and communal agencies in 1940, and the trend in receipts was upward: in 1941, $28.2 million was raised; and in 1942, $29.3 million.

Eichmann arrived in Budapest with his staff on March 19, 1944—the same day Nazis took over Hungary. The one thing he wanted to avoid

* They never got the payment.

† Several other Hungarian-Jewish industrialists also offered up large sums but were less fortunate than the Weisses. Dr. Albert Hirsch, Frigyes Ribarye and his family, Dr. Heinrich Hercz and his wife, and the widow of a managing director of a textile firm paid between 500,000 and 1 million pengös each to depart with foreign currency and jewels. Through Gestapo connivance they were attacked by thugs en route to the airport. Robbed of their valuables, they were then sent to death camps.

was another Warsaw Ghetto uprising. Hauptsturmführer Dieter Wisliceny, who took bribes from Slovak Jews, told the Zionist Relief and Rescue Committee* that Himmler might spare all the Jews in Europe except those in Poland and Germany for between $2 and $3 million. Baron Philip von Freudiger, an Orthodox Jew who was an important member of the Judenrat, or Jewish Council, thereupon handed over 10 percent of the ransom, $250,000; Zionists paid $20,000 to meet Wisliceny and his henchmen. At this meeting, each Nazi received an additional $1000 tip. The baron's money came from local sources; Zionist money came from JDC via Lisbon and Geneva. The Nazis soon learned where both parties got their funds and preferred to do business with Zionists rather than with the baron, because they thought international connections were much better than local ones.

Acting on Himmler's orders, Eichmann summoned Joel Brand, a founder of the Zionist Committee, to Budapest's Hotel Metropole late in April. Eichmann outlined a ransom plan to be kept secret from the Hungarians, who were themselves thinking up ways to prevent Jewish wealth, estimated at 8 milliard gold pengös, from going to the Germans. Instead of trading Jews for money, 1 million Jews could be traded for 10,000 trucks and trailers and 200 tons of tea, 200 tons of coffee, 2 million cases of soap, and varying amounts of tungsten and other war materiel. The trucks would be used only "against the Russians on the Eastern front." No doubt Jews thought he was a crook, grumbled Eichmann, but "a German officer keeps his word." The "World Jewish Organization" could itself choose the Jews to be saved.

Brand was encouraged, although he doubted that the Allies would actually hand over trucks. During a two-week period Eichmann allowed him in Istanbul, Brand hoped to contact the Jewish Agency in Palestine and work out some arrangement.

On May 25, the American ambassador in Turkey, Laurence Steinhardt, advised the State Department that Brand and a Hungarian suspected of being a double agent had just arrived bearing a proposal from the "commissioner for Jewish Affairs, Eichmann [sic]." Brand told a group of

* The committee, formed a few years earlier, maintained a remarkable network of contacts with Germans and had intelligence agents throughout Hungary. It was able to smuggle a few people into Palestine; unlike other Hungarian-Jewish groups, its members had few illusions about Nazis.

Jewish Agency officials what was happening in Hungary; many wept openly, but to Brand's dismay he learned that they were low-ranking and powerless. Turkish authorities would not permit Moshe Shertok, a top-level Zionist official, to enter the country.

Shertok tried negotiating in London with Anthony Eden, whom he found "maddeningly hesitant." Brand was taken to Haifa and then to Cairo, where he was interviewed by Ira Hirschmann, of the War Refugee Board, who advised Washington that Brand be returned to Hungary with instructions not to mention trucks but to indicate that "money and possible immunity [for Nazi war criminals] might be offered."

While Hirschmann met with Brand, Winston Churchill wrote Eden that there could be no negotiations for Jews between Nazis and the Allied governments, although the massacres were "probably the biggest and most horrible crime ever committed in the whole history of the world. . . ." The most that could be done was to issue a warning to Nazis that everyone connected with the trucks-for-Jews ransom attempt would be "hunted down and put to death" after the war.

In Budapest, Jews anxiously awaited Brand's return. As the days and weeks went by, attempts were made to hold off deportations with more bribes.* In mid-June, Himmler was offered 20 million Swiss francs, of which 5 million actually found their way to the Reichsführer. Freudiger received $100,000 from American sources on June 21. Between early May and mid-June, however, Eichmann sent half the Jews in Hungary to gas chambers. As many as 14,000 people arrived daily on railroad sidings near death camps.

With Brand stalled and Russian armies smashing into central Europe, the Germans now shifted their demands from trucks to cash and food. They were encouraged to do so by Dr. Reszö Kastner, a co-founder of the Zionist Committee, who sought to keep a dialogue going.† Some 300 prospective victims destined for Bergen-Belsen paid $1000 each and were guarded by the SS from Hungarian fascists, members of the green-shirted Arrow Cross. Money could also bribe nonfascists to provide false

* Hitler consented to free 1000 Jewish children holding entry certificates to Palestine in exchange for Hungarian willingness to resume transports to death camps. Eichmann, extremely displeased, requested a change in policy so that the children could be killed.

† Kastner later was accused of bargaining with Nazis to save his own family. In 1955, the Israeli Supreme Court found him innocent after a libel trial; ten months later Kastner was assassinated in Tel Aviv.

papers and hideaways. Freudiger pleaded with the Union of Orthodox Rabbis in America: "If you can and will help us then we can perhaps be partially or totally saved. If not, we are lost." But between May 15 and July 7, five trains arrived daily in death camps that were operating day and night to complete the destruction of Hungarian Jewry. In Auschwitz, crews constructed a new railroad siding so that victims could be moved more rapidly from trains to gas chambers.

In the midst of the inferno, Raoul Wallenberg, a thirty-two-year-old Swede who was himself Jewish, was posted in the Swedish legation in Budapest and given War Refugee Board authorization to use JDC funds for relief. Performing a Herculean feat with the help of bribed officials and anti-Nazis, Wallenberg fed, clothed, and found medical supplies for thousands of people, besides issuing 4000 Swedish passports to Jews, many of whom were literally about to board transports. In a miracle of organization, he created a network of hospitals, nurseries, and soup kitchens staffed by Jews. His energy was contagious; Swiss, Spanish, Portuguese, and Vatican officials began to help.*

While the Western Allies raced through France and the German armies disintegrated, the Nazis initiated new ransom feelers. Himmler contacted JDC's European Director, Joseph Schwartz, in Lisbon, suggesting a meeting with a Nazi representative in some neutral place. In the United States it was agreed that leadership for all Jewish agencies involved in rescue operations should be concentrated in JDC. Washington prohibited discussions between American and enemy nationals, and a substitute for Schwartz was found in Saly Mayer, a retired Jewish lace manufacturer who served as Swiss JDC representative. The German spokesman was Kurt Becher, who dressed in civilian clothes when speaking with Jews.

Sensing the possibility of large cash influxes from America and an imminent end to the war, Nazis attempted to show good faith by releasing 318 Orthodox Jews from Bergen-Belsen. Mayer could not reciprocate with money because the War Refugee Board would not permit ransom payments. The Russians were highly suspicious that a separate peace might be in the making between the Western Allies and Germany, and such transactions could encourage this view. It was felt the best that could be

* After Budapest capitulated, the Russians refused to permit JDC operations to continue. Wallenberg, arrested by the new conquerors, was never again seen alive.

done to ease Russian fears and establish credibility in German eyes was for JDC to place $5 million in a Swiss National Bank account for Mayer —money he could not spend.

Mayer was extremely cautious by nature, and JDC remained circumspect about government regulations. The range of negotiating options was thus limited to one: delay further deportations by tantalizing the Nazis, but not delivering goods or money. Meanwhile, Hitler was determined to press his war on the Jews, and Eichmann outdistanced orders executing the Final Solution to the Jewish Question.

On October 14, Horthy resigned after a German panzer division entered Budapest. His son was kidnapped, and the old regent was told that the boy might be sent to the Mauthausen death camp. Three days later, back from supervising the roundup of any Rumanian Jews he could still lay his hands on, Eichmann began a final cleanup with the help of Hungarian underlings. In mid-November, before Auschwitz was abandoned to the Russians, about 30,000 Jews, including women of eighty and children of ten, were assembled by the Arrow Cross in a tile factory and marched out of Budapest. Eleven days later a second group was marched away. Few survived either death trek.

Mayer kept the SS wondering by insisting on specific lists of foodstuffs and other goods Nazis wanted traded for Jews. Every time the device was used, Becher was forced to return to Berlin to check with superiors. As time passed and German prospects of ending the war short of unconditional surrender grew dimmer by the hour, individual Nazis became increasingly amenable. Mayer was joined by Roswell McClelland, a War Relief Board representative, who dropped all pretenses, flatly telling Becher that the only money Nazis received would be for refugee relief. Liquidations must cease immediately. Becher acquiesced, and the Germans got thirty to forty Swiss centimes a day to pay for each survivor's food.

Thus ended JDC's attempts to ransom European Jews. In the final analysis, Saly Mayer's negotiations succeeded in bringing 1673 Jews to Switzerland from Bergen-Belsen, diverted 17,000 more from Auschwitz to camps in Austria, and possibly staved off the deportation of 170,000 others to Auschwitz. In Budapest the SS permitted the International Red Cross to shelter 3000 Jewish children and to distribute food and clothing to 7000 Jews in labor camps near Vienna. The talks also inspired other ransom attempts, including one in which a Swiss friend of Himmler, Jean-Marie Mussy, negotiated with the SS for release of 1200 Jews from Theresienstadt for $1 million. Mussy asked the World Jewish Congress for money and the World Jewish Congress asked JDC, but only a small sum found its way into Nazi coffers.

On the other side of the ledger, Rudolph Höss, who commanded Auschwitz, claimed that 400,000 Hungarian Jews had been killed in that camp alone during the summer of 1944, when negotiations began. Any Jews who remained alive in Hungary after this whirlwind did so not because of Nazi hesitation, Allied purposefulness, or Saly Mayer's tactics, but because the Germans simply retreated so quickly. There was barely time to blow up the camps and destroy evidence.

Measured in terms of Jewish lives saved during World War II, the results of all the ransom and bribery efforts, including the one in Hungary, were negligible. In August 1943, Riegner cabled the American Jewish Congress that four million were dead; twenty-one months later, when the killings finally ended, probably more than 6 million were dead. In Warsaw, Lodz, and Lublin, prewar centers of Jewish life, 1120 Jews greeted liberators. In Czechoslovakia, 51,000 survived out of 360,000. Six out of every 7 European Jews alive in 1939 were dead in 1945.

On the other hand, Germans and east Europeans were lavishly enriched by the expropriation of Jewish property. Estimates of the loot between 1933 and 1945 range from $12 billion to $32 billion. Whole new middle classes came into existence in Germany, Austria, Poland, Czechoslovakia, Hungary, and Rumania. Jewish apartments, houses, and farms were occupied; tools, furnishings, and personal belongings were seized along with the real estate. New owners quickly approved the "aryanization" of property, and if by chance the original owners returned after the war they were killed or driven away by their successors. Neither relief nor reconstruction solved Jewish problems in Europe. Against genocide, ransom and philanthropy were also ineffective.

5
The Promised Land

DURING THE EARLY 1900s, America's great Yahudim hoped socialism and labor unions were aberrations that assimilation would cure. Characteristically optimistic and confident, Jacob Schiff, Louis Marshall, Oscar Straus, and top ranks of the American Jewish Committee were still positively unhinged by political Zionism, a late nineteenth-century movement arguing for a Jewish Risorgimento, for the establishment of a Jewish state, and against assimilation as *the* solution to Jewish problems. The establishment cried out that Jews were Jewish by religion and not by nationality. It was divine intent that Jews be concerned with eternal verities, not with specifically Jewish politics. Jews had no dual obligations, in theory or in fact, to the countries in which they lived and to some distant organization of Jewish nationalists nobody ever heard of.

Fortunately, Zionism's prophet, Theodor Herzl, was as far away as his movement. Herzl was a tall, thin, elegant, intense Hungarian with melancholy eyes and a black beard so full that he resembled an Assyrian monarch. Judged by his family history, Herzl would have fit into any group of American Yahudim. His Budapest family was assimilated, his Jewish education ended when he was thirteen years old, and although he witnessed anti-Semitic incidents during his student years in Vienna, he did not overreact to them. He turned from the law to theater, writing dramas and a series of trivial comedies, one of which was performed by a German troupe in New York. As a playwright, he was not very successful in Europe or in America.

Herzl bitterly resented his early creative failures, although he was to do considerably better as a freelance writer for newspapers. In the fall of 1891, Vienna's *Neue Freie Presse* offered him a position as its Paris correspondent. He quickly accepted.* The following year, Herzl attended the libel trial of Édouard-Adolphe Drumont, the red-faced "pope of anti-Semitism" and founder of the National Anti-Semitic League, which railed against Rothschilds and international Jewish financiers. "Down with the German Jews! France for Frenchmen!" shouted Drumont in the courtroom. "Down with the Jews!" followers roared back.

Two years after that, Herzl attended pre-trial sessions in the court-martial proceedings against Alfred Dreyfus, a Jewish artillery officer accused of high treason. Convicted behind closed doors, Dreyfus was publicly degraded on the parade ground of the École Militaire and sent to Devil's Island. "I am innocent! Long live France!" he shouted as he was led away. "Death to the Jews!" howled a mob.

Like many others, Herzl soon suspected that Dreyfus was innocent and that the army's high command was using him as a scapegoat. But if a Dreyfus trial could happen "in republican, modern, civilized France a century after the Declaration of Human Rights," reasoned Herzl, "it could happen anywhere."†

Ideas of the most limpid quality formed in his mind. He would inspire Jews to a new political unity and lead them to the Promised Land. Securing funds from the rich and blessings from the rulers of western Europe, he would finance land purchases in Palestine. Jews would "build houses, palaces, workingmen's homes, schools, theaters, museums, government buildings, prisons, hospitals, asylums—in short, cities. . . ."

Herzl was one visionary who realized the value of money if anything was to be accomplished, and he asked Baron Maurice de Hirsch for an appointment. Still the richest Jew in the world, the baron had set up the

* Herzl had marital problems, and the post also offered him the opportunity for a trial separation.

† Whether or not the Dreyfus trial fully explains his conversion to Zionism is another matter. For most historians, it does not.

Jewish Colonization Association scarcely four years before. In a letter, Herzl modestly suggested a "Jewish-political conversation" that would "have its effect when you and I are no longer here." Hirsch, not unnaturally curious, requested details. "You have hitherto been only a philanthropist . . . I want to show you the way to become something more," responded Herzl.

Dressing with "discreet care" and breaking in a new pair of gloves, Herzl called on the baron to say that the whole concept of Jewish philanthropy was wrong. "If we had a united political leadership—the necessity for which I need not stress and which in no case should take the form of a secret association—if I say, we possessed this leadership, we could proceed to the solution of the Jewish question. We could tackle it from above, from below, from all sides. The aim we would have in view, once we possessed a center and a head, would determine the means to be pursued."

"You breed beggars," continued Herzl. "It is characteristic of the situation that no other people shows so much philanthropy and so much beggary as the Jews. Plainly there must be a close connection between those two phenomena. Philanthropy, it is apparent, debases the character of our people."

Hirsch, who was having troublesome problems with philanthropy, interrupted to say that Herzl was "quite right." Nonetheless, he could not agree with Herzl's assertion that the Jews needed "general uplift," less charity, and more involvement in politics. "No, no, no!" said the baron. "I do not want to raise the general level. All of our misfortunes come from the fact that the Jews want to climb too high. We have too much [sic] brains. My intention is to restrain the Jews from pushing ahead. They shouldn't make such great progress. All of the hatred against us stems from this." Continuing in the same vein, Hirsch reported that he was successfully recruiting Jews in Russia for Argentinean colonies. "After a few prosperous years, I could show the world that the Jews after all are fitted for agriculture."

Herzl thought that it would serve no useful purpose to further explain Zionism; without hearing more, Hirsch labeled Herzl's views "visionary notions." Stung by the remark, Herzl retorted that he would go to the German emperor and say "let our people go. We are strangers here. We are neither permitted nor are we able to assimilate with the people. Let us go! I will procure for you the ways and the means—which I will use for the exodus—whereby no economic catastrophe will follow our departure."

This raised the question of financing. "I will raise a Jewish national loan of ten million marks," said Herzl. "Fantasy," responded Hirsch. "The rich Jews will give nothing. Rich people are worthless; they care nothing for the sufferings of the poor."

This was not true, as Hirsch well knew and was himself proving. Before him, Sir Moses Montefiore, one of England's richest Jews, had put large sums into Palestinian colonies and requested the Turkish governor of the province to allow him to rent land and permit instructors to teach husbandry to resident Jews. In 1854, James Rothschild built a Jewish hospital in Jerusalem, and in 1870, Edmond de Rothschild actually began the modern era of Jewish colonization in the Holy Land by establishing an agricultural school near Jaffa. Palestine had eighteen villages and 4500 Jews in 1897; two years later Rothschild had already invested about £2 million, amalgamating French colonial interests with Jewish philanthropy.

The rich, including Hirsch and Edmond de Rothschild, were willing enough to support Jewish settlements in the Holy Land. What they were unwilling to do was to make major capital investments in a Jewish political entity. This, Herzl found intolerable. How was it, he later wrote Hirsch, that "mints of Jewish money can be found in large amounts for a Chinese loan, for Negro railroads in Africa, for the remotest undertakings—but for the deepest, most immediate and crying need of the Jewish people itself, is there none to be found?" On July 5, Herzl dejectedly wrote Hirsch that "our political lethargy clearly betrays the degeneration of our once vigorous race."

Driven by his vision of the truth, Herzl remained unshaken by the Hirsch setback. He returned to Vienna as literary editor of the *Neue Freie Presse.* Attempting to keep up with both this work and Zionist activities, he ruined his health. At the beginning of 1896, at age thirty-six, Herzl had only eight years more to live. That year he began the momentous course that would change the history of the Jewish people: On February 14, *Der Judenstaat* (*The Jewish State*), henceforth the bible of the movement, was published. This ninety-six-page pamphlet, "an attempt at a modern solution to the Jewish question," originally intended to serve as a text for a speech to the Rothschilds in family council assembled, aimed at nothing less than restoration of the "ancient" Jewish state.

Herzl assessed the status of Europe's Jews and concluded assimilation was a failure. Jews were patriots and superpatriots in every European country. Yet "majorities" perceived Jews as "aliens" and would not leave them in peace. "The Jewish Question" existed wherever there were large numbers of Jews; where it did not currently exist, Jewish immigrants were sure to bring it. The only solution was a Jewish state, a "democratic monarchy" that would be created by two instrumentalities: a "Society of Jews," which would provide a plan and a political structure, and a "Jewish Company" capitalized at £50 million, which would finance the exodus from Europe and commerce in the new state. Further thoughts on working hours, architecture, and other subjects were provided in the brief compass of the work.

Der Judenstaat surprised Herzl's friends, readers of the *Neue Freie Presse*, and Zionists in the Pale, not to speak of Jewish assimilationists. To his friends it made no sense that a sophisticated, attractive, worldly man who frequented literary salons, wrote light comedies, and penned witty essays on various topics of the day for one of the world's great newspapers should argue against assimilation. Readers accustomed to the latest news from Paris found a new and surprising subject. Zionists were hardest hit; Theodor Herzl, who wanted to lead the Jews out of Europe and said he knew how to do it, was totally unknown in Jewish, let alone Zionist, circles. Further offending believers, Herzl thought it ridiculous to tie a Hebrew cultural renascence to a political movement: "Who among us would be capable of buying a railway ticket in Hebrew?" he scoffed.

Labeled a visionary even by his most significant convert and advisor, Vienna's chief rabbi, Moritz Güdemann, Herzl sought diplomatic successes to establish credibility among Zionists and the rich. In April 1896, he was introduced to Frederick, Grand Duke of Baden, a sympathizer who would later help him to meet Kaiser Wilhelm II. In June he hurried to Constantinople, where he met the grand vizier and proposed a deal: Jews would oversee the Ottoman Empire's financial affairs and find a way to ease its huge debt, in return for Palestine as an independent or even a vassal state. Herzl received an Ottoman decoration; otherwise things went badly. The Turks rightly guessed that he had neither Jewish legions nor Jewish funds behind him.

This result would hardly seem to presage a triumphal return to Europe. Yet Herzl was hailed as a hero in the Jewish press for presenting the Zionist case to the sultan. On his way to Constantinople, he was received enthusiastically by crowds of Jews in Serbia and Bulgaria. On his way back, it probably first occurred to him to appeal directly to the masses for financial support, going over (or under) the heads of the rich and powerful. Herzl went to London, which he had visited the previous year. Well-to-do British Jews found excuses to avoid him; only 160 copies of the English edition of *The Jewish State* had been sold. On the other hand, thousands of Jews living in the East End, London's Lower East Side, came to see and hear him at a mass meeting. The experience made a profound impression. "I am the little people's man," Herzl wrote in his diary.

Adulation might be gratifying, but it still left the Zionist movement without a "Jewish Company," which meant that little headway could be made in forming a "Society of Jews." Herzl laid plans to renew fund raising with a declaration of Zionist aims to Baron Edmond de Rothschild, in Paris. But Herzl had little talent or insight for fund raising—the spotlight always had to be on him rather than on the prospective donor—and he was totally unprepared to be tactful when the baron attempted to refute his ideas.

Rothschild had little faith in the Turks and thought a huge influx of refugees to the Holy Land would be impossible to control. As many as 150,000 schnorers would have to be fed, a task to which the philanthropist was not eager to address himself. Herzl pleaded that Rothschild was the "keystone of the entire combination." Without him, everything would "fall to pieces." Herzl declared he wanted to turn the entire project over to Rothschild, "the philanthropic Zionist." At this point in the conversation, the "philanthropic Zionist" was unwilling to accept any assignment and was, in fact, becoming angry. Both men then said they were delighted to make each other's acquaintance, and Herzl left. Edmond de Rothschild, he wrote in his diary, was a decent but faint-hearted man with the same attitude toward Zionism that a coward had toward necessary surgery. "And the fate of many millions is to hang on such men!"

For Herzl, the Rothschild meeting settled the matter of fund raising, at least for the time being. The rich would not help, the masses were interested. He would therefore set up a worldwide fund-raising organization, and the masses would somehow provide money to finance a homeland. In May 1897, Herzl met with representatives of Hovevei (Orthodox) Zionist groups in Germany, Austria, and Galicia and decided with them to convene an International Zionist Congress in Basel. The non-Zionist reaction to this proposed assembly was enough to permanently depress any less determined prophet. Assimilationists claimed there was no Jewish Question, hence no Jewish congress was necessary to solve it. Enthusiasts were not sure how to answer them. Nobody knew exactly what Herzl wanted discussed.

Forging ahead anyway, Herzl chaired the first Zionist Congress, which began on August 28, 1897. After receiving a fifteen-minute ovation, he announced two principal goals for World Jewry, just as he had done in *Der Judenstaat.* The first was the establishment of a Jewish national home through negotiations with Turkey and the great powers; the second was the creation of a financial instrument capable of providing funds for a state. Herzl did not criticize the rich, but found the philanthropic approach to Jewish colonization useless. At the current rate of progress it would take 900 years before all the world's Jews could enter the Promised Land.

"If you only will it, then it is no fairy tale," said Herzl. The World Zionist Organization was founded with Herzl as its first president. As he intended, the meeting stimulated wide discussion in the Jewish and non-Jewish press, and gave the movement a stature it had never before had. Now he could get to work on financing. As he wrote sarcastically in an issue of *Die Welt*, a Zionist periodical he edited and paid for, the Zionist movement would avoid "the graciousness of benefactors and the kindness of philanthropic institutions" by launching a sales campaign for 2 million shareholders paying £1 each. This money would be used as a basis for negotiations with the Turks.

To initiate this campaign, it was deemed essential to secure wealthy backers who would set the pace by purchasing large amounts of stock. Herzl likened the financial campaign to a military operation, complete with mobilization, skirmishes, and a battle. Plans went awry as early as the mobilization phase. Months were spent with a London banker, who would not make up his mind what he wanted to do, a Polish banker who suggested that the capitalization be increased to £10 million and then did nothing to raise it, and German bankers who listened carefully and also did nothing. Before the Second Zionist Congress in 1898, Herzl bid a sales campaign begin without bankers. "As it is we are like the soldiers of the French Revolution who had to take to the field without shoes or stockings."

This made for stirring statements, but continued failure to gain support from the rich was a serious obstacle in Herzl's path, effectively blocking political success. As late as the Fourth Zionist Congress in 1900, a minimum goal of £250,000 could not be raised, despite the most dedicated efforts. Herzl, who spent his own earnings and the larger part of his wife's fortune on the movement, was, at forty-one, "old, tired and poor"; symptoms of the heart disease that would kill him were growing worse. A November 1898 meeting with Kaiser Wilhelm II in a tent on the outskirts of Jerusalem was a failure, partly because the German foreign minister, Bernhard von Bülow, reported the anti-Zionism of Jewish bankers. Later meetings with the Turks turned on Jewish financial aid, which could not be offered without the interest of Jewish financiers. At one meeting, the astronomical sum of £30 million was proposed to liquidate the Turkish national debt.

Herzl went from one European capital to another, from Vienna to London,* to Rome, to Sofia, and after the Kishinev massacre in 1903, to St. Petersburg. Minister of the Interior Phleve offered to "support" the Zionist program if Jewish nationalism did not increase in Russia. Nicholas II, told of the talks, took the opportunity to express shock that anyone believed his government abetted murderous acts; the czar had good will for all his subjects. There is no evidence how much of this nonsense Herzl accepted, but Phleve admitted the Imperial aim was to assimilate Jews of superior intelligence and to drive other Jews out of the country. The Zionist movement could serve a Russian purpose by dumping unwanted millions of nonpersons in Palestine. Phleve understood why Russian Jews hated the Russian government, but he ascribed the problem to the presence of too many Jews in the Pale.

Horrified by Kishinev and aware of the urgent need for Jewish emigration from the Pale, Herzl continued negotiations begun with the British government on the possibility of settling Jews in East Africa. The

* Where another attempt to interest the English Rothschilds failed.

"Uganda Scheme" presented to delegates at the Sixth Zionist Congress in 1903 was intended as a temporary measure, not to replace the ultimate goal, a return to the Holy Land, but to afford terrified people an immediate refuge.

Herzl had already aroused envy and antagonism among fellow Zionists, a contentious lot always ready to vent frustrations on each other, but he was totally unprepared for the storm of abuse that greeted the Uganda Scheme. Matters were not helped by his statement that the government of Nicholas II would not hamper Zionist development if Zionists acted within a "legal" framework.

Delegates from the Pale were enraged. How dare Herzl meet with Phleve, this repulsive creature, this instigator of murder and rape? The president of the World Zionist Organization was indeed a visionary if he believed that anti-Semites would act on behalf of Jews, or that Russian Jews, after their frightful experiences, would settle for anything less than Palestine. Herzl had not only offended by negotiating with the arch-enemy, but had struck at the very core of east European Zionism, the eschatological belief in redemption through a return to the Promised Land, Palestine. Utterly unconvinced by Herzl's rationale for Uganda, 177 Russian and Polish delegates withdrew as a body from the congress.

This represented the largest number of delegates from a single country and offered the real possibility that the movement would fragment once and for all. Yidn furnished the overwhelming mass of Zionist followers and paradoxically had been drawn to Herzl because he represented sophisticated European culture in contrast to their own modest and provincial ways. Despite their poverty, they also provided much of the money. In 1902, 500 delegates at the first all-Russian Zionist Conference in Minsk represented 75,000 members. There were 1572 Zionist groups on the local level in Russia a year later, and the number of shekel-holders (members) and local groups was increasing.

The quarrel was patched up, but less than a year after the Sixth Congress Herzl was dead, his last months spent in acrimonious debate with Russian Zionists. Herzl had been vain, brash, arbitrary, self-centered, and wildly impractical. He provoked storms that threatened to end the Zionist movement. Sympathizers recognized that he was no closer to securing Palestine as a national home at the Sixth Congress than when he published *Der Judenstaat* in 1896. His travels appeared pointless; after all his exhortations, Europe's rulers were still only mildly interested in Zionism, and then only if Zionism could be used to further their own interests.

His fund-raising record was equally dismal. Almost to the end of his life, he naively hoped that the Rothschilds would contribute large sums. Theoretically, Edmond de Rothschild would turn over direction of his Palestinian colonies to Zionists, and Hirsch's Jewish Colonization Association would "capitulate" and help with the financing. In 1902, the Jewish National Fund (Keren Kayemeth) was created to buy land in small parcels. During the first three years of its existence, only £41,300 was collected, "all in small sums from the less wealthy." The year of Herzl's death, collection boxes with a white Star of David on a blue background became the chief fund-raising device for the acquisition of a Palestinian homeland by Zionists.

Wrong as he was on a host of organizational and fund-raising problems, Herzl was unquestionably right on the issues that mattered most. In *Der Judenstaat*, he unflinchingly faced the insecurity of Jewish life in Europe and with uncanny prescience warned Jews of an impending catastrophe. To Jews in the Pale he was a modern Moses, giving form to their thoughts and searching for the way to the Promised Land.

After Herzl's death, who would lead them forth?

Certainly no American *shtadlanim* had faith in Herzl or his philosophy while he was alive. Oscar Straus, who met Herzl in 1900, found him "untrained" for the task of seeking international support. Jacob Schiff declined to meet Herzl in 1904 despite Rabbi Stephen Wise's urging. Although attached to fellow Jews in "faith and race," Schiff was "an American pure and simple and [could not] possibly belong to two nations."

Yahudim made their position abundantly clear in the press. Anti-Zionism became editorial policy for Adolph Ochs's New York *Times.* Belittling Herzl, the *American Hebrew* caustically noted that the first Zionist Congress rated "less than two inches of space per day" in the daily press. The *Jewish Chronicle* saw "no good thing" in Zionism, and New York's *Jewish Messenger* doubted Herzl's sanity. The *American Israelite* considered Zionism a political creed suitable only for eastern Europe's unwanted multitudes. At the 1897 convention of the Central Conference of American Rabbis, spiritual leaders proclaimed their "total disapproval of any attempt for the establishment of a Jewish state," which would confirm the anti-Semitic assertion that Jews were foreigners wherever they lived.

Among those to sound the loudest alarm against Zionism and Herzl was Rabbi Isaac Wise, who leaned to a belief that Jews should turn to agriculture as a means of building character, but should not till the soil in a Jewish country. Wise thought Herzl a mere politician trading on the misery of east Europeans. The first Zionist Congress was of minor importance, a "farce." Americans need not concern themselves with "all this agitation. . . ."

On the other hand, Yahudim could rightly claim an interest in Jewish settlements stretching back to 1825, when Shearith Israel's inimitable Mordecai Manuel Noah, who had seen Jewish misery in Europe and Africa, announced plans for an American-Jewish "city" on Grand Island in the Niagara River. Made possible with funds from a Christian friend, "Ararat" was to be a temporary substitute for Palestine. Noah issued an invitation to Jews from an Episcopal Church in Buffalo, explaining that an American experience would mature Jews politically.* Few responded, some thought he was a lunatic; Noah concluded that only the Holy Land could inspire a large-scale Jewish migration.

Yahudim also cheered the Palestinian beneficences of Sir Moses Montefiore and Edmond de Rothschild, and listened to "messengers" who traveled to America from the Holy Land to raise funds for assorted yeshivas, hospitals, and other institutions. In 1849, Shearith Israel resolved to send an annual gift of $25 to the poor of the Holy Land, and in 1853, a North American Relief Society for Indigent Jews in Jerusalem, Palestine, was organized by Sampson Simson; it received a $10,000 bequest in Judah Touro's will.

Like their counterparts in France, Germany, and England, American Yahudim of the early 1900s thought that more Jews might go from Russia to Palestine if there were no flag-waving nationalist or noisy Zionist congresses. Emphasis should be put on making arid land fertile through new technologies, not by agitating for autonomy. All this talk

* At least it couldn't hurt, thought Noah: "The effort may be successful, but otherwise, can never be injurious."

about colonial trusts, national funds, and Jewish financial advisors was useless and irritating. In 1908, Schiff contributed $100,000 to establish a technical institute in Haifa.

Nonetheless, there were Yahudi defectors, including several Reform rabbis. Professor Richard Gottheil of the Semitics Department of Columbia; his father, Gustav, senior rabbi at Temple Emanu-El; and young Rabbi Stephen Wise attended the first Zionist Congress in Basel and came away deeply impressed. They were later joined by such eminent clerics as Rabbi Bernard Felsenthal, Rabbi Solomon Schechter of Jewish Theological Seminary, and the redoubtable Judah Magnes. Thanks to their enthusiasm, the Federation of American Zionists, a miscellany of some 100 synagogues, Jewish societies, and other groups, was organized.

Downtown, the movement was made up of intellectuals sharing an antireligious bias with socialists, but unwilling to channel alienation into militant trade unionism and class struggle. Their exemplar was Louis Lipsky, who had a brilliant talent for articulating the faith. Downtown Zionists had no money, little prestige, and precious little influence within their own precincts. They were more interested in ideology than in financing. Their favorite activity was arguing tactics and philosophy in cafes and cafeterias, and dues payments were always in arrears.

Zionist federation life was not made easier by the continual hue and cry Yidn raised against Yahudim who headed the movement. The major charge was despotism: with characteristic Yahudi arrogance (according to Yidn), uptown rabbis made all major policy decisions and awed downtowners "into a peculiar state of submissiveness. . . ." Jacob de Haas, Herzl's secretary and a neutral, came to America in 1902 to serve as federation secretary and editor of its publication, the *Maccabean.* Neither Haas nor Magnes, who later replaced him as secretary, could inspire unity. Nor could they recruit Yahudim with big money. The organization was too insignificant, too troublesome, and too uninfluential to command respect or interest. Yahudim resigned; even Magnes drifted away.

Lower East Side Zionists, as yet unprepared to assume overall responsibility, were literally forced into leadership positions in 1911 because no alternatives were left. The downtowners were ready to try anything to increase popular and financial support. To pacify leftists, socialism and

Zionism were declared compatible philosophies. To bewitch Yahudim, the announced goal was Palestinian colonies, not the victory of Jewish nationalism. To inspire the Orthodox, ancient Jewish glories were recalled.

Nothing worked. Labor groups were negative, *landsmanschaften* were disinterested, and the *Forward* was openly hostile. The masses, eager to move upward in the social order, remained indifferent; if they were at all disposed, they joined Mizrachi (Religious Zionists), Paole Zion (Labor Zionists), or Hadassah (the Women's Zionist Organization). Political Zionism remained a cause that appealed to intellectuals. In 1901, only $50 was raised for the National Library in Jerusalem. In 1914, the budget was $12,150, and out of two-and-a-half-million American Jews there were little more than 12,000 members. Leaders considered giving up and moving to Palestine.

Like many major organizational successes, the Zionist breakthrough was an accident. Within weeks after the outbreak of World War I, Turkey joined the Central Powers, and Palestine was completely cut off from allies and neutrals. The World Zionist Executive, with headquarters in Berlin, was similarly cut off from national Zionist groups in England, France, Russia, and the United States. In the breach, Louis Lipsky called a meeting at the Hotel Marseilles in New York on August 30, 1914, to form an emergency Provisional Executive Committee for General Zionist Affairs, which would function until some word came from Berlin. Aside from the fact that one member of the World Zionist Executive, Schmaryu Levin, happened to be in New York and approved, the committee had no legal basis for existence.

It was at this meeting that Louis Brandeis suddenly became a Zionist leader—indeed, chairman of the provisional committee—after a series of attempts to recruit him for the movement had failed. Brandeis had formally joined the Federation of American Zionists only three years before. As late as April 1913, he refused membership on the board of directors of the Zion Association of Greater Boston, although he had served on a committee honoring a visiting Zionist, Nahum Sokolow. He had not been intensely interested in affairs Jewish or Zionist, and up to 1912, by which time he was a millionaire, his total contributions to Jewish causes were probably less than $1500.*

* Brandeis's conversion to Zionism, like Herzl's, has never been fully explained.

For thirty-five years, from the mid-1880s until his death in 1920, Jacob Schiff's approval was necessary for successful Jewish communal efforts. (*Edward M. M. Warburg*)

elix Warburg, Schiff's son-in-law, eventually
ad "57 varieties" of philanthropies.
dward M. M. Warburg)

In 1914, the Joint Distribution Committee's founders included the ever-present (seated, foreground, left to right) Marshall, Warburg and Schiff. (*Joint Distribution Committee*)

Louis Marshall, probably the mo:
articulate spokesman in America
Jewry's history.
(*Zionist Archives and Library*)

Justice Louis Dembritz Brandeis
(about 1914). He urged Zionists
"Organize, organize, organize" a
to forgo the delightful pleasures
ideological disagreement.
(*Zionist Archives and Library*)

Chaim Weizmann in the 1920s. Perhaps more than any other man, Weizmann understood East European Jewry's need for redemption in the Holy Land. (*Zionist Archives and Library*)

Emanuel Neumann engineered Zionist fund raising campaigns during the 1920s, while others provided a "machinery of jazz." (*Zionist Archives and Library*)

David Ben-Gurion, at his best, got to the heart of a matter with incredible speed but brooked no opposition.
(*Zionist Archives and Library*)

Henry Morgenthau, Jr., was secretary of the treasury and later chairman of the United Jewish Appeal's great post-World War II fund raising campaigns.
(*Zionist Archives and Library*)

Rabbi Abba Hillel Silver simultaneously served as pastor, fund raiser, and Zionist spokesman until the great American Zionist schism of 1948. *(Abba Hillel Silver Memorial Archives)*

Henry Montor, the post-World War II model for Jewish fund raisers. Much to their surprise, Montor kept proving that American Jews could do things they said they couldn't do. *(United Jewish Appeal)*

Joseph Willen invented card calling and, like Montor, served as a model for Jewish fund raisers.
(Ike Vern, United Jewish Appeal-Federation of Jewish Philanthropies)

Nahum Goldman's 1950 negotiations with representatives of the Federal Republic of West Germany resulted in billions of dollars in reparation payments, which financed Israel's industrial growth.
(Zionist Archives and Library)

Almost sixty years old in 1914, Brandeis was a charismatic character with appeal to non-Jews, as well as to Jews. Born and raised in Kentucky, his scholastic record at Harvard Law School was legendary. His reputation as a New York corporation lawyer was among the best, and his earnings, among the highest; in 1891, he was earning the enormous sum (for the time) of $50,000 a year. As a man of means he could afford to take up causes he favored.

Whatever downtowners had thought when they elected him chairman, Brandeis was no figurehead leader. "Organize, organize, organize," followers were commanded, "until every Jewish-American must stand up and be counted, counted with us, or prove himself wittingly or unwittingly one of the few who are against their own people."

Symbolizing a shift from ideology to action, federation offices moved uptown from Henry Street on the Lower East Side to Twenty-third Street in the business district. Administrative inefficiencies were not tolerated. Brandeis arrived at the office early each morning and held meetings, received visitors, assigned tasks. Cultural development took a backseat to fund raising, organization, and indoctrination. Concrete accomplishments were sought, believers were expected to cooperate, and abstract discussions were rare. Brandeis had a mania for reports on all phases of activity, including fund raising, and he personally supervised office operations. Everything was bent to the supreme goal: a thriving Zionist movement. Good Zionists, Brandeis wrote the Zionist Council of Greater New York, would prove themselves "only by producing Members, Money, Discipline."

Brandeis's prestige, enthusiasm, and energy were irresistible. Early Yahudi leaders—among them Richard Gottheil and Stephen Wise—returned to the fold. A brilliant new leadership group was recruited: Judge Julian Mack of Chicago; Felix Frankfurter, a professor of law at Harvard; and Louis Kirstein, a stalwart contributor to Jewish causes in Boston. Under Brandeis's leadership, the provisional committee became a coalition of all Zionist groups. The masses were fired by a newfound vitality and efficiency. Downtowners flocked to the banner, and the number of members would reach 22,000 in 1917.

"[Democracy] means that every Jew in this land, preeminently every Jew in the Zionist Movement, has a right to be heard, what is more, he has also a duty to be heard," Brandeis told the 1916 Convention of the Federation of American Zionists. It was really simple. To be a Zionist was to be in the midst of a glorious adventure. To be Jewish was to be the inheritor of a glorious tradition. To become better Americans, Jews had to become better Jews, Zionists, and contributors. The Zionist program would provide a haven for all Jews in Palestine, a "legally secured home."

But this was contradictory. Could Zionists avoid becoming hyphenated American Jews in spirit if they joined a sectarian political movement? Could a Jew remain loyal to America and yet work for and contribute to the creation of a Jewish country? Yes, argued Brandeis, an advocate of total commitment to the secular culture of his native land. Ancient Jewish values underlay the basic principles of both Zionism and American progressivism. Far from being incompatible, they were mutually uplifting.

Unable to take philosophical leaps from Judaism to Americanism to Zionism, Zionist ideologues on the Lower East Side did not share Brandeis's views. But they were afraid to voice dissent, lest Brandeis, interpreting criticism as ingratitude, depart. For great Yahudim the problem was even more frustrating: They believed Jewish nationalism was being masked by Americanism and Judaism.

In August 1914, Brandeis's first task appeared to be philanthropic rather than political; twenty-odd settlements in Palestine had to be helped to survive war and blockade. Eighty-five thousand Jews were isolated, the vast majority dependent on doles from overseas. Kibbutzim* earning their way through exports of wines, oranges, and almonds were cut off from markets and from imports of foodstuffs. Suspicious of Jews in their midst, the Turks arrested Zionist leaders wherever they could be found and expelled thousands to Egypt,† thus hoping to foil incipient local revolts by Jews seeking an autonomous state. In August 1914, Henry Morgenthau, the anti-Zionist American ambassador to Turkey, cabled Jacob Schiff that $50,000 was urgently needed to save colonies from collapse. The provisional committee voted $100,000 for relief; Brandeis made a $1000 contribution, but Zionists could raise nowhere near $100,000 despite Brandeis's plea that "the European Jews are now prevented from contributing practically anything. Upon us falls the obligation and the privilege of providing the needed funds."

* Jewish agricultural settlements.

† One activist named David Ben-Gurion fled to the United States.

Money for Palestine would come mainly from where money always came—the Yahudim. Of the $50,000, the American Jewish Committee sent $25,000; Schiff sent $12,500, and the Zionists sent $12,500.

Brandeis, an exceedingly shrewd tactician, realized that the provisional committee could deal on equal terms with Yahudim only when it reached a position of strength. For obvious reasons, financial equality was not a realistic goal. The counter to money was a large membership. Before socialist, Orthodox, and Yahudi relief committees were fully operational in JDC, the remittance system permitted American Jews to help relatives in the Pale. Brandeis recommended that the provisional committee process private remittances and thus bring the masses into closer contact with the movement. At first Yahudim and the Orthodox opposed Zionist supervision, but in the end Zionists at home and abroad handled the transmittals under JDC's aegis. Full advantage was taken of publicity; in July 1916, the Zionist office for New England sent letters to 450 remitters, urging them to join the Zionist cause.

It is not surprising that friendly collaboration between Zionists and Yahudim was short-lived. Yahudim wanted Zionists to work under close observation through the American Jewish Relief Committee. Brandeis preferred an independent course. This prompted Louis Marshall to dismiss Zionists as "self-advertisers." Not unperceptive, Marshall thought Zionists wanted to make it appear to the masses that they were taking the initiative in relief while Yahudim followed their lead. Zionists retorted that the rich were once again seeking domination of the Jewish community, imposing their views on the Lower East Side.

Victories over Yahudim made headlines in the Yiddish press, but they did not help raise money for Palestinian settlements. Zionists improved campaign techniques—$135,000 was collected in 1915 for "ordinary disbursements"—but the expenses of an emergency fund, plus operations of a larger organization, were increasingly burdensome. By mid-1916, Brandeis was calling for a minimum of $20,000 a month in addition to relief contributions.

These sums were not comparable to the large contributions Yahudim could muster. A *modus vivendi* between Zionists and JDC was essential. The provisional committee decided to drop philanthropic work, continue processing remittances, and concentrate on membership drives. Relief would be given over to JDC.* Relief, the *Maccabean* explained to Zionists, "does not come within the scope of the original program of the Provisional Committee."

While the explanation may have satisfied believers, it was hardly elucidating. The provisional committee had originally been called into existence as a holding operation and few specific aims had been outlined. It had no defined scope, nor did Brandeis cast light on the matter, except to say vaguely that a Jewish heritage and the Jewish People must be preserved.

Yet Brandeis grasped more quickly than anyone else that the outbreak of war presented a superb opportunity to unite American Jewry on political grounds; philanthropy was just one aspect of this opportunity. The day after the Hotel Marseilles meeting, Brandeis began his campaign for an American Jewish Congress, a representative body of organizations whose delegates, elected by the masses, would work toward international solutions of Jewish problems.

This was exactly what *shtadlanim* did not want to see and what they had worked diligently through JDC to avoid. Money gave them control over overseas relief, and overseas relief gave them control over the Jewish community. Everything might be lost in free elections, with power going to the Yiddish press, radicals, Zionists, and that arch villain, Brandeis. If *shtadlanim* refused to participate and to continue giving, they would be accused by the masses of yet another betrayal; if they acquiesced and continued giving, they would be aiding mortal enemies and possibly, as Schiff feared, promoting anti-Semitism. "Jewish Wall Street does not want this congress," a pro-congress speaker told a Lower East Side crowd. Schiff and Marshall journeyed downtown to defend oligarchic rule and to convince the masses of the demogogic nature of Zionist leaders, of the "blatant and flamboyant" style of Zionist oratory. The American Jewish Committee, they explained, already represented Jews; no further representation was necessary.

Occasionally Schiff and Marshall were tempted to abandon the struggle and leave Lower East Siders to their own devices and just deserts. "If you run counter to our [American Jewish Committee's] best judgment, if you desire to take the . . . terrible risks which I see and which you apparently

* JDC spent $200,000 annually in Palestine for a medical unit, in addition to its other efforts.

do not behold . . . I say, if you shall persist in this course, let yours be the responsibility. I will have none of it," Marshall warned the sixth convention of the New York Kehillah (Jewish communal agency) in April 1915. Schiff told Magnes that he would withdraw financial support from the Kehillah if Magnes supported the congress movement.

The specter of Zionist sovereignty over American Jewry spurred Yahudim to renewed efforts, yet negotiations between the groups were fruitless. A stalemate lasted until late March 1916, when a well-attended preliminary congress meeting took place in Philadelphia. Compromise proposals were heard: The congress would serve as a "temporary" organization to represent Jews at the peace conference at the end of the war; it would commit no one "to the adoption, recognition or endorsement of any general theory or philosophy of life."

For Yahudim these were sops, followed by a ray of sunshine when Brandeis's nomination to the Supreme Court was confirmed by the Senate in June 1916. "I take it, you will then no longer be able to continue as leader of the Zionist and nationalist movement in this country," suggested Schiff in a hopeful letter of congratulations. But in July the new justice led a congress delegation to a meeting with the American Jewish Committee at the Astor Hotel. This aroused the ire of Adolph Ochs's *Times*, which noted editorially that Brandeis "has discharged his duty" and no further Zionist obligations were necessary. Yielding to public pressure, Brandeis resigned from the provisional committee, but, to the consternation of Yahudim, continued to command cohorts from a new base in Washington.

Brandeis masterfully put Zionists on the right side of most issues. As happened frequently in Zionist affairs, succeeding political breakthroughs were accidental. During two momentous months, March and April 1917, revolution broke out in Russia and the United States entered the war on the Allied side. In June, 335,000 Jews voting in a national election chose 300 delegates to an American Jewish Congress. Delegates, Zionists, Marshall, Schiff, and the American Jewish Committee were now all on the same side, euphoric about the downfall of czarist oppressors, carried along by the rapid sequence of events.

In November, the Balfour Declaration provided another rallying point. Brandeis's influence on President Wilson was a crucial factor; without the president's approval, the British would never have issued the document. True, exactly what Zionists got was vague: the "National Home" to which it referred could mean anything from a retirement colony to a political state. A statement in Lord Balfour's letter about not prejudicing the rights of others could also nullify everything that preceded it. Yet within three weeks the provisional committee discussed a chartered company* to maintain law and order in Palestine until a Jewish government was set up.

The succession of events was too much for *shtadlanim*. They could not continue to be obstructionists, opposing the popular will to develop Palestine, and still maintain standing in the Jewish community. Writing Israel Zangwill, Schiff conceded that the time might be at hand to seriously consider Palestine as a Jewish homeland in which the "best elements" of world Jewry could gather. It was impossible to continue "alms-giving" forever. Writing Judge Mack, Schiff explained that his opposition had never been to Zionism, which had developed "a greatly needed self-consciousness," but to an independent political and sovereign Jewish nation in Palestine. Never resolving these inconsistencies, Schiff called for an amalgamation of JDC and Zionist fund-raising appeals in December 1919, urging American Jewry to "forget its differences" and find a solution for the Jewish Question "of which I verily believe Palestine has become the cornerstone."

The walls of the rich had been breached.

By any measure, Zionist organizational achievements during the war were remarkable. Brandeis took the ideas of a distant prophet named Herzl, some talky Lower East Siders whom nobody knew, and a few marginal Yahudim, and welded them to American liberalism. He then produced a dues-paying membership large enough to influence Lower East Side Jews, non-Jews in Washington, and members of the American Jewish Committee. Not satisfied with that, he raised $5,739,000 by 1920. Skillfully playing his cards, he made the provisional committee the most powerful Zionist group in the world. Never strong on Zionist ideology and exasperated by followers who wanted to discuss it in depth, he was able in 1917 to rid himself of ideologues questioning his heavy emphasis

* "The utmost vigilance," said Brandeis, "should be exercised to prevent the acquisition by private persons of land, water rights or other natural resources, or any concessions for public utilities. These must all be secured for the whole Jewish people."

on pragmatism. A Zionist meeting in Baltimore to form a permanent organization to succeed the provisional committee heard both Mizrachi and Paole Zion representatives demand proportional representation on the new executive committee. "General Zionists" (Brandeisists) would not agree to the demand; both Mizrachi and Paole Zion then quit the meeting and Brandeis's leadership. A year later, the General Zionists convoked a meeting in Pittsburgh to create the Zionist Organization of America (ZOA), its program downgrading nationalism and strongly weighted in favor of Palestinian economic development.

In Europe, Chaim Weizmann was the chief Zionist leader. Like Brandeis, he had filled a breach left when the British branch of the movement was cut off from the hierarchy in Berlin. Weizmann cultivated David Lloyd George, the wartime British prime minister, and persuaded Arthur James Balfour, the foreign secretary, to issue the Balfour Declaration. Around him gathered prominent British Jews, including Harry Sacher, Israel Sieff, Joseph Cohen, and Simon Marks. Strictly speaking, Weizmann had no legal authority to speak for the World Zionist Organization or to negotiate in its behalf. Yet he was an unquestioned leader, acting with the same commanding authority that Brandeis exuded.

Born in a *shtetl* in 1874, trained as a chemist in Germany and Switzerland, Weizmann had arrived penniless in England in 1904. While making his way to a modest fortune in his profession, he found time to attend prewar Zionist congresses. By turns concise and contradictory, mercurial and stable,* he understood as no other man of his time the psychology and yearnings of the Jewish masses. He was infinitely patient with their petty bickerings, their inclination to see world history as a conspiracy against the Jews, their endless theoretical discussions, their fears and hesitations, their humility in meetings with great Yahudim. He was unafraid to accept responsibility for the realization of their aims, and he was unwilling to trumpet hollow, meaningless victories to build his own image.

Brandeis met Weizmann during a London stopover on a trip to Palestine in 1919. During the encounter, Brandeis struck Weizmann as cold, calculating, unyielding in his "Puritan" attitudes, and naive about the difficult political road that lay ahead in the struggle for a Jewish state.

* "He was no organizer. He was a soloist," said Felix Frankfurter.

Brandeis found Weizmann neither "as great" nor "as objectionable" as he had been portrayed.

To insure that Brandeis arrive at the first postwar meeting of the Actions (Executive) Committee of the World Zionist Organization speaking from a position of strength, a ZOA campaign to raise funds "for the restoration of Palestine" was launched in 1919. Schiff's name was listed as a committee member, along with such distinguished non-Jews as William Jennings Bryan, Gov. Alfred E. Smith of New York, and the president of Harvard University. Zionist stalwarts in key posts were asked to move aside for influential people who could solicit big gifts. Three million dollars was raised—to the rank and file, a fantastic demonstration of fund-raising prowess; to Zionist intellectuals, a source of concern that the ZOA would soon devote itself only to fund raising.

On July 7, 1920, the meeting began in London, its major purpose to decide how to further the cause and develop Palestine in light of the Balfour Declaration. Typical of Zionist meetings organized by Yidn, there was no formal agenda and accommodations were uncomfortable. Delegates drifted in late and promptly began arguing with each other in a babble of tongues. Parliamentary procedure was haphazard at best. No feasibility studies had been prepared on immigration, hydroelectric power, or agricultural projects in Palestine, and thus no recommendations could be made. Orderly discussions appeared impossible.

American delegates, accustomed to the discipline and efficiency of the Brandeis years, were appalled by the confusion and lack of preparation. They also had some surprises of their own to spring. For Brandeis, Zionism's political work was complete with the Balfour Declaration.* The next job was the economic development of Palestine for Jews who wanted to live there.

He was not one of them. Not only did he lack the intense personal commitment to the Holy Land born of daily anti-Semitic experience in the Pale, but he was hard put not to accept assimilation and a Jewish country as equally desirable goals. In London as in New York, Brandeis tied Zionism to liberalism. Weizmann was willing to resign an important post at the University of Manchester to devote full time to Zionist de-

* "The effort to acquire the public recognition of the Jewish Homeland in Palestine, for which [Herzl] lived and died, has been crowned with success," Brandeis said in an address at the conference's opening session.

velopment; Brandeis had no intention of leaving the Supreme Court for any assignment.

After the long and rambling discussion that traditionally opened Zionist meetings, the Americans proposed to abolish the Zionist Commission (which advised the British government in Palestine) and replace it with a seven-member Jewish Advisory Council. The administration of the World Zionist Organization would be overhauled completely in the interests of economy and efficiency. Each national Zionist group would be autonomous, and the movement's headquarters would be moved to Palestine. A Greater Actions Committee, consisting, in Brandeis's words, "of members possessing those qualities which especially fit them for specific tasks in Palestine," would be created. Superannuated Zionists would be pensioned off "just as governments and public bodies do."

To Europeans who saw the movement's American branch as its major financial reservoir, this was more than alarming; it was potentially disastrous. "I do not agree with the philosophy of your Zionism, . . ." Weizmann angrily told Brandeis. "We are different, absolutely different. There is no bridge between Washington and Pinsk." Weizmann could not accept a Zionism inspired mainly by libertarian ideals, devoid of a messianic fervor. The only goal worth working toward was Jewish political sovereignty in the Holy Land, the salvation and the hope of the eastern European Jewish masses.

All this set the stage for an angry debate about financing and fund raising, the subjects on which the conference foundered. Brandeis thought European Zionists wastefully extravagant, unable to disburse large sums of money efficiently. He disliked fund raising and wanted Palestine to escape "schnorerdom." Economic development was to be stimulated through investments on which annual returns would be paid. Philanthropy would be downgraded in favor of solid American business practices.

To the Europeans, the American view represented a "premature emphasis on private enterprise and profits," reflecting a "lack of belief in the cooperative system of agriculture" developed in the Holy Land. As Weizmann was later to tell American businessmen, "We must have money to sink in Palestine, to reconstruct what has been destroyed. When you drain the marshes, you get no returns, but you accumulate wealth for the generations to come."

Weizmann's counterproposal was Keren Hayesod, an economic development fund for Palestine to which world Jewry would contribute £25 million. The money would come from the masses as well as from the rich. Every Zionist would set an example for coreligionists by tithing 10 percent of his assets and income. About 20 percent of receipts would go to the Jewish National Fund to purchase land, a third would pay for immigration, education, and other welfare services, and the balance would be spent developing utilities, agricultural settlements, and economic enterprises.

Antagonisms might have been resolved had differences merely revolved around financing. But differences between Brandeis and Weizmann were basically philosophical and precluded compromise. In fact, their positions on fund raising were fairly close. Brandeis acknowledged the paramount need for economic stability if prospective investors, including great Yahudim, were to be attracted. Neither stability nor profits were immediate possibilities in Palestine, and philanthropic funds were therefore a necessity. Moreover, on key issues such as nationalization of agriculture, land, and industries, both men were in agreement.

A final break was heralded by Weizmann's announcement that Palestine needed $10 million a year from American Jews. It was now Brandeis's turn to be stunned. The goal was "astronomical," he insisted; at best, American Jewry could supply $500,000 a year. For European Zionists, to whom it was an uncontestable truth that American Jews grew wealthy during the war years, this smacked of indifference. JDC's receipts were no secret. "If this is all you can find in America, I will have to come over and try for myself," Weizmann retorted.

Angered in turn, Brandeis refused to serve on the executive committee of the World Zionist Organization (WZO). Changing his mind, he was willing to be named honorary president of the World Zionist Organization, helping the cause during annual four-month vacation periods from Supreme Court duties. Changing it back again, he was reluctant to offer any services. Once again reversing himself at the urging of the Rumanian delegation, he agreed to serve, provided no budget was adopted and the Zionist Commission was dissolved. These demands the Europeans would not accept, and the London meeting ended with both sides hostile and antagonistic. Final refusals by Brandeis and his delegation to serve on the executive and to support Keren Hayesod rankled Weizmann and his aides and were interpreted as evidence of secessionist tendencies.

American bitterness was given full vent in strict Brandeisist positions taken the following November at the ZOA convention in Buffalo, New York. No specific commitments were made to the World Zionist Organization. Seventy-five thousand dollars monthly had previously gone to London, but only $25,000 monthly was henceforth to be sent, "with instructions that it be used for the budget expenditures in Palestine only." At home, budgets for the Hebrew Bureau and Zionist publications were cut from $56,000 in 1920 to $6,000 in 1921; funds for general educational work were pared from $88,000 to $38,000.

In London, cuts were passed down the line. Forty-eight people were discharged from the WZO staff. Allocations for the Zionist Commission, the Hebrew Language Committee, and Zionist-sponsored Arabic newspapers were reduced. Reforms were made, though grudgingly. But news that Americans were unyielding on the issue of autonomy and about to launch their own fund-raising plan for Palestine made an open break inevitable; Weizmann kept his promise and embarked for America.

On Saturday, April 2, 1921, Weizmann and a party including Albert Einstein, who was raising funds for Hebrew University in Jerusalem, arrived in New York. Because it was the Jewish Sabbath, debarkation was delayed until sunset; Einstein and Weizmann talked to reporters about relativity and Zionism. When they left the ship, the visitors found "the whole of New York Jewry" waiting at dockside. Thousands came from the Lower East Side, from Brooklyn, and from the Bronx to pay homage.

At 11:30 P.M., the two men arrived at the Commodore Hotel, "tired, hungry, thirsty . . . completely dazed," still accompanied by well-wishers and horn-blowers. Weizmann was carrying a memorandum delivered on the ship by Judge Mack, president of the ZOA, setting forth conditions under which Americans would cooperate in raising funds for the Keren Hayesod. Zionist finances were to be tied to principles of public budgeting (monies could not be transferred from one account to another), and strict budgetary controls were deemed essential. Private investments as well as philanthropic funds were to be sought.

Buttressed by aides and encouraged by welcomers proving that not all

American Jews shared "the attitude of their leaders," Weizmann considered unilateral action. Yet American leaders were powerful, and Weizmann foresaw "difficulty in doing anything substantial" without their cooperation. For weeks he wavered, unable to reject compromise, equally unable to accept it. In public he called on the American leadership to "lay down [its] weapons," but in private he was more amenable.

Events in Palestine were the deciding factor. At the beginning of May there were Arab riots. Sympathy for Jewish victims could be channeled for Keren Hayesod's benefit. Weizmann decided to break with Brandeis, and Keren Hayesod was declared established.* A showdown came in June after both sides launched campaigns to recruit supporters. At the ZOA convention in Cleveland, rival positions were put forth with great skill by Felix Frankfurter and Stephen Wise for Brandeis and by Louis Lipsky for Weizmann. Heavily laced with pro-Weizmann delegates, the convention voted down Brandeis, 153–71; the jurist, his lieutenants, and Nathan Straus resigned from the ZOA executive committee to become "humble soldiers in the ranks. . . ." Weizmann then launched a fund-raising campaign, making loyalty to the "Jewish People" the key issue and scheduling as many personal appearances as possible.

"To anyone who has not actually been through it, it is difficult to convey any idea of what this experience meant," he was to write later. A pattern emerged. For months on end, Weizmann traveled from city to city, arriving on early trains and being greeted by hosts of noisy enthusiasts. From the station he would be taken to a hotel or to the city hall, "to breakfast with anywhere between twenty-five to fifty local notables, including, usually, the mayor." At about 10:00 A.M., when ceremonies were over, cameramen and reporters waited for a press conference. "For some unfathomable reason they always billed me as the inventor of TNT. It was in vain that I systematically and repeatedly denied any connection with, or interest in, TNT."† Then there would be a formal luncheon followed by meetings with local Zionist workers to en-

* In an unpublished autobiography, Emanuel Neumann, the new organization's campaign director, makes no mention of the disorders that influenced Weizmann and ascribes the decision to pressure from aides, including himself. It is difficult to see, however, how the outbreaks could have been ignored.

† Weizmann was the discoverer, during World War I, of a vegetable substitute for acetone, an acid used in the manufacture of TNT. The discovery was particularly timely for the British because acetone had previously been obtained from Germany.

courage them in their labors. A formal dinner, "very like lunch, only more so . . ." would be followed by a mass meeting, and finally a rush to the station for a train to the next city.

Weizmann, habitually late for appointments, found himself on regular schedules for meetings with big givers,* many of whom considered themselves experts on Zionism. He listened to Brandeisist criticism and responded to "crank schemes for the overnight creation of a Jewish homeland." He found American givers surpassed their counterparts in *shtetls* when it came to *koved*: "a big donor would often make his contribution to the fund conditional on my accepting an invitation to lunch or dine at his house. Then I would have to face a large family gathering—three or four generations—talk, answer questions, listen to appeals and opinions, and watch my replies carefully, lest I inadvertently scare off a touchy prospect. I would sit through a lengthy meal and after it meet a select group of local celebrities and again listen and answer till all hours of the night."

Thanks to the experience, Weizmann grasped fundamentals of American Jewish philanthropy that had escaped Brandeis: There was no need to explain all the reasons why one should be a devout Jew, a committed Zionist, a loyal American, and an intelligent investor. For Yidn once removed from the Pale, guilt-ridden by their great fortune while brethren suffered and died in Europe, atonement could be made in the form of contributions. "You will have to sweat and labor and give money on which you will not get any return, but which will be transformed into natural wealth," Weizmann told prospects.

Yidn rallied everywhere, particularly in New York. In Brooklyn's Brownsville section, local Zionists who supported Weizmann in the struggle with Brandeis arranged a Keren Hayesod mass meeting. But one detail was overlooked—consent from the national Keren Hayesod headquarters, which subsequently ruled against the meeting because of a presumed lack of local big givers to justify the use of Weizmann's time. The news outraged Brownsville. Brooklyn Jewry had been disgraced. The national leadership relented; there could be a parade, but no appeal for funds.

This, too, was considered a slur, and determined Brooklynites scheduled an appeal. A week before the event, a builder named Jacob Goell advised

* At that time, contributors of $5000 or more were considered big givers.

local Zionists of a devotion to their cause so great that he would contribute to Keren Hayesod $2,000 a year for five years. Goell promptly produced the first payment. On the night of the rally, the local Liberty Theatre was packed with "an audience that only Brownsville could produce." Goell's generosity was acclaimed, the theater rocked with applause and excitement, pledge followed upon pledge, and $125,000 was raised.

This was but one example of Weizmann's success among Yidn, achieved despite opposition from Brandeisists. Yet only two million dollars was raised; a rival drive directed by Judge Julian Mack never got off the ground. But Weizmann paid a stiff price for the achievement. He learned that a service once offered might later be considered an obligation: fund raising became part of his regular duties in America. "As the years passed, and my visits to America were repeated almost annually, a sort of tradition was established, . . ." he writes in his memoirs, *Trial and Error.* Weizmann traveled from New York to San Francisco soliciting gifts.

Contributors avid for *koved* even followed him to Europe. He dared not avoid big givers who happened to know his whereabouts, lest they become offended and then disaffected. "It was not that I minded very much giving umbrage on my own account," writes Weizmann, "but I learned that there were people who, having tried to see me in Europe and failed—I am sure through no fault of mine—went back to the States to cancel their pledges to the Keren Hayesod!"

At the end of 1921, Weizmann's hold on American Yidn appeared unshakable; Keren Hayesod's fund-raising apparatus was literally built around him. He provided charisma, and his lieutenants—Lipsky, Neumann, who engineered fund-raising campaigns, and Meyer Weisgal, who handled publicity—provided a "machinery of jazz." Despite Weizmann's charisma and American Jewry's guilt feelings, however, $10 million was not raised. New York's *Jewish Day* calculated that collections averaged something less than two cents a month per American Jew. Moreover, Lipsky noted that an increasing number of Yidn, become rich during the war, were seeking association with great Yahudim in causes favored by establishment givers. There was a distinct possibility that rich Yidn might be lured away from Zionism by artful anti-Zionist Yahudim.

This left Weizmann's Zionists roughly where Brandeis's Zionists had been: growing in numbers, but bereft of support from great Yahudim who were implacably hostile to Zionism and Jewish nationalism and alone possessed the big money that could assure success. The key Yahudim were Louis Marshall and Felix Warburg, whose services at the head of JDC and Federation had made him a Jewish folk hero after Schiff's death. From Marshall and Warburg's standpoint, Weizmann replaced Brandeis as the man to see about Yidn and Jewish nationalists. Significantly, Marshall and Warburg were among Weizmann's visitors at the Commodore Hotel when he arrived in 1921.

Weizmann had not been successful everywhere as a fund raiser. Cincinnati was a "difficult" city; Chicago resisted him largely because of opposition from Julius Rosenwald, in Weizmann's words, a philanthropist willing to contribute "to a Negro university, for a *Volksmuseum* in Munich, for a Berlin School of Dentistry. . . . But the only Palestinian institutions to share in his benefactions were the Teachers Seminary in Jerusalem and the Agricultural Station in Athlit. He read most of our material, and his stock answer whenever I met him was: 'If you can convince me that Palestine is a *practical* proposition, you can have all my money.' "

Weizmann found Warburg "a man of sterling character, charitable to a degree, a pivotal figure in the American Jewish community, if not in very close touch with the rank and file." Invited by the financier to lunch at Kuhn, Loeb in the spring of 1923, Weizmann was treated to sordid accounts of life in Palestine, but he allowed Warburg to wax emotional. He then dismissed the entire monologue as "backstairs gossip."* Stunned by the response, Warburg's reaction was to offer a contribution. Weizmann suggested that he visit Palestine instead. To Weizmann's surprise, the next news from Warburg was a postcard from the Holy Land expressing approval of "every phase of our work."

Warburg's trip, thought Weizmann, was a good beginning, albeit to nothing of immediate significance. For Yidn, Zionism was a movement for national regeneration; for Warburg, Weizmann discovered, it was "one

* "A more fantastic rigamarole, I have, to be honest, never heard from a responsible quarter: bolshevism, immorality, waste of money, inaction, inefficiency, all of it based on nothing more than hearsay."

among the fifty-seven varieties of his philanthropic endeavors. . . ." Moreover, the philanthropist's aides repeatedly warned him against close identification with Jewish nationalists.

Yet Weizmann badly needed accommodation with great Yahudim, men "doing magnificent relief work for European Jewry . . . [who were pouring] millions into a bottomless pit, when some of the money could have been directed to the Jewish Homeland. . . ." Between 1921 and 1925, four Keren Hayesod appeals yielded $6 million. During the same period, JDC raised $20.8 million.

Convinced in the mid-1920s that a Jewish commonwealth in Palestine was merely theoretical, impractical, and nowhere in sight, Marshall and Warburg were amenable to a Weizmann offer to join the Jewish Agency, the World Zionist Organization instrumentality set up to replace the Zionist Commission. Through the Jewish Agency, *shtadlanim* could see themselves exercising a restraining influence over zealots who rattled on about a Jewish state. Weizmann could see himself controlling non-Zionists through the World Zionist Organization, which would in turn control the Jewish Agency. Only the Zionist rank and file, unaware of these political subtleties, were perplexed by the maneuver. Stalwarts asked why, if rich Yahudim wanted to decide Zionist policy, they did not join the ZOA like everybody else. Weizmann's answer was that the Jewish Agency must be "a body representative of the [entire] Jewish People." Developing Zionist plans for non-Zionists, Weizmann was authorized to proceed by the Fourteenth Zionist Congress, which met in Vienna in 1925.

The same year, Warburg announced a $15-million, three-year JDC "United Jewish Campaign" to finance eastern European reconstruction, including Agro-Joint. The news threw Zionists into an uproar. It was immediately seen that Yahudim were unveiling a counter-colonization plan in Europe with communists, no less, as allies. The future of Palestinian colonization might be jeopardized.

Attempting to find common ground, JDC invited Zionists to a meeting in Philadelphia in September 1925. Delegates were told that compromise was essential to Jewish unity. JDC funds would be used only for purposes as "heretofore and up to this time," including agricultural settlements and excluding "any new or untried task in the field of social amelioration and reconstruction." A resolution committee drafted a peace treaty, which did not satisfy Neumann and other Zionist leaders who feared that Zionist agencies would be swept into the background.

Neumann sounded out Keren Hayesod, the Jewish National Fund, Hadassah, Mizrachi, and Hebrew University on mounting a separate Zionist campaign, its goal $5 million for 1925–26. Rabbi Stephen Wise agreed to serve as chairman, provided Neumann direct the effort. Executive committees of participating agencies would be autonomous, but would jointly decide overall policy. At a meeting in November, Neumann's plan was formally adopted.

The announcement of a United Palestine Appeal (UPA) in 1925–1926 threw non-Zionists into an uproar. They claimed unity had again been thwarted by hot-headed nationalists. As proof of Yahudi perfidy, however, Zionists produced a letter written to prominent Jews throughout the country by David Brown, head of JDC's fund raising. Soliciting contributions for the United Jewish Campaign, Brown neglected to mention any commitment to Jewish settlements in Palestine, but carefully described Crimean settlements.

Marshall and Warburg attempted to pacify both sides. One-and-a-half-million dollars of the first year's $5 million JDC goal would be channeled to Palestine for economic development through a Palestine Economic Corporation. Two $500,000 contributions to UPA, one from Warburg and the other from Mrs. Sol Rosenbloom of Pittsburgh, made possible the creation of Hebrew University. Nonetheless, controversy carried over into 1927, when Weizmann was dragged into the struggle through the refusal of Judge Otto Rosalsky, the prospective UPA chairman, to accept an assignment unless non-Zionists and Zionists reached an agreement.

An exchange of letters clarifying issues between Marshall and Weizmann was proposed. Louis Lipsky wrote a draft for Weizmann, which was rejected by a committee including Rosalsky, and the entire group went to work on a new draft. Simultaneously, David Brown presumptuously drafted a letter of his own for Weizmann's signature* and presented it for approval at a luncheon meeting attended by Judge Irving Lehman.

* Whether Brown actually wrote the letter is seriously questioned by Neumann, who told me that he did "not think [Brown] was capable of drafting such a letter," and by James Marshall, who wrote me that Weizmann "was not a man to deny the realities of the situation." On the other hand, Rabbi Herbert Parzen, an authority on Zionist organizations during the period, is certain that the letter was Brown's work.

Brown blamed the ZOA leadership for recent difficulties. Weizmann refused to approve the draft, and Judge Lehman admitted to Marshall that the letter was unsatisfactory.

Marshall and Warburg either would not or could not repudiate Brown. Referring the problem back to his committee, Weizmann was told that Brown's draft was not only unacceptable, but insulting. However, if Weizmann wanted to take responsibility and sign in the interests of peace, neither Rosalsky nor anyone else would protest publicly. Another meeting with Marshall was rejected by Weizmann, but in the end all parties agreed that the letter should be signed for the sake of the Jewish Agency and fund-raising campaigns for both camps. Following an exchange of letters between Weizmann* and Marshall, the JDC effort did predictably well. At first the UPA effort faltered; by October 1927, however, $6 million had been pledged by 150,000 donors.

As Zionist prospects improved, Brandeisists returned to the fold. Efficient and energetic, they occupied high ZOA and UPA offices by 1928. Their 1920 defeat in Cleveland still rankled; loyalty to Brandeis ran strong, and as the dust from their confrontations settled, they maneuvered to rid the movement of Weizmann and Lipsky, whom they detested. Charges of mismanagement and unauthorized financial transactions were leveled against Zionist officials. Wise criticized as inadequate Weizmann's plans for the Jewish Agency, noting a lack of British assurances that a Jewish National Home would be established. Marshall-Warburg forces, thought Wise, would reduce a Zionist Palestine to a mideastern Agro-Joint.

Weizmann needed a victory to hold down Brandeisists. In August 1929, when the constitution for the Jewish Agency was submitted to the Sixteenth Zionist Congress in Zurich, Brandeisists and Lipsky-Weizmann adherents were both maneuvering for ZOA control. Reflecting the strife, UPA was close to disintegration: The Jewish National Fund and Hadassah announced they would mount separate campaigns. Weizmann's personal magnetism could not hold the coalition together.

Yet Weizmann carried the day in Zurich. During a two-week period, the

* "Although we Zionists have consecrated ourselves to the task of rebuilding and remaking Palestine, I am urging upon all Zionists the importance of realizing that every Jew has the right to his own opinions as to what is needful for the good of Jewry," Weizmann (or Brown) wrote.

world's outstanding Jews—artists, writers, politicians, businessmen, scholars, leaders of Palestinian settlements—met and called for the creation of a Jewish National Home under the leadership of Weizmann and the Jewish Agency. Half the agency's 224 members would be chosen by Zionist groups, half by non-Zionist groups. Forty-four non-Zionist seats, the largest single bloc, would go to Americans. Weizmann was elected president and Marshall, who received an ovation, was elected chairman. The *shtadlan* suspected "that the burden of money raising [for the Agency] and of planning would be imposed upon the [non-Zionists] to a disproportionate extent." One reading of events even led to the interpretation that financial responsibilities would pass completely from Zionists to non-Zionists.

But what else was there to do? The grim experiences of Jews in postwar eastern Europe demanded political as well as philanthropic unity. Three days after the congress adjourned, Albert Einstein, Sholem Asch, Leon Blum, Louis Marshall, and other stellar lights met with Weizmann to sign the "Pact of Glory," a formal declaration of cooperation between Zionists and non-Zionists. Marshall and Warburg assured Weizmann that his money troubles were over; no longer would he travel "making innumerable appeals and addresses in order to help create the means for the limited budget of the Zionist Organization." But within weeks Marshall, the last of the great *shtadlanim*, died in a Swiss hospital following emergency surgery. The loss was irreplaceable. No Jew in America could even approach his stature. Again, gloom pervaded Zionist councils.

One subject Herzl never thought about in *The Jewish State* was Arabs, 90 percent of the Holy Land's population during the 1890s. A man in a hurry, he remained indifferent to the Arabs during his trip to Palestine in 1898. For fifteen years after Herzl's death, until the end of World War I, Zionists continued to ignore Arabs,* who similarly tried to ignore Zionists.†

Meanwhile, the Jewish National Fund purchased land from Arab rulers who liquidated themselves as a class but still earned fortunes. Huge

* "I consider that it is unnecessary to bother any more with the Arabs at present," Weizmann wrote his wife in 1918, "let them take it or leave it."

† The Arabs busily concentrated on playing off the British against the Turks and Germans and vice-versa.

estates changed hands. Privately, sheiks were willing enough to do business with Zionists. In 1919, King Faisal of Saudi Arabia and Weizmann actually signed an agreement with the provision that "all necessary measures shall be taken to encourage and stimulate [Jewish] immigration into Palestine on a large scale."*

Publicly, Arab leaders took extreme anti-imperialist and anti-Zionist positions, embodying the outlook of Palestinian Arabs. *Fellaheen*—laborers and peasants—bitterly resented change in general and the British and Zionists in particular. Antagonisms were fanned by Muslim religious leaders. In 1920, the first clash between Arab and Jew occurred, with deaths on both sides. In 1929, the new Jewish Agency was viewed as a direct affront, and the Grand Mufti of Jerusalem deliberately instigated disorders. After sporadic incidents near the Wailing Wall in mid-August, a young Jew was stabbed. This signaled riots in which 133 Jews and 116 Arabs were killed.

Yahudim and Yidn were still far from united in favor of the Jewish Agency, and Marshall's death had been a shattering loss. Yet violence did not paralyze Jews with fear as Arab leaders hoped it would; Palestine was one place where Jews had hope. Settlers struck back, and in New York a Palestine Emergency Fund was organized while UPA postponed its drive. Within weeks, $2.1 million was raised. Felix Warburg, Julius Rosenwald, and Adolph Ochs were among major contributors.

This set the stage for the Allied Jewish Campaign in 1930, the first joint Zionist–non-Zionist drive for funds. The goal was $6 million, $3.5 million for reconstruction in eastern Europe and $2.5 million for "further upbuilding" in Palestine. JDC would be the conduit for money to Europe; Zionist participants included Keren Hayesod, Hadassah, and Mizrachi.

Despite Warburg's encouragement and careful omission of the words "Zionism" and "Jewish National Homeland" from all campaign literature, the Allied Jewish Campaign was a failure. Less than $2 million was raised before JDC and Zionist agencies parted company. Launched at the worst possible time—shortly after the financial crash in October 1929—its leaders had to contend with widespread fear and unemployment. Yahudim were also reluctant contributors to a cause from which Zionists benefitted. Attempting to strengthen its own ranks, the ZOA encouraged

* The Jewish population grew slowly, from 11 percent in 1922 to 31 percent in the 1940s.

Brandeisists to return. After a meeting with the justice, agreement was reached: Twelve of eighteen ZOA Administration Committee members were to be Brandeisists, sworn enemies of Weizmann and Lipsky.

Late in 1930, Weizmann badly needed another victory to bolster followers oscillating between extremes of euphoria and despair. This time the British solved his problem. Official committees investigating Holy Land riots put responsibility squarely on the Arabs, but added that there had been Zionist provocation. A British policy statement, the Passfield White Paper, called for immediate curbs on Jewish immigration and the Jewish Agency. Zionists protested vehemently in the newspapers and through spokesmen in Parliament. Weizmann resigned from the presidency of the Jewish Agency. Knocked off balance by the furor Zionists had created, the Ramsey MacDonald Labor government backed down and rescinded the White Paper.

But this time a major political victory did not neatly solve Weizmann's fund-raising or organizational problems. Zionist dissidents wanted more than paper triumphs—they wanted a tangible sign of progress. Since the end of the war, no wholesale exodus of Diaspora Jewry to Palestine had taken place.* Money for large-scale economic development was still hard to raise from obstinate Yahudim.

Failures were blamed on Weizmann's conservatism and his nonactivist, collaborationist approach to British politicians. Zionism had become Weizmann's diplomacy; pompous speakers at smoke-filled banquets congratulated themselves and diners on the Balfour Declaration. The Zionist leadership talked mostly about raising money, while the movement seemed to be going around in circles. At the 1931 Zionist Congress in Basel, Weizmann was forced to resign the presidency of the World Zionist Organization. Stephen Wise delivered a particularly stinging attack.†

Zionist activists were taken in hand by Vladimir Jabotinsky, like Weizmann a dazzling speaker in several languages, like Herzl an adept and perceptive writer. Small, ugly, and utterly charming, Jabotinsky was born in Odessa and lived in Italy, where he was strongly influenced by the Risorgimento. During World War I, he organized a Jewish Legion, which boosted Jewish morale but arrived in Palestine too late to do much

* Between 1919 and 1931, immigrants totaled only 108,536.

† In 1935, Weizmann was again elected president with the help of American Zionists, now among his strongest supporters.

damage to Turks. Though he was not a militarist, Jabotinsky was convinced that Jewish armed forces were necessary for the creation of a state, much to the shock of Brandeis and Mack in America, not to speak of Weizmann, who was with him in Basel.

Jabotinsky had expressed his positions before, but could never muster enough votes to take leadership from Weizmann. Nor could his revisionist Zionism convince a majority of members to quit the World Zionist Organization in 1931. Jabotinsky was labeled a "Jewish fascist"; all factions seesawed back and forth trying to avoid an open break. Abandoning hope of ever reaching agreement after a "discipline clause" was passed by the Zionist General Council, Jabotinsky formed an independent organization of revisionist Zionists four years later with himself at its head.

In 1934, with renewed strife in Zionist ranks and confusion over anti-Nazi tactics, a low point in American Jewish morale was reached. It was at that time that JDC and UPA decided to try a second combined Zionist–non-Zionist fund-raising drive, the United Jewish Appeal (UJA). Warburg, Lipsky, and Julius Rosenwald's son, William, were national co-chairmen. The goal was $3 million, and drives were scheduled in 247 cities.

Less than $2 million was raised. JDC leaders doubted that the Jewish Agency would survive, and hoped that the entire Zionist structure would fragment and disappear. Under no circumstances could Yahudi big givers be convinced to support emigration to Palestine as a central point. A $5000 check arrived from Spokane, Washington, with specific instructions that the funds not be used for "Zionistic" purposes. Confirming the worst fears of the rich, David Brown, who directed the campaign, told Warburg that ZOA members were using fund-raising meetings for propaganda as well as for solicitations.

Nor were Zionists happy. "The 'yahudim,'" Samuel Margoshes wrote in the *Day*, a Yiddish daily, "are opposed to . . . [anti-Nazi] protests. . . . We will continue to fight and let them, the 'yahudim' continue their silence." Yet when a break came late in October 1935 and UJA was dissolved, the *Day* was shocked: "The JDC by failing to renew the agreement for a new drive . . . is simply trying to sacrifice the Jewish refugees to its own prejudices without regard to the Jewish National Home."

As if the loss of Yahudi contributions were not bad enough, the break caused complex new problems among Zionist groups. Even with

Brandeisists back, the ZOA was in danger of losing supremacy in the movement to subsidiaries actively raising funds for Palestine. Busy with Weizmann-Brandeis and Weizmann-Jabotinsky confrontations, its leadership had little time for members. Organizationally, local districts went their own way, feeling no great ties to the national office. In 1929, collections were $500,000 behind schedule. A belated National Zionist Roll Call to recruit 250,000 members at $1 each in 1935 attracted fewer than 20,000. Attempting to raise $100,000 the same year, the ZOA actually got $13,500.

Whether Brandeisists or Weizmannites were at the helm, the ZOA needed to reassert leadership, if possible in a restored United Palestine Appeal. This time the tail would not wag the dog. All fund raising for Keren Hayesod and the Jewish National Fund—to be united in one agency—would be controlled by the ZOA through a central executive committee. For 1936 the goal was $2.5 million and Wise was named chairman. At a Washington meeting in early February, the committee received a cable from Weizmann that an additional $1 million was needed for German Jews emigrating to Palestine, and the goal was subsequently raised to $3.5 million.

Two trends in 1936, one domestic, the other Mideastern—in addition to the ever-increasing Nazi terror—made inevitable another attempt to combine Zionist and non-Zionist appeals.

At home, JDC, the ZOA, the American Jewish Committee, B'nai B'rith, and some 300 other national organizations were individually soliciting gifts from federations and welfare funds* around the country. Local agencies complained to the Council of Jewish Federations and Welfare Funds (CJFWF) that the competition for dollars was unmanageable. Suppliants were specifically warned not to solicit funds in competition with local agencies. Rather than provoke a complete breakdown, JDC and Zionists accepted a council formula in 1937, with allocations based on percentages of funds raised. Attempts at renewal the following year led to bitter quarrels while Yahudim and Zionists maneu-

* Welfare funds intended to raise money for overseas relief came into existence during the $15 million JDC campaign of 1925–28. The following year, Detroit introduced a "double-barreled" federation campaign combining appeals for overseas and local causes. This was soon standard procedure throughout the country with the exception of New York City, where Federation and UJA held separate annual drives until 1973.

vered for higher percentages; the problem was further complicated when the National Refugee Service, which helped refugees in the United States, was also given an allocation percentage.

In the Middle East, Arab violence resumed in 1936 with a general strike and terrorist acts. In mid-November a British commission headed by Lord Peel arrived in Palestine and heard testimony from Arabs and Jews. The Zionist position, elucidated by Weizmann and Ben-Gurion, was conciliatory: Arab and Jew could live together peacefully, and no special emphasis was put on the creation of a Jewish state. Weizmann made a masterly presentation, perhaps the greatest of his career, on Zionism, its history, and the perils to European Jewry.

Arabs were unimpressed, insisting that Jewish emigration and land purchases stop. British investigators leaned toward the Arabs, hoping to discourage them from leaning toward the Nazis. The Peel Commission's solution satisfied no one. It proposed a Palestine divided into three states: Arab, Jewish, and British mandate. London used the recommendations as a basis for the 1939 White Paper in which the Balfour Declaration was effectively repudiated, Jewish immigration halted, and an Arab state scheduled for creation.

The combination of the Peel Commission Report, the growing tragedy of German Jewry, and Arab violence was too much for many Yahudim. In 1937, the Central Conference of American Rabbis, which represented Reform religious leaders, pledged full cooperation to Zionists. Similarly, the Union of American Hebrew Congregations called on Jews everywhere to regard "financial and moral support" for Jewish settlers as an obligation. B'nai B'rith, peppered with first- and second-generation members of eastern European heritage, began raising large sums to help resettle German refugees in Palestine. On their part, Zionists played down demands for Jewish sovereignty in order to quiet animosities.

JDC, still committed to reconstruction—although the concept was now meaningless—resisted pressures to rejoin Zionists in fund-raising campaigns. On November 9, 1938, another JDC-UPA venture was voted down by the executive committee. That night, the Nazis launched the *Krystallnacht*. Within a month, JDC reversed itself, opting for a United Jewish Appeal.

With Reform Rabbi Abba Hillel Silver, Zionist and UPA chairman, as its major tactician and orator, UJA raised over $15 million. Yet the equitable division of funds continued to concern each partner. Zionists claimed that relatively few refugees were in need of assistance from the National Refugee Service. In 1940, UPA received 23 percent of funds raised; late the same year, its administrative committee voted to withdraw from UJA and conduct a $12 million campaign in 1941. Federation and welfare fund leaders brought secessionists to a halt, warning that no allocations would be made to Zionists unless the United Jewish Appeal continued operations.

Silver attempted to flank the CJFWF, suggesting each community hold its own referendum on the issue. While the proposition was referred to 166 cities and towns, UJA was reconstituted. Referendum results were indecisive; 40 percent of the communities were unwilling to commit themselves. Unable to get a clearcut decision in their favor and fearing the results of a complete break with local fund-raising agencies, Zionists opted to continue the shaky alliance, and UJA was reborn in March 1941 with a $25 million goal.

On the political front, Weizmann and Ben-Gurion were in the United States in 1940 and 1941 encouraging support for the British. France had dropped out of the fighting, and Russia was not yet in it. During one terrible year, the British alone faced Nazis over the skies of Europe and in Africa, from which Rommel advanced toward Palestine. On the eve of American entry into the conflict, a few Yahudim, including Julius Rosenwald's eldest son, Lessing, were prominent members of the isolationist America First Committee. The overwhelming majority of Jews tried to spare the British embarrassment. Rabbi Solomon Goldman, president of the ZOA, decried anti-British statements by Jews. Silver vehemently opposed illegal emigration to Palestine, and Weizmann addressed Zionist meetings in New York, Baltimore, Chicago, Detroit, and Cleveland, "always with the utmost caution." It was insane to denigrate the British, the sole hope of European Jewry, thought Zionist leaders. A Palestinian settlement would have to await the end of the war.

This certainly sounded realistic. At this stage of the fighting a rupture with the British over immediate and open immigration appeared suicidal for the Zionist cause. Moreover, caution fit the general mood of timidity that characterized American Jews. Still, it left unanswered the question, what actions could be taken for European Jews?

To Vladimir Jabotinsky, visiting the United States in the spring of 1940, the answer was a Jewish army fighting alongside the Allies as an independent unit like the Free French. Addressing thousands of cheering people in Madison Square Garden, Jabotinsky called on Jews to give the lie to the assertion that they made good soldiers only when propped up between Christian comrades. Zionists and the British Foreign Office were less thrilled. Louis Lipsky and Stephen Wise hurried to Lord Lothian, the British ambassador in Washington, to clearly disassociate themselves from this revisionist militancy. In London, it was properly feared that what revisionists really had in mind was a brigade formed, trained, paid for, and equipped by Britain, to be used ultimately to seize Palestine as a Jewish homeland.

To assure smoother public relations, Zionists formed an Emergency Committee for Zionist Affairs to serve as a "clearing house for information." With Wise as chairman,* the committee decried revisionist Zionism as a "viciously fascist" ideology. "Americans are first, last and all the time American citizens eager to spend all they have and all they are to insure the victory of America, . . ." stated a manual for the organization of local Zionist public relations committees. "American Zionists continue to be interested in Palestine *because Palestine is an important outpost in this indivisible war.*"

In August, Jabotinsky died of a heart attack. The idea for a Jewish army marched on. A brilliant Palestinian named Hillel Kook, who took the name Peter Bergson† and worked for Irgun Zvai Leumi‡ in London during 1939 and 1940, took charge. Bergson recruited Ben Hecht, a highly impractical Hollywood writer, producer, director, and newspaper columnist, to help develop a publicity campaign that would "raise millions." Hecht had come to Bergson's notice through his column on Ambassador Joseph Kennedy, who had bid fifty of Hollywood's Jewish movie-makers to play down Jewish rage against Germans lest the world think that a "Jewish war" was being fought. Hecht retorted that "the

* The name was later changed to the American Zionist Emergency Committee and Rabbi Silver joined Wise as co-chairman.

† Kook, the son of a rabbi and nephew of the chief rabbi of Palestine, wanted to spare his family any embarrassment brought on by his activities.

‡ Irgun, or Etzel, was an illegal terrorist group that carried out attacks on Arabs, was condemned by the Jewish Agency, and refused to accept restraints by Haganah, the Jewish self-defense force in Palestine.

sound of moral outrage over the extinction of the Jews would restore human stature to the name Jew."

Hecht and Bergson launched the Committee for an Army of Stateless and Palestinian Jews. In Hollywood, Jewish moguls turned down appeals for funds, fearing anti-Semitic reactions. Others pledged, but did not pay; at one meeting, $130,000 was promised, but only $9000 collected. Hecht wrote fifty prominent American Jews, seeking workers. He received a reply from only one, Alfred Strelsin, an advertising tycoon who traveled with Bergson to Washington to cajole cabinet members, congressmen, and bureaucrats into backing a Jewish army.

Unlike ZOA leaders attuned to congresses, meetings with each other, and after-dinner exhortations, Bergson, Hecht, Strelsin, and coworkers concentrated on arousing the Jewish masses. Full-page newspaper advertisements excoriated Nazis, the British, and American Jewish leaders, Yahudi and Zionist. A show business following was attracted—Stella and Luther Adler, Billy Rose, and other stage and screen celebrities. Non-Jews were encouraged to participate as well.

Success was all out of proportion to Bergson's and Hecht's standing in official Zionist circles, which was nil. Fearful that the masses might stray financially as well as ideologically, the Zionist Emergency Committee issued additional pamphlets. In *A Warning to the Zionists of America*, the faithful were told in upper-case type, "DO NOT BE MISLED BY [Bergson's and Hecht's] PUBLICITY—REMEMBER THAT FULL PAGE ADVERTISEMENTS WILL NOT REBUILD THE JEWISH NATIONAL HOME. MOBILIZE PUBLIC OPINION BEHIND THE ACCREDITED ZIONIST BODIES." Wise led a Zionist delegation to Washington urging legislators to reject militant visitors, then traveled to Albany where Governor Thomas Dewey was given an identical message. Prospective Bergson contributors were urged to withhold funds.

Yet Bergson forced the ZOA to greater militancy.* Zionist attacks on British policy in Palestine increased in frequency and hostility, even though the British were fighting the Nazis. In May 1942, an Extraordinary Zionist Conference was convened; Weizmann, Ben-Gurion, and 600 delegates assembled in New York's Biltmore Hotel. Weizmann's views

* Bergson met Ben-Gurion in Emanuel Neumann's New York apartment. The future premier of the Jewish state argued that Bergson's militant positions were completely unsound, but he later adopted many of them.

had been heard before: Only an Allied victory in which Britain played an important role could advance the Zionist cause. To antagonize the British while they fought the Nazis was not only totally unrealistic, but morally unconscionable.

With far greater approval, delegates heard Ben-Gurion call for immediate British reaffirmation of the Balfour Declaration. This was hardly original, but under the circumstances it was direct and inspiring. Short, testy, and authoritarian despite his professed socialism, Ben-Gurion's principal asset was something most Zionist leaders lacked: the understanding that in political life the right things seldom get done for the right reasons. The "Biltmore Program" he espoused called for immediate immigration and a Jewish Army fighting in defense of its own country. It proposed a Jewish Agency vested with control of Palestine, which would become a Jewish commonwealth.

Ben-Gurion scored a great personal victory at the conference, which was hailed in the Jewish press as a clear-cut call to battle, a great step forward, and a decisive turning point. Yet he was unable to overthrow Weizmann, who still had the support of ZOA leaders, and nothing turned decisively among non-Jews, who controlled Palestine and money, and had all the guns. Churchill, a Zionist sympathizer, continued to regard the White Paper as a mistake, but did nothing to rescind it. Roosevelt reassured Wise and anti-Zionist Yahudim with customary statements of sympathy and moral uplift.

The effect on American Jews was startling. Zionism as the major influence in American Jewish life can be dated from mid-May 1942. The United Jewish Appeal of JDC, UPA, and the National Refugee Service might march forward unsteadily, threatening to shake apart almost daily, but dissolution was unthinkable. Jews took heart that it might be possible for them to actually control some events.

A group of Reform rabbis passed a resolution supporting the creation of a Jewish army fighting under a Jewish flag. But the Biltmore Conference threw other Reform rabbis into a state of shock. In June, diehards meeting in Atlantic City formed the American Council for Judaism, the only American Jewish agency created to combat Zionism. A "Statement of Principles by Non-Zionist Rabbis" stressed "how dear Palestine is to the Jewish soul," but emphasized that Jewish nationalism would engender anti-Semitism. The council's basic arguments were the same that had been used by *shtadlanim* for a half century. Judaism was a religion, not a nationality. Jews were citizens of the country in which they lived and owed no loyalty to an international Jewish government.

After formal organization in August, council rabbis recruited members among Yahudim in the American Jewish Committee, likewise in the throes of shock over Biltmore, but unwilling to go as far publicly as the council. Sidney Wallach, executive director of the committee,* was hired by the council to organize a fund-raising campaign. Wallach in turn enlisted several renowned Yahudim, including Lewis Strauss, Arthur Hays Sulzberger (who featured council statements in the New York *Times*), and Lessing Rosenwald (who contributed large sums, but did not take over total support). A credible job was done securing gifts from rich Yahudim, but efforts to recruit a mass following were unsuccessful. The council claimed 15,000 members throughout the nation. Zionists believed the number was 8,000; actually it was around 6,000.

Matching the Zionist Emergency Committee in energy if not in effectiveness, the council loosed on the American public, Jew and Gentile, a flood of books, brochures, magazines, press releases, and statements. Its officers and its chief spokesman, Rabbi Elmer Berger, foresaw shifts in public opinion that momentarily inspired despondent Yahudim to larger gifts. Operating on an annual budget of about $300,000, the council made no impression on the Jewish masses and little on Christians, despite relays of delegations to Washington. Its premises were utterly unrealistic. Few people were inclined to return to 1900.

The council frightened Zionists who were concerned that Jewish communal disputes might fragment political action and successful fund raising among big givers. Operating on an annual budget increased to $500,000—which came from the Jewish National Fund and the Palestine Foundation Fund via the Jewish Agency—the American Zionist Emergency Committee became the spearhead of a drive to counter council activities. By 1944, 130 local versions of a Committee on Unity for Palestine distributed hundreds of thousands of brochures and letters to

* Yahudim had a penchant for fund raisers recruited from the ranks of Yidn, who were thought to have an intuitive expertise in the field. Wallach was born in Poland; in 1939, the committee's sole field representative was Rabbi Abba Abrams. In the future, ex-UJA men were deemed especially desirable by both the committee and the council.

Zionists and to non-Zionists. Big givers were urged not to contribute to the council and to exert pressure on pro-council rabbis to alter their positions. Over half the council's sponsoring rabbis were forced to withdraw by September 1943. Three years later, no more than a dozen were still on the council's roster.

Meanwhile, neither Weizmann, Wise, Ben-Gurion, Silver, or missives could entice to the fold the movers and shakers of American Jewry, the biggest big givers of all, the hierarchy of the American Jewish Committee. One wing of the committee, headed by Maurice Wertheim, president in 1943, opted for negotiations with Zionists partly on grounds that it was inconsistent to support a United Jewish Appeal and then decry Zionist objectives. James Rosenberg, Lewis Strauss, and the committee's incoming Alabama-born president, Judge Joseph Proskauer, adamantly opposed Wertheim's "whole enterprise as a tragic error." An intermediary between Zionists and Yahudim was sought. Henry Monsky, the first president of B'nai B'rith with eastern European forbears, was the choice. Monsky proposed to bridge the gap between Zionists and non-Zionists with an assembly that included representatives from every major Jewish organization.

To embattled Yahudim, the idea for an assembly leading to a new unity sounded suspiciously familiar: They would get to pay overseas bills while Zionists controlled policy through the membership. Morris Waldman, the committee's secretary, warned Proskauer that the assembly was a Zionist trick and Monsky was nothing more than a stooge. On the other hand, the committee itself was losing financial support and members because it appeared arbitrarily to flout popular opinion in the Jewish community. If it were to have any influence on the masses, it would have to participate.

Thus braced for action in two directions—for *and* against the assembly—the committee ignored an invitation to an organizational meeting in January 1943. But after Proskauer took office, an olive branch of "friendship and fellowship" was proffered Zionists in an effort "to cooperate with those many vital Jewish institutions and movements in this country—religious, cultural, philanthropic. . . ." The committee agreed to send representatives if the meeting were retitled the American Jewish Conference. Zionist leaders agreed to change the title and to play down demands for a Jewish state. Out of 502 delegates, 240 were members of the ZOA. More than 100 others were members of Mizrachi or Paole Zion.

The American Jewish Conference began peacefully enough with a declaration of unity by Monsky: It made no difference whether Judaism was a religion or a nationality, Jews were an integral group. Proskauer added that compromise was necessary, and the "gates of Palestine" must be kept open. The meeting was proceeding along smooth lines when Rabbi Silver, who strongly opposed any retreat on the statehood issue, managed to get to the rostrum even though he was not scheduled to speak. Defying the tacit agreement between Yahudim and Zionists, Silver roused delegates with a call for immediate statehood and open immigration to Palestine. How this could be accomplished in the middle of a war was not made clear, but Silver's rhetoric, rather than his substance, counted to listeners. Pent-up emotions were set free. Silver urged a commonwealth resolution, which passed 498–4; the American Jewish Committee walked out of the American Jewish Conference; and the unity movement collapsed, leaving rich and poor in separate camps, as before.

For Proskauer and the committee, this was not the only bad news Zionists offered in 1943; 34.6 percent of UJA receipts going to UPA were being used to pay for pro-Zionist propaganda, some of it distributed by the Zionist Emergency Council. Through their contributions, Yahudim were, in effect, paying for Zionist advancement. Nothing could be done to halt the practice without risking UJA's demise. Under the circumstances, that could not be allowed to happen.

With Bergson, Zionists had less happy results in 1942 and 1943. The Committee for a Jewish Army kept American Jews in a constant state of ferment. At ZOA headquarters, it was feared that militants were on the verge of capturing the imagination of American Jewry, in addition to diverting badly-needed funds.* Wherever possible, Bergson supporters were located and told that militants were adventurers, "pistol-packing" extremists representing no reputable political party.

Bergson and Hecht countered with advertisements, pageants—an entertainment-propaganda event developed into an art form by Zionists,†

* They were right to worry about American Jewry: Bergson claims 700,000 *proste* Yidn responded. Financially, he was hardly a threat. His committee never developed substantial ties with big givers.

† Max Reinhardt, the great German director, had been recruited for the Zionist production, "The Eternal Road."

—and an Emergency Conference to Save the Jewish People of Europe, which was held at the Commodore Hotel in New York a month before the American Jewish Conference. At the five-day meeting attended by 2000 people, the theme was "Action now to save the Jews of Europe." Non-Jews, including Will Rogers, Jr., of California and Rear Adm. Yates Sterling, Jr., Rtd., were prominently featured as speakers.

Bergson delivered the Emergency Conference recommendations to Treasury Secretary Morgenthau. They were dismissed as impractical, as well as inconsistent with United States policy. At the end of August, Bergson wrote Morgenthau that Cordell Hull, Eleanor Roosevelt, and Attorney General Francis Biddle had also been given the plans. He wondered why a special United States Commission had been set up to save European art and monuments, yet no "specific government agency" could be created to save 4 million European Jews.

Blocked at the cabinet level, Bergson wrote Roosevelt to request United States intervention "in the conflict between the policy of the Government of Great Britain and the interests of the Hebrew nation." Displaying the *chutzpah* for which he was renowned, he proposed that since there was no recognized "Hebrew National Authority," the "Hebrew Committee of National Liberation," which he headed, be invited to comprise "the Hebrew representation, which would include those members of the Jewish Agency who are Hebrew nationals, barring, of course, the participation of those members of the Jewish Agency who are nationals of other nations. . . ."

Such antics were easy to deride; indeed, this became a popular sport among Zionists when they were not worrying about Bergson's next venture. Far from influencing the government, Hecht's and Bergson's conference produced little in the way of solid results. A march of Orthodox rabbis in Washington ended up antagonizing Roosevelt. But for thousands of American Jews, the Hebrew Committee, no matter how far-fetched, seemed to be doing something. A Jewish Brigade was finally activated in the British Army in September 1944. When Bergson's committee raised a flag with a blue Star of David over its Washington "embassy" on Massachusetts Avenue, hundreds of thousands of Jews were thrilled. Remembering Jabotinsky and reading newspaper advertisements written by Bergson and Hecht, they bought tickets to extravaganzas and sent in one-, five-, and ten-dollar checks.

In October 1944, a major Zionist counterattack began. The Washington *Post* claimed that Bergson could not account for $1 million in contributions. He was described as a "nuisance"; it was further claimed he had evaded military service. The committee responded that all funds were used for its work and that the *Post*'s publisher, Eugene Meyer, was a stooge for Zionists. The attack petered out, and in a subsequent editorial Meyer retracted much of what had been printed.* In January, Bergson announced "open defiance" of the British government's policy limiting Jewish immigration in Palestine.

To the average Jewish citizen of the United States, fissures between Bergson and Zionists, the council and Zionists, and Ben-Gurion and Weizmann appeared deep and unbridgeable as the war drew to a close. Much time and money had been spent in Washington advancing various ideas for a Jewish homeland. Yet Roosevelt and the State Department were not greatly concerned with the issue. In a test of strength in 1944, Gen. George Marshall and Secretary of State Cordell Hull were able to have a strongly pro-Zionist resolution defeated in Congress.†

On the other hand, signs of an emerging Jewish unity were missed by Jews and non-Jews alike. American Jewry was far stronger and more courageous than anyone was giving it credit for being. The opposition of people in high places no longer cowed it; thousands had become activists. Two years after the war ended, nearly a million American Jews, one in every five, were to pay dues to a Zionist organization. Thousands contributed increasingly larger amounts to UJA—hardly a portent of failing confidence. Between 1939 and 1945, campaigns in New York City alone raised $50.3 million. What American Jews despairingly sought was a unified, affirmative leadership.

For American Jewry, the inability to prevent the holocaust, to mitigate it at any point, or to help coreligionists escape, would forever haunt those who spent the war years in safety. There were uncountable sub-catastrophes. Among them, the *Sturma*, a ship loaded with 769 persons that sank in the Black Sea, unable to proceed to the Holy Land because "the [British]

* Just why Meyer, ostensibly thoroughly assimilated after a Zionist past, and with little interest in Jewish causes, became involved is something of a mystery. According to Bergson, an anti-revisionist Washington rabbi engineered the original story.

† Roosevelt congratulated Sam Rayburn, the House majority leader, for this.

High Commissioner fears that admission of these Jews into Palestine would provoke tension. . . ." After German armies retreated, but while the war was still being fought, pogroms broke out in Poland; a right-wing partisan group declared killing Jews a sign of patriotism.

To quote Amos Alon, what this proved was that "without a country of your own you are the scum of the earth, the inevitable prey of beasts." Nothing happened immediately after the war to bolster the survivors' confidence in non-Jews or in Diaspora Jews, for that matter. Through May, June, and July 1945, JDC, like other relief agencies, hewed to official regulations: Only U.S. Army teams could operate in displaced persons camps. No representatives of Jewish agencies, Zionist or non-Zionist, arrived to offer help or encouragement. Because of Morgenthau's influence, Truman ordered Jews transferred to their own camps. Once these were opened, JDC swiftly provided relief.

In March 1945, Ben-Gurion met in Paris with associates to formulate plans for an underground task force securing arms. In June, Ben-Gurion was in the United States, where Jewish communal leaders were not sure what to do next. Saudi Arabia's Ibn Saud had convinced Roosevelt that Zionist-Arab amity was impossible.* Saud suggested that Jewish refugees be settled in Germany "on the choicest lands and houses of the Germans."† Truman appeared too new in the job of president to make solid judgments. UJA had just been reconstituted for a third time after threatening to shake apart in 1944, when JDC and UPA fought bitterly over allocations.

From ZOA leaders, Ben-Gurion heard nothing but skepticism about schemes for Palestinian immigration and illegal arms purchases and shipments.‡ It was with relief that he turned to Henry Montor, UJA's executive vice-president,§ a facile writer, a daring innovator, and an aggressive fund raiser with an unmatched knowledge of Jewish communities.

* At one point, Roosevelt and Churchill tried to convince Saud to permit western Palestine to become the site of a Jewish state—at a price of £20 million to world Jewry.

† The president said he learned more about the Middle East in five minutes with Saud than he had learned during all his years in office. So much for the influence of his close Zionist friends, Frankfurter and Wise.

‡ Nor was Ben-Gurion himself always realistic. At one meeting he was overheard to say that he would seek $15 million from Bernard Baruch, whose affinity for Zionists and Zionism had not theretofore been noted.

§ He simultaneously served as executive director of UPA.

Montor's professional life had been spent on the barricades of Jewish organizations, after a brief period of study at Hebrew Union College in Cincinnati. He was a Zionist of sorts,* he was an organization man, and he was a super hustler. To everything he did he brought messianic devotion that tolerated no indifference to details. Montor dressed in black suits and white shirts, forbade smoking in his presence, addressed everyone as Mister, arrived first at the office each morning, worked harder than anybody else, loathed Yahudim who blocked from leadership positions in Jewish communal agencies ambitious Yidn willing to raise money, and was a close friend of Ben-Gurion's aide, Eliezer Kaplan.

In late June, Ben-Gurion summoned Montor to his suite in the Hotel Fourteen on East Sixtieth Street, a few doors up the block from the most fashionable Yahudi club in New York, the Harmonie. Ben-Gurion wanted nothing less than a group of men who could raise money to smuggle Jews into Palestine and provide arms for Haganah. Montor made thirty-five telephone calls, repeating Ben-Gurion's request, asking each man to come to New York on a date to be set later. He then told Rudolph Sonneborn, with whom he was in close touch at UJA, about Ben-Gurion's plans, and asked to use his apartment for the meeting.†

Sonneborn, the wealthy scion of Baltimore Yahudim, was chairman of UJA's finance committee. In his youth he had been a football player and World War I naval aviator. Still wearing his uniform, he became a member of the American Zionist Commission that went to Palestine in 1918. As dedicated a worker as Montor, Sonneborn had met Ben-Gurion in 1919 at the Versailles peace treaty meetings, but had not been closely in touch with him.

The all-day meeting in Sonneborn's elegant living room on July 1, 1945, has since been hailed as important in Zionist history as the Biltmore Conference.‡ Among those present were Ben-Gurion, three aides, Sonneborn, Montor, Meyer Weisgal, and seventeen Jewish businessmen.

* Early on, Montor had aspirations for a literary career and served on the staff of the Zionist periodical *New Palestine*.

† The idea of fund raising for Jewish armed forces was not new to Montor or to Sonneborn. Years earlier, Montor had flatly turned down Bergson's request for help. Sonneborn actually became a member of Bergson's Committee for a Jewish Army.

‡ On the same day, forty-one Jewish delegates from twenty DP camps in Bavaria met to form the Central Committee of Liberated Jews and demand annulment of the 1939 White Paper. "[Those] who freed us from slavery and death," hoped the survivors, "will also aid us in the reconstruction of a peaceful and secure home."

Exactly who was in the latter group varies from account to account. Exactly what was said also varies, since no minutes were taken.

In any case, around 9:30 A.M. on the blisteringly hot day, sweating and in shirtsleeves, Ben-Gurion began talking about the worldwide Jewish situation. What was left of European Jewry was utterly demoralized. No country, including the United States,* would take refugees. Britain, making efforts to maintain a military presence in the Middle East, was economically exhausted. After the British left Palestine, Jews would face Arab armies bent on destroying them. These armies could be defeated —if rifles, machine guns, tanks, airplanes, heavy artillery, and enough people to use them were available. At best, there were two years during which to prepare.

Manpower could be obtained through illegal immigration. A tiny munitions industry in the Holy Land could be expanded. Ben-Gurion's three aides then elucidated where arms could be procured. Yaacov Dori, Haganah chief of staff, said large quantities of arms-making machinery as well as surplus arms would be available in the United States after Japan was defeated. Eliezer Kaplan, treasurer of the Jewish Agency, outlined potential costs. Moshe Shiloah, chief of Haganah intelligence, described how materiel could be smuggled out of the United States.

At the end of the meeting, Ben-Gurion suggested no specific actions, except that everyone be ready to act quickly and attract like-minded men of means to create an American arm for Haganah. Evidently, he did not intend to work through the ZOA, the World Jewish Congress, or the World Zionist Organization; he would control fund raising. No one made a formal pledge of funds, and no one declined to contribute. Ben-Gurion admonished invitees not to spread the word that he or any other Palestinians had been in Sonneborn's apartment.

At that point, Ben-Gurion, his aides, and his listeners all sounded like characters in a second-rate spy novel. A stumpy man with a Winged Victory haircut, three Palestinians, and influential Jewish businessmen were thinking about moving hundreds of thousands of people from one continent to another and of raising and equipping armies in defiance of the British navy, the armies of several Arab countries, and the laws of the United

* Anti-Semitism, as measured in public relations polls, reached an all-time high in 1944.

States. Nothing less than B-17 Flying Fortresses were to be obtained, in addition to tanks, heavy artillery, and other equipment that could hardly be hidden in crates. Ben-Gurion's listeners felt intuitively that they had been present at a historic moment. Despite the lack of clear-cut directives, the appraisal made sense. This *was* what was going to happen.

In September, Sonneborn heard from Ben-Gurion that "the time has come." An innocuous office was opened at 250 West Fifty-seventh Street in New York. Within weeks, seventeen similar offices were opened around the country to form a nationwide clandestine fund-raising, arms-purchasing, and shipping agency with side ventures in espionage and sabotage. It was known as the Sonneborn Institute.* It had no letterheads, no board of directors, and no officers. Every Thursday, the institute held a luncheon meeting in New York's Hotel McAlpin. There, Palestinians reported on needs and Americans discussed shipments.

The institute's first assignment was to raise over $1 million for the purchase of machine tools. Sonneborn's campaign plan, based on that fundamental of federated fund raising, the commerce and industry drive, was easily understood by fellow conspirators. "In each of thirty-five or forty industry groups we want one man to act as our representative," he told a group of institute members. This man would chair meetings of a trade division, solicit contributors, and help recruit additional cochairmen. By December 31, the money was raised, but Sonneborn asked more of his cochairmen: They were next to solicit prospects in homes, offices, country clubs, and factories for more money.

This was broadly interpreted to mean wherever prospects could be found. In a midwestern city hall, crap shooters in the basement contributed ten straight pots. Across the Hudson from Manhattan, $10,000 was raised from revelers in a nightclub. Throughout the country, accountants and attorneys advised clients how gifts could be disguised and channeled through Swiss bank accounts to return through fictitious corporations. By mid-April 1947, additional contributions totaled $505,177.

While Sonneborn and his institute were energetically arming Haganah,

* A grisly contribution was made by Jews who had died in gas chambers. Their gold teeth, collected by the Nazis and confiscated after the war, were purchased from the U.S. Army; the gold was then used to purchase arms.

Bergson and Hecht were raising money to purchase weapons for Irgun, which was already attacking British troops in Palestine.* They headed no commerce and industry drives and held no luncheon meetings. Full-page advertisements called for an "eye for an eye, a tooth for a tooth, and an English soldier on the gallows for every Jewish soldier who is hanged." In a "Letter to the Terrorists of Palestine," printed in fifteen newspapers at "usual advertising rates" and later reprinted gratis in hundreds of other papers, Hecht told Irgun members that a "certain small percentage of the Jews of America are not behind you." This percentage included "practically all the rich Jews of America, all the important and influential ones, all the heads of nearly all the Jewish organizations whom the American newspapers call 'The Jewish Leaders.' They want a sanctuary where the Jews of Europe can all stand on a rock and eat philanthropy fish, till the Messiah arrives. . . . [They] are pouring millions into the business of feeding the survivors of the German massacre," when "they" should be purchasing arms. Hecht bid Irgun "hang on," promising "to raise millions."

Much of this was true. Jewish leaders were perplexed and angered by Irgun and by Hecht's open advocacy of violence, which was not a "Jewish trait." UJA leaders, Zionist and non-Zionist, condemned terrorism as "injurious to the best interests of the Jewish community in Palestine." They feared such attacks would stiffen British resistance and alienate sympathetic non-Jews. But instead of bemoaning the fate of murdered people, Hecht was calling for action and willingly giving up his own earnings.†

Mickey Cohen, the bookie emperor of California, and his bodyguard visited Hecht. Cohen wanted to help Irgun, but sought assurances; Los Angeles, complained the bodyguard, was full of thieves. Cohen was leery

* Under Menachim Begin, a Polish immigrant, Irgun attacks were made on British troops and military installations beginning in February 1944. In October, 251 Irgunists captured by the British were deported to Eritrea. After the assassination of Lord Moyne in November, Haganah turned Irgunists over to the British. Neither measure quelled terrorism. In July 1946, British headquarters in Jerusalem was blown up along with the King David Hotel, and in one of the most daring prison breakouts in history, sixty extremists escaped from the Acre fortress in May 1947.

† Hecht was one of the highest-paid screenwriters in Hollywood. His films were officially banned in Britain.

of being swindled by "phony Jews." A "Jewish" patriot who had sold him a bronze plaque for $200 turned out to be a Chicago con man.*

Cohen had other problems, too. A rival syndicate was about to start tossing bombs into his home and sending associates to mortuaries. Nonetheless, he agreed to host an Irgun fund-raising party. Hecht asked about invitees. "You don't have to worry," responded the bodyguard. "Each and everybody here has been told exactly how much to give to the cause of the Jewish heroes. And you can rest assured there'll be no welchers."

Under these circumstances, Hecht thought that he might forego oratory. "The speech," objected Cohen's associate, "is what Mr. Cohen wants to hear."

Hecht addressed Cohen and "a thousand bookies, ex-prize fighters, gamblers, jockeys, touts and all sorts of lawless and semi-lawless characters; and their womenfolk." After guests announced their contributions, Hecht retired from the stage. "Make another speech and hit 'em again," ordered Cohen. Hecht protested that he had already spoken for forty-five minutes. "You tell 'em," Cohen ordered the bodyguard. "Tell 'em they're a lot o' cheap crumbs and they gotta give double."

The message was dutifully roared over the microphone. Cohen came to the edge of the stage and stood in the floodlights, saying nothing. Each contributor again rose to "[double] the ante for the Irgun." "We raised two hundred G's," said the bodyguard to Cohen, mopping his face. "Furthermore, we been here three hours and nobody's taken a shot at us."†

Irgun exploits captured headlines through 1946 and 1947. Alarmed by Bergson's and Hecht's success, the Sonneborn Institute formed a rival committee, "Americans for Haganah."‡ Purposely low-keyed, it lacked the opposition's drawing power. Anti-Irgun brochures, Palestinian "truth squads," and local Zionist Emergency Committees likewise had limited

* The bodyguard added that when "Mr. Cohen's friends catch this thief they will break his head."

† Cohen was later prosecuted for income-tax evasion. He claimed large philanthropic contributions, but the only ones that could be authenticated were those made to Bergson's group.

‡ Some Zionist leaders were not hostile. Rabbi Silver rejected Bergson and Hecht, but told one Irgun member that Irgun was "entitled to the help of all Jews irrespective of affiliation."

success. When a Bergson "Sons of Liberty Boycott Committee" published sixteen pages of British goods to avoid purchasing, ZOA leaders debated supporting it, then backed off because of inevitable British economic reprisals in Palestine.

Meanwhile, Ben-Gurion's predictions came true. In July 1945, the Labor Party won a resounding victory in Britain, which was followed by a deepening economic recession brought on by the profound dislocations of the war. Arabs and Jews both wanted the British to withdraw from Palestine; Jews pressed for partition and Arabs pressed for an Arab-dominated country. Neither side would accept a British trusteeship. When Truman strongly urged the immediate admission of 100,000 Jewish refugees to the Holy Land, British Foreign Secretary Ernest Bevin angrily denounced the proposal and the open solicitation of funds in America to pay for emigration.

In late October 1947, word went out from the Sonneborn Institute to Jewish communities throughout the country that another $1 million was needed. Besides cash, contributors sent World War II souvenir pistols, rifles, machine guns, bazookas, mortars, and hand grenades. At the Hotel Fourteen, Teddy Kollek, later the mayor of Jerusalem, coordinated fund raising, purchasing, and shipments, while another Palestinian named Yehuda Arazi stalked the halls thinking about buying a surplus aircraft carrier. In a dingy building on One Hundred Twelfth Street, Haim Slavin, Phil Alper, and Elie Schalit furtively arranged for munitions to be crated and stored in an old warehouse in the Bronx. Elsewhere, hundreds of unsung workers scoured the country for arms, machinery, hiding places, and larger gifts. Boxes labeled "Czechoslovak crockery," but in reality containing weapons, reposed in the basements of synagogues and Jewish centers. "We have today at least one person in virtually every community in America," said Sonneborn at an institute meeting. "There are perhaps eight or ten thousand of us throughout the country and we represent here the energyzing [sic] force." A worker found that individuals who had hitherto given nothing to UJA would make substantial gifts for arms.

On November 29, 1947, the United Nations voted 33–13 for partition. There was dancing in the streets of Tel Aviv, London, and New York. Next day the Arabs proclaimed a three-day protest strike, and on December 1 there was rioting in Jerusalem. Within days, Arab countries neighboring Palestine announced they would march in as British troops marched out; within weeks an "Arab Liberation Army" consisting of ex-Nazis, British fascists, and native irregulars was formed under the command of Fawzi El Kaukaji, whose World War II days were spent recruiting Muslims to serve in Hitler's armies.

It was now a race between Arabs and Jews as to which side would be the best equipped when the mandate officially ended on May 14, 1948, three months earlier than the deadline set by the United Nations.* At a regular Thursday meeting at the Hotel McAlpin in October, diners learned that $1 million more would be needed in two months. On December 11, they were told that by the end of the year $5 million more would be needed. This amount could never be raised, said Sonneborn. Returning to Tel Aviv from New York, Eliezer Kaplan told Ben-Gurion and other Zionist leaders that increasing commitments to overseas relief campaigns, plus the waning of wartime prosperity, had set limits to what American Jews could do.

Ben-Gurion was aghast. Thus far, the Sonneborn Institute had produced a fraction of necessary arms, and nowhere near the money needed to procure heavy weapons and fighter planes in Europe, where major purchases would be made. He and Kaplan would leave immediately for the United States. But this, objected the others, would remove the strongest Zionist personality in Jewish ranks from the Palestinian scene at a critical time.† In his stead, Golda Myerson‡ was dispatched.

On a bitterly cold January day, with no luggage except a handbag, Mrs. Myerson stepped out of an airplane in New York. She was in the wrong city to plead the cause. The rich and their representatives were in Chicago, where the Council of Jewish Welfare Funds and Federations was holding its annual meeting. Proceeding to the Midwest, she was squeezed into a program through Henry Montor's influence, but warned by Zionists to avoid upsetting big givers with stories about prospective Arab attacks.

Speaking extemporaneously and paying little heed to warnings, she bluntly said that "we have no alternative in Palestine. The Mufti and his men have declared war upon us. We have to fight for our lives, for our

* This was no act of British generosity. By advancing the date, they ensured that Jews were given less time to prepare, and Arabs ample notice to position their troops.

† Moreover, Ben-Gurion was noted neither for tact nor for diplomacy. That his aggressiveness might antagonize givers was also a possibility that occurred to colleagues.

‡ In 1956, she would change her last name to Meir.

safety, and for what we accomplished in Palestine, and perhaps, above all, we must fight for Jewish honor and Jewish independence." Having thus moved the argument from Palestine to the survival of World Jewry, she sarcastically nodded in the direction of the faint-hearted—"It would be audacity on our part to worry the Jewish people throughout the world because a few hundred more Jews were in danger."—but reiterated that so long as Palestinian Jews remained alive, the Jewish people would remain alive.

There was no despair in Palestine. Nor was there any chance American Jews could dissuade Palestinian Jews from fighting. "Don't be bitterly sorry three months from now for what you failed to do today," she urged. "The time is now." Between $25 and $30 million was needed within two or three weeks to purchase arms.

Where would this money come from? Incredible sums, $131.7 million in 1946 and $157.8 million in 1947, had been raised for overseas relief through UJA. It was impossible to organize a special campaign in so short a time. The money would come through loans, said Mrs. Myerson. Federations and welfare funds would go to banks, take out loans, and repay them as money was actually raised. This left many big givers speechless. How would they meet overseas responsibilities the following year? "Let's ask for $50 million," she suggested. "Then you can have your $25 million and I'll have my $25 million."

In defiance of all accepted procedures in finance and fund raising, she turned out to be right. The money was borrowed and the money was raised. Traveling around the country at a frantic pace with Henry Morgenthau, Jr., William Rosenwald, and Edward M. M. Warburg, she convinced communal leaders to participate. "Not only did we make it in January," Mrs. Meir later said proudly, "but we made it again in May, after the state was established." A weapons purchasing office was opened in Geneva.

With armaments now financed through banks and William Levitt, a mass producer of homes who advanced $1 million for twenty-five Messerschmitt 109Fs, the Sonneborn Institute switched from weapons to dry goods: 10,000 coats; 10,000 pairs of boots; 1000 binoculars; and 200 typewriters. Plus 7000 olive drab brassieres, Bach and Beethoven records for Haganah rest centers, a Bible for Ben-Gurion, a telescope for Moshe Dayan's good eye, Waring blenders to shred papers if Arabs captured command posts, and dozens of other items.

In April, Ben-Gurion inventoried Haganah's weapons and manpower. Jewish striking forces still consisted of a mere 3000 men and women in the Palmach, the trained commando force, and 14,000 hastily trained recruits, many of them competent only to fire revolvers and rifles. The Haganah leadership feuded with Ben-Gurion over how defenses should be organized. Opposed to this force, Arab armies were estimated at 23,500 men equipped with British tanks, heavy weapons, and 100 aircraft.

On May 14, one day before the British left Palestine, Ben-Gurion signed a Proclamation of Independence under Herzl's portrait in the Tel Aviv Museum. Eleven minutes later in Washington, Truman recognized a *de facto* Israeli provisional government. In a less congratulatory mood, five Arab armies crossed Palestine's borders eight hours after independence was announced, expecting a quick victory and much loot.

The expectations were not realized. On June 11, a United Nations peacemaking team arranged a temporary truce. In Amman, Arab leaders tried unsuccessfully to reconcile divisions and rivalries. In Tel Aviv, Israeli leaders also argued with each other, but thought it miraculous that defenders held out as well as they did. Two-thirds of the territory earmarked in the partition plan was in Jewish hands.

In the next phase of fighting—and no one doubted it would be renewed—the preponderance of arms on one side or the other would be decisive. In Europe, Haganah representatives continued feverishly making deals for weapons. Ben-Gurion screamed to American Jews for more money. Three B-17s, flown from the United States via the Azores, arrived in Czechoslovakia in late June and picked up arms.*

Haganah was not the only Jewish force seeking weapons. Bergson's Hebrew Committee purchased a surplus LST to take 5000 refugees from France to Palestine in February. Named the *Altalena* (a pseudonym used by Jabotinsky in his early writings), it was captained by an American navy veteran who offered his services after seeing the pageant, *A Flag Is*

* They also loaded 500-pound bombs. On their way to Tel Aviv, after fighting broke out again, they dropped the bombs on Cairo taking Arabs completely by surprise.

Born. It was destined to carry, instead of refugees, $5 million worth of armaments* for Irgun, and 800 volunteers. On June 11, the *Altalena* put to sea from Port de Bouc near Marseilles, closely watched by the British, who alerted the United States State Department. It sailed in defiance of a cease-fire provision halting the importation of munitions by either side during the truce.

As the *Altalena* neared the Israeli coast, the final act in a struggle that had wracked Zionist politics for a decade was about to be played. Menachim Begin offered 80 percent of the munitions to Haganah, on condition that the balance go to his Irgun forces in Jerusalem and the weapons be stored in Irgun armories. Volunteers could serve in either army. Begin boasted that the *Altalena* carried enough equipment to outfit ten battalions.

Men and materiel were badly needed; at the Israeli cabinet meeting on June 20, a proposal was considered to lower the draft age to seventeen. But ministers also learned that in preparation for the *Altalena*'s arrival, Irgunists had broken into a Haganah camp and intended to hold it as a reception center.

Ben-Gurion was faced with a double challenge to his authority. Begin had evidently decided he could defy the government and the United Nations; he might also break an agreement to incorporate Irgun troops into the Haganah. The *Altalena* was kept at sea while negotiations continued. Ben-Gurion demanded weapons and men be surrendered. If fighting erupted between Jewish forces, the government would claim it was upholding the UN truce.

On June 20, the *Altalena* was beached near Tel Aviv, watched by UN observers, Haganah troops, and bystanders. Fighting broke out between Jewish forces after an attempt to unload arms from a launch. A detachment of Haganah troops poured a withering fire into the ship, then blew it up with a cannon shot in the hold. Hearing gunfire, Irgun troops began leaving their positions and engaged Haganah units in a chaotic action. The Irgunists were crushed.

Bergson, who arrived in Tel Aviv on a chartered flight, was clapped into jail, not to be released until the end of August. But carried along by momentum, the Hebrew Committee in New York kept raising funds. At the Waldorf-Astoria, Leonard Bernstein conducted an orchestra at a

* Bergson told me that these weapons were donated by the French government.

"Wings for Victory" Irgun benefit and said that pressure had been put on him not to appear. In July, August, and September, Begin was addressing rallies in Israel, and in October, the Sons of Liberty Boycott Committee was still banning British goods. In December, Begin came to America on a goodwill mission.*

On July 8, fighting between Arabs and Jews broke out again, but was stopped by a second truce on July 18, which was in turn shattered by Egyptian and irregular offensives in the north and south of Israel in October. Not until July 20, 1949 were armistice negotiations between Egyptians and Israelis completed on the island of Rhodes. From its Fifty-seventh Street office, the Sonneborn Institute continued sending materiel. It finally closed its doors in 1955, and remaining funds were given to a seamen's home in Israel.

* Begin and Bergson were elected members of the first Knesset, after the state was proclaimed.

6
A Golden Age

AMERICAN JEWRY had three major characteristics in 1948. First and most important, it was the only Jewry left with major resources of manpower and money. Second, descendants of Yidn were rapidly taking key leadership positions from Yahudim, deciding Jewish destiny worldwide. Third, its outlook was different from what it had been in the 1930s, although not from that of other Jewries in the Diaspora. It was largely disinterested in Orthodoxy, in *Yiddishkeit*, in the particulars of Zionist philosophy, and in calls for Jewish exclusivism. As American Jews entered a "Golden Age of Jewish Security,"* differences between them and Christians grew increasingly blurred.

Many Jews no longer knew what they believed except that Orthodox Judaism was incompatible with newly-discovered life styles. Searching for common bonds with coreligionists, they found the quasi-American conviction that money can solve any problem could be tastefully joined to the ancient concept of *zedekah*. Federations assisted the sick and the old while government provided unemployment compensation and social

* A phrase denoting the 1950s and 1960s and used for the first time, to my knowledge, by Norman Podhoretz in a 1972 *Commentary* article, "Is it good for the Jews?"

security benefits. Jewish poverty was a thing of the past.* American-Jewish money would create a haven for refugees in Israel and support a vast network of hospitals, old-age homes, and other facilities at home. Philanthropy became the core around which Jewish life was organized.

Figures tell the story in one way. From 1939† to 1942, between $27 million and $29 million was raised annually for UJA and domestic agencies. In 1943 and 1944, $35 million and then $47 million were raised. In 1945, the figure shot up to $57.3 million. A turning point was reached in December 1945 when UJA's Henry Montor proposed a $100 million goal for 1946. A hesitant leadership agreed because of urgent overseas needs, because a vast fund-raising machinery was in existence, and mainly because Montor said it could be done. In a campaign since legendary for its intimations of Jewish wealth, $101 million was raised for UJA, in addition to $30 million for domestic needs. The following year the combined domestic and overseas figure was $157.8 million. In 1948, it was $205 million—nearly three times the amount raised by the American Red Cross in the same year.‡

The Red Cross had a constituency of 150.7 million Americans, including Jews, to solicit. UJA's constituency in 1948 was 5 million people, 3.5 percent of the total population. Two-thirds of American Jews were first- or second-generation descendants of east Europeans and lived within 200 miles of New York City, but increased giving was the rule everywhere. New York raised $7 million for UJA in 1943 and $56.2 million in 1948, an 803 percent increase. Sioux City, Iowa, raised $43,860 in 1943 and $387,000 in 1948, an increase of 886 percent.

The amounts raised surprised Jews almost as much as non-Jews, who sought to learn the "secrets" of Jewish success. Superior fund-raising techniques and aggressiveness were generally held responsible. But techniques and temperament did not wholly account for the phenomenon.§ A major factor had to be the emergence of Jewish middle and upper classes capable

* Or so it was thought. Jewish poverty was suddenly rediscovered in the early 1970s after a quarter century of supposed eradication, as we shall see.

† The second largest contribution made in the United States during 1939 was Julius Rosenwald's $100,000 for fellowships for Southern blacks.

‡ The Red Cross goal for 1948 was $73.5 million.

§ The ZOA's former fund-raising director, charmingly mild-mannered Dr. Sidney Marks, used a YMCA fund-raising handbook as his guide, claiming that it was his best source for ideas.

of contributing large sums. And by midcentury, the great emphasis in immigrant families on education bore fruit in hosts of new professionals—doctors, accountants, lawyers, dentists, pharmacists, and entrepreneurs.

A lucid study by Nathan Glazer, "Social Characteristics of American Jews," published for the 1954 tercentenary observance of Jewish settlement in America, offers statistics. In a single generation, Jews increased their professionals by 400 percent. In New York City, scene of big money and big opportunities, Jews formed 26 percent of the population, but 33 percent of the professionals and semiprofessionals and 45 percent of the proprietors. In San Francisco, 18 of every 1000 gainfully employed Jews were lawyers or judges and 16 were doctors; among non-Jews, there were 5 per 1000 in each category. In Charleston, 2000 Jews included 8 doctors, 7 dentists, 18 lawyers, 5 pharmacists, 9 teachers, 18 engineers, 7 social workers, 4 accountants, 3 radio commentators, 3 writers and editors, 3 artists, and 1 orchestra leader.

How did earnings of Jews and of non-Jews compare? The lack of accurate data rendered it impossible for Glazer or other sociologists to do more than offer a semi-educated guess. Yet in small towns and cities, in professional life and in commerce, Jews appeared to be surpassed in earning power only by Presbyterians and Episcopalians. In 1951, 12 percent of New York's Jewish households had an income of $10,000 or more, as compared with 5 percent of non-Jewish households; 29 percent of Jewish households earned less than $4000, as compared with 49 percent of non-Jewish households. In Los Angeles, the median income for Jewish families was $5077; the corresponding figure for the total population of the United States was $4000.

Higher earnings were just one indication of postwar Jewish affluence. In the 1920s and 1930s, downtowners in New York had begun leaving the aging and congested Lower East Side. In the early 1950s, one development more than any other speeded and shaped an exodus to suburbia: William Levitt's mass-produced houses, first unveiled in 1947 on 1000 acres of potato farms near Hicksville, Long Island. Most builders produced 1 house a year; a bare 26 percent could manage 2. On an assembly line basis, Levitt turned out 60 houses a week, then 100, then 150.

Levittowns sprang up near Chicago and Philadelphia; imitators in other cities picked up the pattern. Central cities continued to empty, and by 1958, 85 percent of Cleveland's Jews lived outside city limits, as did virtually all Jews in Detroit, Newark, and Washington, D.C. Coincidental with this movement, Los Angeles increased its Jewish population from 151,000 in 1945 to 500,000 in 1970. Miami went from 7500 Jews in 1937 to 40,000 in 1948 and to 150,000 in 1970.

The movement was not without its critics. Mobility led to further acculturation, and further acculturation might not stop short of a complete loss of Jewish identity, despite increased giving. In transit, a great deal had already been jettisoned. Jewish theater, Jewish literature, and Jewish culture were left to wither on the Lower East Side along with Orthodoxy and socialism.

The saving grace was that as areas of Jewish concentration disappeared in the central cities, areas of Jewish concentration sprang up past the outskirts. Cleveland had University Heights, Westchester had Scarsdale, Long Island had Lawrence, and Detroit had Southfield. A continuation of life on some past models was sought. Suburbanites wanted their children to remain Jewish; it was intolerable that tradition and ritual could be completely abandoned.

Houses of worship obviously represented the ultimate in Jewish identity. Thus it was that the early 1950s saw the beginning of the greatest synagogue and temple building boom in history, with hundreds of new places of worship—Reform, Orthodox, Conservative—where before there had been meadows. While sanctuaries in the inner cities were sold to blacks or left to rack and ruin, religion and family counseling were provided in gorgeous new palaces that served as community centers. Lavish catering facilities were available for bar mitzvahs, bas mitzvahs, and weddings.

Perhaps $200 million was spent on construction in the 1950s and 1960s, or the true figure could be four times that amount.* No one has reliable figures. Nor can anyone guess the number of hours spent by tens of thousands of worshippers raising funds or selling tickets to dinners and bazaars to pay off mortgages. Only the most backward clerics did not subscribe wholeheartedly to the building craze.†

Standard fund-raising procedures were developed. During eighteen- or

* By 1970, estimates ran as high as $800 million for 800 new synagogue buildings in twenty years.

† Except in a few cases, the amount earned by a rabbi depended on the size of his congregation and the grandeur of its building, as well as the state of his religious learning.

twenty-week campaigns (forty weeks for big jobs), "pacemakers"* made their contributions while rabbis encouraged their flocks, calling first for "fair share" gifts, second for "sacrificial giving," and, as a last resort, setting minimum "contributions" for congregational membership. Campaign chairmen, chosen for their ability to make large gifts and to ask for as much as they could conceivably get, were driven by an insatiable need for success. Almost anything could be a dedication opportunity, ranging from a kitchen tile to the parking lot to the whole sanctuary. In some places, air conditioners sported plaques. In one New England town, twenty-eight appeals for funds were mailed within thirty-five days.

Yet the major campaigns were mounted not in the suburbs, to which the middle class and many of the rich fled, but in the cities where they worked.† When wartime restrictions on construction were lifted in 1945, federations began raising hundreds of millions of dollars to build, expand, and modernize hospitals, homes for the aged, and community centers. Five years after the war, the shift was noticeably away from emphasis on dependent Jews—those unable to pay for services—to a broad view of philanthropy with emphasis on communitywide services. Social security and governmental welfare programs influenced the change; no longer were the few Jewish poor to be a drain on Jewish resources.

Affluence meant that medical, counseling, and educational costs could be partly financed through fees. But no social service agency or hospital could exist solely on income from its services. By 1956, Jewish communities would be spending more than twice as much as in 1946; allocations for the aged alone rose by 215 percent. Moreover, a Jewish civil service‡ was needed to provide and supervise programs for religious, educational, cultural, leisure-time, vocational, and community relations activities, as well as for fund raising.

Local agencies and institutions were invariably linked to local federations. These were linked, in turn, to the Council of Jewish Federations and Welfare Funds in New York, the supra-agency. CJFWF coordinated

* Big givers whose contributions, it was hoped, would inspire others to increase their contributions and carry the campaign over the goal.

† This gave rise to that now famous retort when a prospect was approached by solicitors at home, in the theater, in a restaurant, or on the golf links: "I gave at the office."

‡ This was made up to a large extent of intellectuals, semi-intellectuals, and quasi-intellectuals who entered the Jewish communal structure during the early and mid-1940s in search of positions.

programs; defined relationships between agencies, institutions, and local federations; established procedures for participation in community chests; and generally offered definitions and rationales for the functions of Jewish communal institutions.

CJFWF's major service to the Jewish community, however, was to provide financial expertise and executive personnel able to direct fund-raising campaigns. In 1935, federations and welfare funds supplied 20 percent of the income of thirty-two national and overseas agencies in addition to operating and building funds for communal agencies; by 1945, 60 percent of all contributions by American Jews, including those received by UJA, came through federations and welfare funds. After administrative costs of about 12 percent were paid, local, national, and international agencies received their allotments. A priority order evolved: United Jewish Appeal, local communal agencies, and the national agencies, in that order.*

Federations had membership fees, but fund-raising campaigns were their financial mainsprings. The campaigns were conducted on a pledge basis with payments on the installment plan. The format developed by New York's federation a half-century before—fund raising among peer groups and the commerce and industry drive—served as a basic organizational tool. To this was added card calling, a product of Joseph Willen's fertile brain. Willen, like Montor, a kingpin of modern American Jewish philanthropy, directed New York federation's campaigns. He could also work long hours, inspire unflagging loyalty in subordinates, speak and write with eloquence, and reach the heart of a problem with intuitive brilliance. Unlike Montor, he did not wear black suits. Like thousands of other Jews, he could only wonder about a Jewry that seemed to have lost its religious bearings in a sea of acculturation. What remained was a Judaism that would be expressed through organizational triumph. In a money culture, the affluent, not the learned, were heroes and focal points.

* Dr. Robert MacIver of Columbia University, an eminent sociologist, was engaged by CJFWF's National Community Relations Advisory Board in 1951 to analyze the welter of American Jewish organizations. The number had continued to increase, although the Jewish population was decreasing as a percentage of the total population. MacIver suggested centralization of services and activities. He was immediately opposed by agency executives who claimed a pluralistic outlook was essential in the Jewish field; flexibility was far more important than any prospective savings. Furthermore, whole bureaucracies might be thrown out of work. While MacIver's recommendations were often ignored, he became popular as a speaker and consultant to Jewish agencies.

The major improvement wrought by Willen was to join *koved* with mass psychology. Testimonial card-calling luncheons and dinners became platforms for philanthropic announcements. Non-Jewish and Jewish big givers had parks, buildings, and plazas named after them. Now, givers with less wealth but equal spirit could get recognition—if not on buildings, then during fleeting moments of glory.

Early experiences with card calling in the late 1920s and early 1930s were not auspicious. When it was first tried, prospective givers were left uneasy. Yidn were afraid they would appear vulgar, making gifts in public. To legitimatize the procedure, Willen convinced great Yahudim—Warburgs, Schiffs, and Strauses—to set examples by making *their* gifts in public. Once big givers endorsed card calling, arrivistes felt it safe and respectable to follow the practice.

By the mid-1950s, the technique had been perfected. This is how card calling works today: Prospective guests at functions receive invitations containing a photograph and biography of the guest of honor. An executive committee headed by a chairman and loaded with the guest of honor's and chairman's associates, employees, accountants, and, above all, suppliers, is listed. How much business a prospect does with the guest of honor or chairman helps mightily to determine whether or not he attends. It is incumbent on a chairman to encourage his committee to work as hard as possible; "volunteers" doing business with committee members encourage additional prospects with whom they are likely to have some influence. Typically, dress buyers solicit dress salesmen. With rare exceptions, all those solicited are Jews.

Luncheon or dinner receipts are not major sources of income. After rubber chicken or plastic roast beef, speeches praising the guest of honor,* stale jokes, monotonous lists of needs, a recital of Jewish woes, and a recital of Jewish victories, the function gets down to business.† The professional fund raiser hands the chairman a set of cards—one for each

* At one function in New York, the guest of honor insisted on supervising all arrangements, including designs for invitations and copy for speeches. No detail was too trivial. Fund raisers were driven to distraction, constantly seeking his approval. When the chairman read the text on the plaque, the guest of honor burst into tears. He had written the text himself.

† I have been told of occasions on which exit doors from the dining room were locked at this juncture.

diner—noting past contributions. The chairman announces his pledge the previous year and his increased pledge for the current year.*

Cards are then read off, with the previous year's biggest givers called first. As each name is intoned a voice floats back announcing the current year's pledge, increased roughly in proportion to the chairman's increase, and done so in honor of the guest of honor! None dare give less than the previous year; few dare give the same amount. Either alternative might be taken by competitors and friends alike as an indication that business is bad, a potentially disastrous intimation in this context. Moreover, can a respectable person maintain a large house in the suburbs or host a lavish bar mitzvah for his son and contribute only a modest sum?

Through the years, card calling has become to American Jewish philanthropy what the nucleus is to the atom. There are variations, but there are no replacements. The technique is as solidly productive in a corporate board room (where I have seen it used) as in a restaurant in New York's garment district (where I have also seen it used). It is described as tasteless, irritating, coercive, and worse. Yet it continues to be used for one reason only—it works better than anything anyone else has thought of. Willen makes an analogy with an observation by Karl Marx. If revolution is inevitable, asked a puzzled disciple, then why the need for constant agitation? Marx replied that he was merely "nudging the inevitable." So Willen made it his task to encourage charitable impulses among givers who would be charitable anyway.

Indeed, card calling, far from antagonizing givers—as might happen among other ethnic groups—is actually the subject of much merriment among Jews. It is viewed as part of the annual rounds, usually following the appearance of forsythia blossoms. Since the vast majority of givers is of east European descent, it is also seen as a modern adaptation of ancient *shtetl* tradition. Big gifts fill the same need for *koved* that less grandiose offerings did in the Pale. Fund-raising functions also offer superb opportunities for social climbing: Membership in a particular country club is often dependent on the size of a prospect's gift; the applicant increases to a figure considered adequate or is denied admission.

Card calling is smooth, efficient, and productive. It inspires those who

* Big gifts are invariably solicited at pre-function meetings, so that no unpleasant or shocking surprises will mar the function.

can to give. By its very nature, however, it makes the size of a check the measure of a person's status. Thanks to the importance of fund raising, big givers now control Jewish communal life in a way that great *shtadlanim*, ceaselessly at war with noisy Yidn, would have envied.

As a result, even during the late 1940s, when millions reacted viscerally to the holocaust and to the establishment of Israel, the number of contributors throughout the country probably never exceeded more than one-third of the Jewish population.* The bulk of funds came from a minority of givers. Contributions of $100 and more were credited with 92.6 percent of funds raised in 1947, as compared with 90.1 percent in 1946. Some 75 percent of $500-and-over contributions in 1947 came from a mere 6 percent of all givers; in 1948, .6 percent contributed $5000 and over. Professional fund raisers estimated that 2000 families were the key to all Jewish philanthropy and provided 80 percent of contributions to UJA.

The broadest participation occurred in small communities where everyone knew everyone else and conspicuous charity was less a matter of religious or ideological commitment than a status symbol. Here it was not unheard of to publish annual listings of gifts, mortifying the less generous. Of about 1800 Jews in Peoria, Illinois, in the early 1960s, 615 people, possibly the head of every household in the town, contributed to the local campaign. Similarly, in 1965, a typical pre-Six Day War year, Cleveland's 80–90,000 Jews collected $6 million, and in 1966, about half of Detroit's 86,000 Jews contributed $5 million to that city's annual Allied Jewish Campaign. Detroit and Cleveland, midway between largest and smallest Jewish communities, set standards for generosity. Year after year, from the mid-1940s onward, they did better per capita than the great metropolitan centers.

But between 40 and 45 percent of all American Jews lived in the New York metropolitan area, and an additional 20 percent lived in Los Angeles, Philadelphia, and Chicago. Only 25 percent of Chicago's donors gave $100 or more, and in Los Angeles only 18 percent gave $100 or more. Philadelphia had the worst record of all: with 331,000 Jews, four times as many as Cleveland in 1958, $770,000 less was raised.

* According to the *American Jewish Year Book* for 1945 and for 1947, it went from 21.1 per 100 in 1944 to 24.9 per 100 in 1946. It possibly reached 30 per 100 in 1948, the highest point in American Jewish philanthropy before the 1967 Six Day War.

In New York, federation and United Jewish Appeal were unusually close-mouthed about divulging information, partly because each was independent of the other* and yet appealed to the same constituency of givers, and partly for the good reason that figures were not always available. Almost certainly, however, fewer and fewer people were making larger and larger gifts.†

In the "Golden Age," costs went up, constituencies went down, and big givers were what fund raising was about. On them depended not merely success or failure, but survival. Certain campaign patterns were noticed. The rich watched each other's contributions; a smaller annual gift from one could begin a chain reaction leading to smaller gifts from others. Conversely, a sizable increase by one could stimulate larger gifts from others. Successful campaigns began with gifts large enough to set the pace for all givers. Any sag in the stock market and major prospects would cry poverty, apparently ready to seek aid, not offer it. Participation by great Yahudi families remained invaluable; charities such as New York's Guild for the Jewish Blind were "in" causes for the newly-enriched because Lehmans, Buttenwiesers, and Loebs attended functions for its benefit.

Under these circumstances it is no surprise that big givers were constantly courted. Like Oriental potentates, they were figuratively borne aloft above madding crowds, with instant access to the executive directors of the agencies to which they contributed, chiefs of medicine in the hospitals they supported, and federation executives wherever they happened to be. New stratagems were devised to attract and to keep the rich in the fold while testimonials, galas, theater parties, and dedication opportunities remained standard. At Brandeis University, the first Jewish-sponsored secular institution of higher education in America, wealthy but unlettered Yidn not only got *koved* but were made alumni. A film unit was set up to produce "This Is Your Life" specials for prospects with

* Except in the matter of fund raisers. Federation "temporaries" (legmen who did the detail work on functions) shifted over to UJA for its campaigns and then back again for federation campaigns. In 1973, a joint campaign was launched for the first time.

† One New York federation board member confessed to me that in 1971 less than 90,000 contributed out of a New York City Jewish population of 450,000 families (figuring four persons to a family); the $104 million "City of Life" building fund campaign in 1961 was carried by gifts from 137 contributors whose $50,000 to $2.6 million donations accounted for over $68 million.

no hope of the real thing on national television, but enough cash for productions on campus in Waltham, Massachusetts. Fund-raising offices were opened in Los Angeles and Miami, where winter crowds were whipped up to hear Abram Sacher, Brandeis University's president and fund raiser *par excellence.*

The authority of big givers was felt in the formulation of communal policy. They thought about causes that would create a better community and also serve their interests.* Since they might become ill or need the services of nursing homes or hospitals, large contributions to hospitals and research support for physicians—occasionally relatives—were always in style. Gifts to nonsectarian causes under Jewish auspices were also fashionable, reflecting approved, acculturated philanthropy. There was an added inducement to contribute to institutions serving people of all faiths: matching federal, state, and municipal funds. In addition to being tax deductible, a $1 million gift could buy a $5 million hospital wing with the donor's name on it. These bargains proved irresistible; the humanitarian motives of the establishment were mobilized for community betterment as its important names were immortalized.

At federation allocation meetings, luckless agencies without glamor got short shrift. The YIVO Institute for Jewish Research, one of the world's great repositories of Jewish learning, was fortunate to come away with $50 contributions from small federations and $500 gifts from the large ones. The biggest big givers were in such demand and contributed to so many causes that they were not always knowledgeable about who was doing what with their money. On the eve of a 1973 building fund drive for $218 million, New York federation held a dinner I attended. Curious about how much they actually knew, I asked eight major contributors the number and the names of federation hospitals. Half knew the number; none knew all the names.†

Israel was at the center of the new perception American Jews had of themselves in the early 1950s, proof of Jewish vitality after the holocaust

* Matters were no different among the gentile rich, of course. The dedicated investigator would have to search hard and long to find a voluntary hospital without plaques.

† There are nine: Beth Israel, Blythedale, Bronx-Lebanon, the Hospital for Joint Diseases, Jewish, Long Island Jewish-Hillside, Maimonides, Montefiore, and Mount Sinai.

and symbol of the Jewish will to survive. No nation had ever begun life with as many problems per person or per square foot. Arab artillery batteries could easily shell every settlement and city. There were few natural resources underneath the sand dunes, and the population shared no common markets, no military alliances, and no political pacts with any other Middle Eastern people.

These were just some of the problems. There were three languages, Hebrew, English, and Arabic; two sets of schools, religious and secular; three bodies of law, Ottoman, English, and rabbinical; and an Orthodox party that held the balance of power, forcing fossilized views on an increasingly secularized public. Israel's leaders, a self-proclaimed elite that considered itself irreplaceable and omniscient, were also paternalistic, contradictory, and condescending.

So much for starters. The most pressing problem was the absorption of hundreds of thousands of European, North African, and Middle Eastern Jews, for which Israel was totally unprepared. Between 1882 and 1947, the population of Jewish Palestine went from 24,000 to 629,000 in six *aliyot.** In December 1949, the population stood at 1 million, and by the end of 1952 it was 1.6 million, an increase of 63 percent in three years and 254 percent in five years. Extrapolating the same rate of increase, the population of the United States would have gone from 150 million to 245.6 million to 382.7 million, straining the most advanced industrial society on earth. In Israel the specter of economic collapse alternated in the minds of planners with the specter of defeat by Arab armies.

Faced with crushing economic and military problems, Zionists reverted to custom; among the first problems attacked was each other. During its heyday, from 1942 to 1948, the American section of the movement had effectively controlled world Zionism's finances through UPA and UJA. American Zionist leaders, admittedly affronted by Ben-Gurion's tactics, looked forward to deciding policy for Israel, but Ben-Gurion would have none of this. No part of his government was to be in other hands, especially not the part that decided finances. This meant an American movement dominated by him and not by Abba Hillel Silver, in 1948 the leading American Zionist and a man of equally charismatic character and supreme confidence in his own judgment.

* The plural of *aliyah*, the Hebrew word for ascent, or immigration.

UJA became a battleground for Ben-Gurion and Silver. Henry Montor, whose loyalty was to Ben-Gurion, or more properly to Eliezer Kaplan, fired early shots. Resigning as executive vice-president of UPA (but not from UJA) in September 1948, Montor charged that the ZOA used UPA funds "as a lever to dominate the social structure of Palestine." Moreover, ran Montor's thinking, needs were so great that Jews of every shade of opinion must contribute: Non-Zionists as well as Zionists would have to be assigned leadership roles. To paraphrase an earlier strategist, fund raising for Zionism was too important to be left to Zionists.

Because it came from the man whose daring, successful, and abrasive tactics made UJA a giant, the statement had a great effect on American Jews. Zionists were unnerved. Silver was shocked. The rabbi had rendered yeomanlike services since UJA's inception and had, indeed, supported Montor in early endeavors. Silver had also helped Ben-Gurion retire Weizmann as president of the World Zionist Organization in 1946;* in a trade-off, Ben-Gurion ostensibly settled for power in Palestine, while Silver was made chairman of the new Jewish Agency-American Section. Silver then made the mistake of not putting his supporters in key posts at UJA and UPA. Recognizing the mistake in 1949, he tried to oust Montor as UJA fund-raising director and Henry Morgenthau, Jr., as UJA chairman, and take the chairmanship himself to thereby regain control of purse strings. A final phase in the power struggle was initiated when Silver and Emanuel Neumann, then president of the ZOA, resigned from the executive of the Jewish Agency, causing sharp divisions on the eve of a UJA campaign.

When considering statements made at the height of this controversy, the relatively unbiased reader is struck at once by the lack of moderation and magnanimity on all sides. Silver and Ben-Gurion were obviously interested in expanding spheres of influence. It was asking a lot of

* Although much evidence points in this direction, it is only fair to add that Emanuel Neumann, another alleged engineer in the dismissal, emphatically denies collusion took place. The issue at the 1946 Zionist Congress was armed resistance to the British. Given the emotions of the time, the movement needed a leader who would aggressively declare for independence, namely Ben-Gurion. In any case, Silver took a major part of the blame for the ouster of Zionism's elder statesman, who continued to play a leading fund-raising role. On January 9, 1949, $38 million was raised for the Weizmann Institute, and Weizmann's arm was in a sling for days because of strain from shaking hands.

American Jews to require that they search for truth amid accusations, counteraccusations, and pleas for unity from Weizmann and Herbert Lehman. As a matter of fact, it was asking too much: Victory went to Ben-Gurion, more because of his superior political tactics, his stronger allies, and the general exhaustion, than because of sounder arguments.

During a two-month period early in 1949, Morgenthau refused to serve again as UJA chairman,* then made acceptance conditional on Montor's ("my good right arm") employment. Neumann and Silver charged that the Jewish Agency wished to give UJA "dictatorial powers," and the UPA board was adamant Montor could not continue in his post. Nahum Goldmann and Ben-Gurion undercut ZOA opposition by winning support for Morgenthau and Montor from Hadassah, the World Zionist Organization, and the Jewish Agency in Jerusalem. By mid-February, UPA split into two factions, each accusing the other of sinking to the "lowest depths of moral bankruptcy." Neumann and Silver tried and failed to rally support from JDC and local federations and welfare funds. On February 20, sixty-two UJA board members backed Morgenthau-Montor; a week later, UPA remained adamant that Montor could not return, Morgenthau refused to be chairman without him, and Silver reminded everyone he was no longer a member of the executive of the Jewish Agency. On February 28, the 1949 $250 million UJA drive began without support from Morgenthau, Montor, UPA, or ZOA.

The situation was obviously untenable. A breaking point was reached on March 1, when fifty-two of eighty-two UPA board members voted to endorse the campaign and thirty (Silver's contingent) abstained. The following day, Morgenthau announced that he would serve as chairman and Montor would direct the effort.

Retiring to his pulpit in Cleveland, Silver ended his official Zionist activity.† For the ZOA his defeat spelled a loss in prestige and power from which it never fully recovered. American Zionist leaders eagerly awaited Ben-Gurion's departure from office. Intuitively gifted at frustrating Arabs, he now offered further proof of similar abilities dealing with Jewish antagonists—sixty-three years old in 1949, he held the post of premier until 1953; he was to return to the cabinet as defense minister

* He was chairman in 1948 and 1949.

† Nonetheless, he continued working diligently for Israel.

in 1955, resume the premiership later the same year, resign a second time, and resume again in 1961.*

Israel's position on the world Jewish scene and Ben-Gurion's dominance in the Zionist hierarchy were now unchallenged; meanwhile, the country was in constant economic turmoil. European, Egyptian, and Iraqi immigrants arrived with a few precious stones or dollar bills hidden over long years. North African Jews arrived with nothing. In addition to transportation, each immigrant cost Israel between $2300 and $2500 to clothe, house, and feed. There was little to export except citrus fruits. The result was a staggering deficit of $861 million† over three years and a reliance on hastily contrived short-term solutions because no one had the time to think through long-term ones.

By December 1948 the economy was in critical condition. Price controls and rationing were introduced, but as late as July 1949 the cost-of-living index stood at 344 points, compared with 280 in November 1947. No firm got raw materials without delivering specified quantities of finished goods. Nonetheless gray and black markets flourished, and the Israeli pound sold on the street for one-eighth the official dollar-pound rate of exchange. Equally alarming, UJA income slipped from previous high levels.

Golda Meir and Eliezer Kaplan made trip after trip to America, meeting with Jewish communal leaders. Ben-Gurion asked financial experts, among them Herbert Lehman, about floating a $1-billion bond issue in the United States over twelve to thirteen years. According to the experts, "such campaigns succeed only when a large part of the contribution is deductible from income tax [and] few would contribute to a loan in which every cent came out of the donor's pocket."‡

Unhappy with the response—"not because [I did] not value their financial know-how but because [I could] not rely on [their] Jewish sensitivity. . . ."—Ben-Gurion convened an assembly of Zionist and non-Zionist representatives from CJFWF, UJA, and South African and British

* This was in addition to numerous threats to leave the government. Ben-Gurion took up yoga and learned to stand on his head. Admirers claimed he thought better upside down than opponents did right side up.

† It could have been $824 million or $960 million—the sources differ.

‡ Meaning that donors would prefer UJA, to which contributions had been tax-deductible since January 1936.

Jewries. In September it heard that the absorption of refugees would probably cost $1.5 billion. At best, Israel could provide $500 million. A mixture of contributions, private investments, and bond issues would have to provide the balance. In Ben-Gurion's words, "the Jerusalem conference unanimously decided to mobilize American Jewry and the Jewish communities in the other prosperous countries to implement the $1-billion Independence Loan. [The meeting] adjourned on September 6 with the singing of 'Hatikvah.' "

Henry Montor resigned from UJA, took over Israel bond sales, and opened an official drive in May 1951. Purchasers viewed the securities as a new fund-raising gimmick.* Rhetoric about investment funds was ignored by most purchasers. Bonds bought with no thought of redemption were used as bar mitzvah gifts (the $100 bond was recommended for this practice) and weddings. On Wall Street, investment banking firms wouldn't touch Israel bonds with a ten-foot pole. Israel had fewer than .5 million employed and a gross national product less than $1.3 billion. Nobody dreamed that a quarter century later State of Israel bonds would be the third most widely-held security in the world.

Without help from Wall Street, Israelis and American Jews set up the American Finance and Development Corporation for Israel to manage "campaigns," a word that did little to remove the fund-raising stigma.† Bonds were registered with the Securities and Exchange Commission, but were sold in operations like no other underwriting effort. Neither volunteers nor managers (the professional fund raisers who directed sales campaigns) took tests usually given security salesmen. Volunteers got testimonial functions, managers got salaries, and State of Israel bonds with headquarters in New York, ended up with a 6 percent commission, a figure larger than the usual spread between price to the public and proceeds to the borrower for bond issues. From each $1000 bond, Israel ended with $940. The large underwriting commission financed operations.

* Some thought Montor had discovered a way for contributors to give to the cause twice, in a stroke of the aggressive genius he so frequently displayed. In fact, according to several givers who prefer to remain anonymous, Israel bonds was Montor's idea.

† The conference became to Israel bonds what the kick-off banquet was to UJA. National leaders assembled in Miami or New York to announce pacemaking purchases. When Levi Eshkol died in 1969, $61 million in bonds was sold as a memorial in a single evening, setting a record.

State of Israel bonds were not redeemable on demand, like United States savings bonds are, nor did they pay high interest rates.* Yet in three years, $130.5 million worth were sold in America.† Union pension funds, management profit-sharing plans, insurance companies, and universities purchased bonds; eventually 220 of the nation's 300 largest banks included them in investment portfolios. Bonds built the Tel Aviv airport, housing projects, hotels, irrigation systems, electric power systems, apartment houses, harbors, and El Al airlines. They financed nearly everything but arms procurement, which was the government's responsibility, and social welfare, UJA's responsibility.

But at UJA headquarters, State of Israel bonds were seen as the competition, a challenge to the accepted order of things. Big givers were now beseeched in four areas—local, national, and two for Israel. Questions were constantly raised in the minds of volunteers impatient to get on with philanthropic jobs. Should a bond campaign precede a UJA campaign or follow it, or was it possible to mount both simultaneously? Which dollars did better jobs, bond or UJA? A coordinating committee consisting of representatives from Israel bonds, UJA, the Jewish Agency, and the Israeli Embassy bogged down in arguments as fund-raising organizations struggled to exceed previous goals. When high-level Israelis visited the United States, UJA and Israel bonds openly fought over their availability as speakers at conferences and banquets.

A climax was reached in 1955, after more than $162 million in bonds was sold. Montor came up against the redoubtable Isidore Sobeloff, director of Detroit's federation. There was a philosophical contretemps between the two men, based on Montor's conviction that Israel must take financial primacy over local causes,‡ a view Sobeloff could hardly endorse. Nor would local bond committeemen forsake Sobeloff, whose influence in the Detroit Jewish community was akin to Willen's in New York.

Montor scheduled a bond dinner for March 1—while preparations were

* The first issue paid 3½ percent; later issues paid higher rates of interest.

† Overextending himself, Montor had predicted $500 million in sales over three years.

‡ In 1949, when a similar situation arose in one city and he was working for UJA, Montor instructed the field man to open a separate office and pull the campaign from under the aegis of the local federation, rather than subordinate Israel's or his own interests.

in progress for the local Allied Jewish Campaign—and the Detroit Jewish community shook apart. Protests were lodged with CJFWF, UJA, Israel bonds, Abba Eban (Israel's ambassador to the United States), and Levi Eshkol in Jerusalem. "In Israel's best interests, it is our sincere hope—with a week's time left for action—that the national bond office will concede the right of local leaders to act on dates to be chosen for bond functions in Detroit," said a message from two local leaders backed by other big givers.

Messrs. Safran, Stollman (the two local leaders), and peers offered to post personal checks guaranteeing the sale of $150,000 in bonds. Montor was not pacified; staff members from New York made necessary arrangements for a bond function. Sen. Wayne Morse of Oregon was recruited as principal speaker; Mischa Elman, the famed violinist, was engaged as an after-dinner recitalist. Adding to the confusion, newspaper advertisements for Montor's bond drive used the name "Committee for the Economic Defense of Israel," instead of American Development Corporation for Israel, as sponsor of the protested event; "Women's Leadership for Israel" replaced "Women's Division of the Israel Bond Organization."

This was going too far. At UJA Montor found Yidn more willing than entrenched Yahudim to part with dollars for recognition and he elevated them to leadership positions. This had not endeared him to the Jewish 400. As Israel bonds, his devotion to duty was such that managers were shifted from city to city even if successful, lest they begin to sympathize with local big givers rather than with national headquarters. Now newly-elevated Yidn were becoming disenchanted. There were complaints, and there was concern in Jerusalem about receipts. At a mid-March press conference in New York, Levi Eshkol said Montor "distinguished himself in mobilizing the material and moral resources that made possible the establishment of the state." Montor then resigned, departing for Rome and a new career in the factoring business.

Eshkol announced termination of the American Financial and Development Corporation for Israel and the creation of a new operation headed by Dr. Joseph Schwartz, kingpin of JDC and executive vice-chairman of UJA.* Two months later, the new Development Corporation for Israel opened offices, Schwartz expressing the belief that Israelis were "within

* Like Montor, Schwartz served two organizations, in this case JDC and UJA. He resigned his UJA position when he joined the bonds operation.

reach of their goal of economic self-sufficiency." Under the circumstances, this appeared rather far-fetched; bonds added to UJA added to United States government aid* still had not made the crucial difference in Israel's economy. But coincidentally with early Israel bond campaigns, the largest single source of Israeli capital was being negotiated.

Long before the end of World War II, German reparations and restitution of Jewish property had been discussed by American Jewish organizations. In 1943, an Allied statement warned Germans that no matter what legalities were invoked, sequestered property would have to be returned after the war. In September 1945, Weizmann asked $8 billion in restitutions, indemnifications, and compensations, as well as the return to rightful owners of real estate, art treasures, and valuables. Where no heirs or principals could be located, property was to be turned over to the Jewish Agency in Jerusalem acting in behalf of world Jewry. The victorious powers were not sympathetic to Weizmann's proposal; at the Paris Reparations Conference later that year, $5 million was offered to nonrepatriable concentration camp victims. A maximum of $25 million in German assets in neutral countries was offered to Jewish organizations in the event victims or their heirs could not be located.

In the immediate post-war period, reparations was an explosive issue, involving German guilt, Jewish unwillingness to deal with the nation responsible for the disaster, and the implications of redemption through cash payments. Germans themselves were not eager to make restitution. In November 1949, after eight weeks in office as chancellor, Konrad Adenauer offered Israel DM 10 million worth of German goods. Four months later the North Rhine-Westphalia Parliament passed a bill legalizing the transfer of prewar Jewish property to non-Jewish owners. In Israel any official move even to discuss reparations with Germans was certain to provoke violent repercussion. In 1950, however, exploratory talks took place between Israelis and West Germans, and early in 1951, Israel sent notes to the Allied powers in Berlin advancing claims of $1.5 billion on Germany. Three occupying powers acknowledged the validity

* Most of the aid took the form of loans or the sale of surplus commodities. Grants were awarded mainly for the resettlement of refugees. It was recognized that Israel assumed burdens previously assumed by the American government in caring for displaced persons.

of claims,* but replied that they could not force West Germans to pay reparations.†

There matters stood, apparently deadlocked, when Adenauer met the Israeli ambassador to France and the governor of the Bank of Israel and heard an emotional description of Nazi crimes. On September 27, Adenauer addressed the Bundestag, acknowledged Nazi guilt, but added that the majority of Germans could not be held responsible for the holocaust. Nonetheless, crimes were committed in the name of the German people, and for that reason moral and material amends must be made. The speech received worldwide approval; in Israel, responses ranged from reserved hostility to passionate opposition to any traffic with Germans.

Ben-Gurion was determined to proceed. Tactically, third parties outside Israel were needed to conduct negotiations. The most powerful figure in the Diaspora was now Nahum Goldmann, destined to be chairman of the Jewish Agency and president of the World Jewish Congress. Goldmann was a dapper, sophisticated figure who had lived in New York since the 1930s and held citizenship in more than half a dozen countries, including the United States. He represented Diaspora Jewry to Israel and Israel to Diaspora Jewry. Oddly enough, he was able to do this because neither saw him as one of their own—he was not an American Zionist, nor did he take his chances in the Israeli political arena. Instead he flayed American Jews for not living in Israel and flayed the Israeli government for its inflexibility. This endeared him neither to American Jews nor to Israelis, but his skill in bridging philosophical gaps through his membership in nearly every Zionist and Jewish organization in existence made him invaluable.‡ Goldmann was an international and interorganizational figure who could not be replaced; nobody had figured out a way to admonish him without fear of awful retribution. He knew every major figure in the Diaspora worth knowing.

* The Soviet Union never bothered to reply.

† East Germany did not acknowledge Israeli claims on grounds that Nazism was eradicated and survivors could return any time they wished. In September 1974, however, the United States made it clear that "normal relations" between the two countries would never be possible unless East Germany agreed to discuss compensation, and talks began.

‡ So varied were his activities that it was said, "like the Messiah he comes, he comes, but he never arrives."

In 1950, at the "urging" of Dr. Noah Barou, vice-president of the British section of the World Jewish Congress, Goldmann had begun to occupy himself with reparations.* A year later, Moshe Sharett, the Israeli Foreign Minister, asked him to call a conference of American, French, and British Jewish organizations to support Israel's claims. The key to success was clearly the American contingent, made up of American Jewish Committee members who suggested to Washington that the price of West German reentry into the family of nations be set at indemnification. The message was conveyed to Bonn—dependent for its survival on Marshall Plan aid—which saw reparations not only in their humanitarian aspects, but as a means of keeping American sympathy.

At the beginning of October, twenty-two major Jewish agencies met in New York and constituted themselves a Conference on Jewish Material Claims against Germany. In January 1952, the Israeli cabinet voted publicly to demand reparations. Meeting secretly with German representatives, Goldmann; Jacob Blaustein, president of the American Jewish Committee; and Moses Leavitt, JDC's treasurer, tried to work out an agreement. Both sides were aware that the official American attitude was the key element. Any suspicion that Washington was negative or neutral on the issue would end talks despite Adenauer's assurances that his government was acting in good faith. When an impasse was reached in June 1952, Blaustein, who wielded considerable political and economic power as head of the American Oil Company, prodded Truman and the State Department. John McCloy, United States High Commissioner for Germany, subsequently pressed for indemnification as a symbolic act for the new, democratic Germany.

On September 10, 1952, Goldmann, Sharett, and Adenauer, respectively representing the Claims Conference, Israel, and Germany, signed an agreement in Luxemburg. Over a twelve- to fourteen-year period, $714 million in goods would be given to Israel. In addition, indemnity laws would be passed to compensate individuals. Israel promised $16 million to the Claims Conference and set aside $130 million for the resettlement of immigrants. In March 1953, the Bundestag ratified the agreement, and in September the Knesset followed suit. Two countries that did not rec-

* Thus he modestly asserts in his autobiography. His involvement actually began during the war. Goldmann raised the indemnification issue as early as 1941, when the Nazis were at high tide in their conquests.

ognize each other politically agreed to massive shipments of goods as a result of talks masterminded by a group that had no status in international law and depended for support on Jewish communal leaders in a third country. "Members of the parties that had opposed the payments willingly benefitted from the goods received," Ben-Gurion comments acidly in *Israel: A Personal History.* Goldmann, Blaustein, Levitt, and others who negotiated the accord were then relieved of travel with a coterie of bodyguards protecting them from Jewish terrorists sworn to murder.

There is little doubt today that reparations were the factors that finally stabilized the Israeli economy in the mid-1950s.* German building materials and industrial and agricultural products made possible continuous development in key industries. "Group II" capital goods, including machinery, turbines, precision instruments, fifty-nine vessels, and one floating dock, provided a new capability to manufacture and to export goods. Israel might have eventually generated equal amounts from UJA, private investment, and the American government. If so, the cost would have been severe inflation. Nor could the gross national product have risen an impressive 12.1 percent between 1950 and 1954 without the huge capital influx.

On the other hand, the very importance of reparations underscored the salient weakness of the Israeli economy, dependence on unearned funds from abroad. Between 1949 and 1965, an import surplus of $6 billion in contributions, loans, and reparations, 70 percent of it from American Jews, the United States government, and West Germany, were to finance Israel. If the state was to endure, industries would have to be created. For this, managers, engineers, and professionals, as well as a large and industrious population, were essential.

"You and I have had the good fortune to see two miracles come to pass," Ben-Gurion told Nahum Goldmann after Luxemburg. "The creation of the State of Israel and the signing of the agreement with Germany. I was responsible for the first, you for the second. The only difference is that I always had faith in the first miracle, but I didn't believe in the second one until the very last minute."

Although the premier—BG, as he came to be known—was an incon-

* Goldmann believed they would make Israel "as economically independent as any state can hope to be in our interdependent world."

sistent believer in the supernatural, he was temperamentally unable to resist nudging the impossible. It was clearly BG's *chutzpah*, rather than his social or economic planning, that kept things together during Israel's early, "heroic" period. The rest of the government followed his example; obstacles were kicked aside or ignored. As architect of the state, Ben-Gurion worried about defense, economic chaos, UJA, bonds, and reparations, but also found time to think about *aliyah*, which alone could provide managerial and professional personnel.

The search for youth and talent was theoretically directed by the Jewish Agency, now a World Zionist Organization copartner. In August 1948, its executive met in Tel Aviv to develop cooperative relationships between Diaspora Jewry and Israel.* While the Israeli government concentrated on defense and economic growth, the Jewish Agency and the World Zionist Organization would concentrate on *aliyah*,† the absorption of immigrants, and fund raising.

Ben-Gurion was soon loath to allow non-Israelis even these responsibilities; early immigration figures from the West were disappointing. Despite intensive Jewish Agency efforts to encourage *aliyah* in the "countries of prosperity," only 1090 American Jews emigrated to Israel between 1948 and 1951, a sizable number of them over sixty-five years old, hoping to live out their remaining years with the help of social security checks mailed from Washington. Crusty as ever, BG heaped equal blame on Diaspora Jewry and Zionists and plunged into the task of changing fate himself.

For Ben-Gurion, one prime nonevent colored *aliyah*: the refusal of World Zionist Organization leaders, up to and including Goldmann, to set personal examples by emigrating to the Jewish homeland. Yet an Israeli policy directly encouraging *aliyah* was fraught with danger. It risked displeasure in Washington if American officials thought there was undue interference in internal affairs. It risked a halt in the flow of UJA and bond dollars if communal leaders were sufficiently alienated by talk

* Ben-Gurion wanted to be premier of Israel and simultaneously to be chairman of the Jewish Agency. The stubborn opposition of American and British Zionists forced him to give up the idea.

† Which went into reverse on some levels. During the early years of the state, thousands of well-educated Israelis left for the United States and Europe in a brain drain.

of dual loyalties. Borrowing from banks against contributions had become a standard procedure*—through 1954, loans totaled $64.8 million—and for this the active cooperation of wealthy non-Zionists was essential. Sharp Zionist observers noted that Yahudim were apt to become edgy about statements on mass emigration and angry about Israeli propagandizing among Jewish youth.

Yahudim tried to anticipate Ben-Gurion's moves. In 1949, a delegation from the American Jewish Committee visited the premier, seeking assurances that the Israeli government was concerned only with its own Jews. This followed an earlier statement issued just after the state was founded that "Citizens of the United States are Americans and Citizens of Israel are Israelis; this we [the Committee] affirm with all its implications; and just as our own government speaks for its citizens so Israel speaks only for its citizens."

Ben-Gurion had scarcely rid himself of Rabbi Silver, was setting State of Israel bonds in motion, and was dealing warily with the Germans when he strongly urged American Jewish youth to emigrate. His statement jolted the American Jewish Committee and threatened to revive the American Council for Judaism, which was at the time hardly breathing, although it was distributing mountains of anti-Zionist materials. Protests were lodged wholesale with handy Israelis at the UN in New York or in the Washington embassy. Judge Proskauer urged a clear-cut break between American Jews and Israel, and Zionists feared the committee might be captured by the council.†

Another series of talks was initiated in Jerusalem. In the summer of 1950, Jacob Blaustein sought a new definition of noninterference. Cajoling and threatening, he got what he wanted, or thought he got what he wanted. At an official luncheon in Blaustein's honor attended by the Israeli cabinet and sanctioned by Chaim Weizmann, Ben-Gurion formally announced that American Jews had "only one political attachment

* During Montor's UJA stewardship, yet another of his achievements was the use of loans as a device to push for higher goals. Town X, for example, might raise $40,000 one year. Montor demanded $60,000 the following year. Field men urged big givers to go to the local bank and jointly borrow $60,000. It was then the responsibility of givers to raise the money to repay the loan.

† While all sides girded for battle, emigration by American Jewish youths remained negligible.

and that is to the United States of America." Israel was dependent on the financial and social strength of the American Jewish community. "We, therefore, are anxious that nothing should be said or done which in the slightest degree undermines the sense of security and stability of American Jewry."*

But disagreements were still bound to occur as JDC-United Israel Appeal† disbursements shifted within the UJA framework, reflecting growing needs in Israel, smaller numbers of displaced persons in Europe, and fewer refugees in the United States. In 1946, JDC got 57 percent of all UJA funds; in 1951, a new contract provided that 67 percent of the first $55 million and 87½ percent of all additional contributions raised each year go to the United Israel Appeal. This agency's by-laws provided that 40 percent of its directors be nominated by the CJFWF. The remaining 60 percent, plus 60 percent of its executive committee, would be appointed by the Palestine Foundation Fund and would vote as a unit. Since Foundation Fund directors were named by the World Zionist Organization and contributions were channeled through it to the Jewish Agency in Jerusalem, American non-Zionists could be effectively blocked from control of funds they helped raise, or, as some perceived it, from knowing how funds they helped raise were spent.

In an atmosphere of hasty development, Zionist officials took little time to clarify financial matters for the curious. The Twenty-third Zionist Congress in Jerusalem in 1951 passed a resolution that "all funds collected by the Palestine Foundation Fund . . . shall serve the requirements of the World Zionist Organization's budget as laid down by the Zionist Congress or Zionist General Council." This was informative, but not exactly elucidating. In practice, UJA funds, which accounted for most, if not all, of the Foundation Fund's income, went to welfare, to Israeli political parties,‡

* That was another way of saying that he had scant respect for America's Jewish establishment. "I demanded aid for defense, but not from the great public and not from the Zionist leaders," he wrote about his pre-statehood activities. "This aid required un-publicized modest work, and leaders in America are not accustomed to or able to do work without 'publicity.' "

† UIA replaced the United Palestine Appeal as the UJA-Zionist beneficiary in 1953 and considered itself the "fund-raising representative of all Zionist parties as well as the Palestine Foundation Fund [Keren Hayesod]."

‡ Which claimed that they spent the funds for philanthropic programs they sponsored.

and to Zionist workers promoting *aliyah.* UJA funds performed a variety of other nonwelfare services as well. They helped subsidize the World Jewish Congress, the Jewish Telegraphic Agency (a service based in Jerusalem supplying news bulletins and feature articles to the Anglo-Jewish press), and they paid for several publications, including *Midstream*, a first-rate quarterly published by the Theodor Herzl Foundation in New York.

Thanks to these overlaps, Israelis stayed active in promoting *aliyah*, American Zionists stayed active in Israeli politics, American anti-Zionists were hard-pressed to keep track of alleged Israeli interference in American politics, and American Jews became accustomed to Israeli participation in communal decisions. Ben-Gurion periodically ignored the ban on *aliyah* statements, declaring in December 1951 that young Jewish technicians would one day be forced to renounce United States citizenship because of anti-Semitism. By 1959, West German reparations totaled $1.5 billion and UJA contributions passed the $1 billion mark. The American Jewish Committee reaffirmed its opposition to the use of UJA funds to promote *aliyah*, but Jerusalem paid as little attention as possible to non-Zionist complaints. Miss Israel joined the stream of Israeli army officers and ministers on UJA and bond circuits, adding pulchritude to some otherwise esthetically dull experiences.

There were, however, disquieting developments outside Jewish circles. In 1957, United States Sen. Allen Ellender called for a study of UJA's tax-exempt status, and in mid-1958, Sen. Ralph Flanders called for a Treasury Department investigation of UJA.* At the end of 1959, Sen. Jacob Javits denied that UJA funds were used for political purposes in Israel, and in April 1960, Nahum Goldmann startled everyone by claiming the Zionist movement was nonpolitical, describing any political characterization as "purely mythological" and the "remnant" of a past period. This was at some variance with what the Internal Revenue section of the Treasury Department could see for itself. UJA was warned that

* Ellender's interest stemmed from Arab inquiries about UJA's status, and Flanders warned that further emigration to Israel plus "injustices to the Arab landowners" would create "such a wave of anti-Semitism as the Jewish race [sic] has never faced. . . ." Considering the substance of charges, it appears that benefits to Arabs, rather than benefits to Americans, motivated both Ellender and Flanders.

unless relationships between it and the Jewish Agency-American Section were changed, its tax-deductibility could be challenged.*

Random anti-Zionist outcries from the American Council for Judaism could be ignored, but an Internal Revenue threat was serious. Big givers were sent copies of a Treasury Department statement describing UJA's tax-exempt status. Four days after Goldmann proclaimed Zionism free of political taint, a major Zionist-UJA reorganization was announced. The Jewish Agency for Israel, Inc.,† a New York corporation, was created to take full responsibility for the disbursement of UJA funds. Theoretically, the Jewish Agency in Jerusalem was detached from control over disbursements, and Zionist activities in America were transferred from it to an American Zionist Council, which became the coordinating group for public relations and educational activities. The Jewish Agency for Israel, Goldmann patiently explained to the press, would be a "purely American philanthropic body, as distinguished from the international Jewish Agency which has headquarters in Jerusalem." It would be headed by twenty-one directors, fourteen of them American Jewish communal fund-raising leaders.

Each year, continued Goldmann, the Jewish Agency for Israel would determine its budgets for "immigration, absorption and resettlement activities which it wishes to support." In Jerusalem, payments would be "strictly supervised" by an American staff supervised by Isador Lubin, commissioner of labor statistics during the Roosevelt years. Israeli political parties would henceforth finance their own philanthropic activities, but could apply to federations and welfare funds for contributions. Their Jewish Agency allocations would terminate at the end of the year.

Internal Revenue dropped its investigation,‡ but many non-Zionists

* The challenge would be on the basis of violation of Section 501e(3) of the Internal Revenue code, which disallows exemptions if a "substantial part" of any organization's activities involve "carrying on propaganda," "attempting to influence legislation," or "taking part in any political campaign on behalf of any candidate for public office."

† This was the third Jewish Agency to come into existence. The other two were the original Jewish Agency in Jerusalem (1929) and the Jewish Agency-American Section (1949), which registered with the State Department under the Foreign Agents Registration Act of 1938.

‡ With no comment in the press, as was proper, since the case never went to court and a reorganization was planned.

suspected "reorganization" was merely a euphemism for the rechanneling of funds. The maze of Jewish Agencies and official and semiofficial Israeli bureaucracies all seemingly devoted to welfare-*aliyah* continued to baffle laymen. It was further noted that seven of the fourteen Jewish Agency for Israel board members were active officers in Zionist organizations and two others were strongly pro-Zionist. Control was seen to be vested in the same group that had held it before reorganization, although lines of interlocking directorates were harder to trace.

Nonetheless, American Jews, Zionist and non-Zionist, defended Israel from criticism while they slowly recovered from reorganization struggles. In late December 1960, the Twenty-fifth World Zionist Congress was scheduled in Jerusalem. At preconference meetings between Ben-Gurion and Goldmann, attempts were made to further clarify relationships between the Jewish Agency in Jerusalem and the Israeli government. Agreement was reached that *aliyah*, Hebrew education in the Diaspora, and *halytiyut* (pioneering) would be prime items on the agenda.

Proceedings began amicably enough. When relationships between Zionists, Israel, and Diaspora Jewry came up for discussion, however, a free-for-all broke out that was reminiscent of Zionist parleys prior to the establishment of the Jewish state. At root were the same sort of hidden motives and lack of definition that had caused earlier difficulties. Stress was evident up and down the line—not only between Israelis and American Zionists, but between ZOA, Hadassah, and American League for Israel* representatives, who exchanged recriminations.

In an unconciliatory mood, Ben-Gurion took the opportunity to smite Diaspora Jewry hip and thigh: "A large part of the [Hebrew religious] laws cannot be observed in the Diaspora, and since the day when the Jewish state was established and the gates of Israel were flung open to every Jew who wanted to come, every religious Jew has daily violated the precepts of Judaism and Torah by remaining in the Diaspora. Whoever dwells outside the land of Israel is considered to have no G - d, the sages said."

For sensitive observers of the American Jewish scene it was hard to measure who was most enraged by this blast—Zionists, non-Zionists,

* The league consisted of dissident Zionists who had left the ZOA in 1957, but did not go so far as to join the Revisionist Zionists of America.

Orthodox clergy, Reform clergy, big givers, small givers, or nongivers.* Further heights of Ben-Gurion's *chutzpah* had been hitherto thought impossible; it was felt he was then displaying the ultimate in colossal nerve. Talmudic scholars objected, not because BG misquoted rabbinic commentary (he had not), but because he implied that they were not fully observant. Also among those to rush forth with objections were big givers,† whose base was the American Jewish Committee and who cried out that he had again violated the 1950 pact, arrogantly trampling men of goodwill, piety, and generosity.

One of the saving graces of the Ben-Gurion–Blaustein entente had been BG's capacity to admit past error, breathe harmony into relations marked by strain, and then do what he wanted to do in the first place. "Your August 1950 Statement did more than anything else to win the goodwill of American Jews toward Israel . . . and to make possible the climate for the successful UJA campaigns in this country and the sale of Israel bonds," Blaustein had written Ben-Gurion in 1960. Repeated outbursts by Ben-Gurion made yet another statement of understanding imperative. In this same context, Blaustein openly discussed claims by Golda Meir, Moshe Dayan, and other Israeli leaders that they had the right to speak for Jews everywhere. These claims encouraged the American Council for Judaism, anti-Semites, and various dissidents to raise the issue of dual loyalties. Fund raising, investment, and Israel's future were all imperiled, said Blaustein.

At the fifty-fourth annual meeting of the American Jewish Committee at New York's Roosevelt Hotel in April 1961, Ben-Gurion offered "strong official reaffirmation" of the 1950 entente. Israel would stay out of American internal affairs; emigration to Israel was a matter of personal choice. Anxious to pacify big givers, he further pledged compliance by other members of his government. "It was admitted that some misunderstandings might have arisen owing to the fact that Mr. Ben-Gurion now and then takes the liberty of expressing views on a variety of topics that are his own rather than those of the government of Israel," said a joint Ben-Gurion–Blaustein communiqué.

* Not to mention Israelis well aware of Ben-Gurion's own anti-Orthodox bias. A statement from him on the necessity for Orthodox observance could cause quite a stir even if it did not relate to Diaspora Jewry.

† Many of them were members of Temple Emanu-El in New York and, like Ben-Gurion, not known previously for interest in strict ritualistic observance.

Unable to please everybody, BG now wounded Israelis, Zionists, and Goldmann with this obeisance to the Yahudi rich. Zionists protested that he was again negotiating with Diaspora Jewry instead of leaving overseas matters to the Jewish Agency and the World Zionist Organization. Worse, he favored American non-Zionists over the faithful. The Israeli cabinet moved to censure him; Ben-Gurion beat back the attack.

The legions were left in utter confusion. Seeking to ease tensions, Max Bressler, president of the ZOA, declared that resolutions made at the Jerusalem meeting "did not imply permanent mass settlement by American Jews [but] suggested a year or two of pioneering activities by enterprising youth of the free world...." Goldmann was mortally offended by Ben-Gurion's negotiations with the committee, which he held "not representative of the Jews of the United States." He was now prepared to recapture Zionism for Zionists by facing down Ben-Gurion in his home territory. In the eye of the storm, BG was notably calm. With complete seriousness he told Zionist leaders that he would have issued the recent statement to anyone who requested it. He had no wish to designate spokesmen for American Jews.

American Zionists and Israelis appeared headed for a major confrontation. To Ben-Gurion, as well as to many Israelis, UJA contributions, bond sales, investments, and support of land reclamation projects had become apologetic charity. *Aliyah* counted most; in 1963, BG again told ZOA leaders that "Zionism can be taught in America, but it can be learned only in Israel."* On their part, many American Jews wondered when dependence would end, whether Israelis could help carry more of the financial burden,† and what could be done to keep Ben-Gurion quiet. UJA and bond income continued to dip; no longer were $100 million campaigns stylish. By 1961, outstanding bank loans totaled $61.5 million, about the annual UJA intake. New borrowing occurred as fast as old loans were repaid.

A new round of official American inquiries into Jewish Agency activi-

* The Eichmann trial, Ben-Gurion wrote in the *New York Times Magazine*, was partly intended to bring home to the Jews of Israel and the world that historically and in the present they lived in a hostile world.

† On October 17, 1962, Dr. Israel Goldstein, who had served as chairman of UPA and moved to Israel, announced an Israeli version of UJA: "... thanks to Israel's present economy, there are thousands of Israelis who can afford to give very substantial sums, ..." he declared in a statement reminiscent of many UJA exhortations he delivered in America.

ties abruptly halted disagreements. J. William Fulbright's Senate Foreign Relations Committee began hearings on the activities of Israel's "non-Diplomatic representatives," with senators confessing confusion at the outset with overlapping and interlocking directorates. Covering his tracks with voters at home, Fulbright made clear his sympathies for resettlement of Jewish refugees. But he found tracing the flow of dollars from contributor to UJA to Jewish Agencies to recipients "very difficult for me to understand and I have tried to. There are so many different affiliated organizations with very similar names and it is almost impossible for me to follow just what happens."

As well as Fulbright could understand, the Jewish Agency in Jerusalem received more than $5 million from UJA between 1955 and 1962; this sum was returned to the American Zionist Council and used to promote further fund raising and *aliyah*—making the council and its constituents guilty of serving as agents of a foreign government without registering with the State Department. The senator, who often waxed repetitive when faced with the array of Jewish agencies, declared this "merely a way of avoiding a disclosure here that should be disclosed."

Briefly, Jewish Agency dollars seemed to have a longer road to travel in the post-reorganization period than in the pre-reorganization period. Raised through hundreds of federations and welfare funds, they were forwarded to UJA's New York headquarters and divided up by partner agencies. Israel's allocation was then sent to the United Israel Appeal, which forwarded its receipts to the Jewish Agency in Jerusalem, which sent part of its receipts back to the United States. Five separate organizations—not counting the original fund-raising groups and the final disbursing ones—handled each dollar. No model of efficiency, this system provided a vast bureaucracy with a great deal of work; dozens of clerks were busy keeping track of the flow of dollars.

On the bright side, Isadore Hamlin, executive director of the Jewish Agency-American Section, told the Senate committee that the Zionist Council had "resolved not to take any more funds from the Agency" as of the previous January. "They were advised by their attorneys to take this action because a problem of their registerability [sic] under the foreign agents act arose." With misunderstandings thus aired, committee hearings ended with no change in UJA's status.

At the beginning of 1967, eighteen and a half years and millions of dollars for *aliyah* had still produced a bare trickle of American Jews bound for Israel. Of 10,000 North Americans who emigrated,* between 40 and 90 percent returned, discouraged by alien customs, high prices, runaway inflation, the constant need to outwit tax collectors, and sheer loneliness. The Jewish life Ben-Gurion promised was not the Jewish life envisaged by many émigrés, a fantasized super-*Yiddishkeit.* To be a good Israeli meant not only learning to read, write, and speak Hebrew, but changing one's surname to a Hebrew one and wiping away traces of past life in the Diaspora.

In America, calls for *aliyah* created a state of affairs unprecedented in Jewish history since Cyrus ended the Babylonian Captivity. After 2000 years of prayer for a return to Zion, there was a Zion to return to. The ritual Passover blessing, "*Le Shana haba be Yerushalyim*" ("Next year in Jerusalem"), needed no theological interpretation by bearded elders.† All it needed was a plane ticket for a flight from New York to Tel Aviv via El Al Airlines. For older Jews—Yidn and Yahudim who had come to terms with each other and with Israel's existence—this posed no problem. Diaspora Jewry's role was to sustain the Jewish State and to help those who wished to go there do so.

For American Jewish youth, however, there were acute problems with Zionism. They were an increasingly well-educated—and radical—group in an increasingly affluent society. By the mid-1960s, about 80 percent of Jewish high school graduates went on to college, compared to 40 percent of the total population. While 57 percent of Jewish families had incomes of $7000 or more each year, 65 percent of all American families earned less. Jews held important posts in government, universities, and corporations. Jewish writers, comedians, and actors were popular; it was chic to be Jewish; and intermarriage rates climbed. The "Golden Age of Jewish Security" had reached its height.

But youthful socialists carrying on the tradition of their fathers could not condone conspicuous consumption in the face of black deprivation

* Estimates run from 6,000 to 20,000 Americans and Canadians between 1948 and 1967; the figure noted is used in most discussions of *aliyah* during the period.

† Unless they were Orthodox, in which case a homecoming to a secular Israel was meaningless. The only true fulfillment could derive from the promised Messiah and God's restoration of His temple.

or a Zionism seemingly bereft of intellectual content. The first post-World War II generation of Jewish radicals rejected "dollar Zionism," Judaism, and "Imperial" America with equal scorn. Memory of the holocaust began to fade into history. Not for the New Left were Israel, bar mitzvahs, the Babbitts of B'nai B'rith, or Jewish princesses. Nor could they support an unending slaughter in Southeast Asia, nor Israel as the American client in the Middle East.

Radicals posed agonizing questions for the Jewish establishment, which could make little of their insurgency and their belief that raising money for civil rights was more important than raising it for kibbutzim in Israel. Who were these upstarts to question whether or not America was the Golden Land? With the dead of the holocaust buried a scant twenty years before, who were these pampered misfits to criticize Israel and her policies while she faced hostile Arab countries bent on her destruction?

The fact that many community leaders themselves had only superficial interest in traditional values and were driven by motivations other than deep faith in traditional Judaism helps explain the fierce attacks on the young. In a 1941 paper, "Self hatred among Jews," the brilliant Gestalt psychologist Dr. Kurt Lewin had described Jews of affluence striving for high positions in Jewish organizations—not because they were deeply committed to the causes, but because these were the only high voluntary offices available in a country where WASPS excluded them from leadership in key voluntary agencies. The Jewish rich were unwilling to risk either the pain of a full break with their past or possible rejection by non-Jews. The safest, albeit ambivalent, role was to render service as ambassadors to non-Jews, becoming leaders and spokesmen for high-minded Jewish enterprises. A tradition begun by "court" Jews and sanctioned by American *shtadlanim* could thus be continued.

Such roles were possible for a select group of big givers, big askers, big entertainers, and big rabbis on an international, jet-set stage. Super-*shtadlanim* commuted between Jerusalem, Washington, and New York, conferring with Israeli premiers, diplomats, and ministers, and with American presidents, State Department officials, congressmen, and businessmen. Politics and philanthropy intertwined until they were almost indistinguishable. In 1956, Ben-Gurion turned Israeli troops back from Egypt when President Eisenhower frightened big givers into warning the premier that he risked serious consequences.* In 1966, President Johnson summoned the Jewish establishment to the White House, where it was flatly warned that too many American Jews were speaking out against the Vietnamese War. American support for Israel might be imperiled, said the president, if the United States was forced to back down in Southeast Asia.†

In Israel, 1967 began with a shaky prosperity. Since 1952, when exact figures were first compiled, the gross national product had increased three and a half times, the number of workers had gone from 544,000 to 900,000, and annual exports had risen from $86 million to $750 million. "We have passed from austerity and rationing to abundance and prosperity," concluded Ben-Gurion. Nearly every home had a radio and a refrigerator, thousands of Israelis were going abroad on annual vacations, and cars filled with young people congested the roads. Tel Aviv's Dizangoff Street, which boasted the prettiest girls in Israel, was crowded with pleasure-bent multitudes.

But prosperity was buttressed by a trade deficit that reached $570 million in 1964. Without UJA, bonds, reparations, and American credits, instant bankruptcy would have been inevitable. Israel, the only country in the world with a net annual import deficit of $500 per capita, was rapidly exhausting the foreign currency reserves it had earned. Economic miscalculations brought on by inexperience and shortages—as well as by the overly large proportion of the labor force in service industries—were weakening growth.

There were ominous signs that the economy was, in fact, petering out. The gross national product decreased from a high 11 percent advance per year to 8 percent in 1965. Agricultural production began to sag. The number of construction starts declined, and 100,000 people, 10 percent of the work force, were out of jobs. Unemployment payments were made for the first time in Israel's history in April 1967.‡

* Eisenhower suspended governmental economic aid and said he was prepared to prohibit private assistance by American Jews. Expulsion from the UN was also threatened.

† In one celebrated instance, an emissary from Gen. Yitzhak Rabin, then Israeli ambassador to the United States, admonished Rabbi Maurice Eisendrath, head of the Union of American Hebrew Congregations, about his antiwar stand.

‡ This was distinct from welfare payments, which Israel offered its citizens immediately after its inception.

This coincided with other bad news. Philanthropic funds from abroad were diminishing, United States government grants-in-aid were gradually being discontinued, and German reparation payments had ended in 1966.* Sales of bonds did not greatly exceed repayment of principal and interest on bonds sold in prior years. In February 1967, Israel recorded a trade surplus, but this was generally interpreted as a reflection of falling domestic demand rather than as a dramatic export achievement.

From both Arab and Israeli standpoints, events during the period immediately preceding the June 1967 war were determined largely by Israel's economic picture. Impatient Arab leaders thought the time to attack was at hand. Cairo's leading newspaper, *Al Ahram*, compared Israel's situation to the symptoms of a man "waking up after a long, boisterous and drunken party." Arabs would later explain that Nasser fell into a series of Israeli traps, which led to a war that deflected attention from Israel's economic crisis.† For Israelis, the military impasse, combining costly call-ups of reserves to the armed forces and loss of income from the tourist trade (the largest single earner of hard currency after citrus exports), was serious enough. Combined with a blockade of the Straits of Tiran, it amounted to a potentially catastrophic political and economic blow.

On June 2, Israel's finance minister, Pinhas Sapir, said enough essential food supplies and raw materials were on hand to last from six to twelve months. Sapir was in New York to confer with Jewish groups in several cities before a campaign that would result, it was hoped, in "the greatest and swiftest outpouring of millions of dollars in UJA's history."‡ In Jerusalem, the government announced that it would raise income taxes by 10 percent over 10 months and float defense loans of $84 million at home and $500 million abroad.

In Egypt, Arabs screamed for a *Jihad*, or holy war, and radio stations promised Israelis that they would be thrown into the sea. On May 15, Jerusalem learned of Egyptian troop movements in the Sinai Desert involving 100,000 men and 1000 tanks. There were demonstrations of concern and solidarity in New York, London, and Washington, but

* Personal restitution from West Germany continued, however, and provided a major source of foreign currency.

† If Nasser was bluffing, as was also claimed afterward, his intention was undoubtedly to hasten an economic collapse.

‡ It did, of course, but ironically not for the reasons offered at the time.

despite later reports of complete confidence in victory, the Israeli cabinet, like the populace, feared the worst. Foreign Minister Abba Eban went to Paris, London, and Washington seeking official pledges of support and returned with requests for restraint. On June 4, the cabinet voted for war.

At 7:10 the next morning hundreds of Israeli jets swept above the Mediterranean at altitudes of less than 1000 feet to avoid radar detection, skimmed the coastline west of Alexandria, and bombed Egyptian air bases. An hour later, Israeli armored forces clanked across the Sinai border, not stopping to catch their breath or regroup until they reached the Suez Canal. In 130 hours it was all over. Jordan and Syria were trounced as badly as Egypt. The Sinai Peninsula, the Golan Heights, the west bank of the Jordan, and all of Jerusalem were in Israeli hands. Had they wished to push further, tanks and mechanized infantry could have entered Cairo, Damascus, and Amman.

During the four-week period beginning in mid-May and ending with a truce on June 10, the American public was caught up in a way no one could have predicted. Public opinion polls were favorable to Israel. Israel was the American surrogate in the Mideastern part of a worldwide struggle with communist or communist-supported forces. Like the public, the press generally supported the Jewish cause, opposing American intervention, but backing Israel. The *Wall Street Journal* and Henry Luce's *Time*, previously cool to Israel, deplored the fact that Israel's neighbors would not permit it to live in peace and work toward a brighter future for the entire Middle East. Thousands of letters and telegrams urging a firm American stand in Israel's behalf poured in on President Johnson, congressmen, senators, and other public officials.

For American Jews, May offered the possibility of a holocaust replay, but June offered a modern version of David and Goliath. Relief had profound psychological effects. Emotions swung so quickly from fear to confidence to pride that many individuals could not keep track of their feelings. Israel's fate dominated discussions; people clung to transistor radios and attended synagogues in droves. Until the very end, the murderous boasts of Arab leaders cast a pall over Jewish homes everywhere.

In this highly-charged atmosphere, tortured by impotence in the face of a second annihilation in a quarter century, American Jews began contributing to UJA and buying State of Israel bonds in amounts no one ever imagined possible. Strictly speaking, there were no fund-raising or bond campaigns in June 1967, but vast collections took place throughout the country. People lined up and pleaded to make contributions. UJA's New York office was swamped with checks, cash, and money orders; banks loaned clerks to keep up with the impossible bookkeeping job.

Fund raisers accustomed to hard-sell card calling could not believe what they saw happening around them. At one luncheon on June 5, $1 million a minute was pledged for fifteen minutes. At a Merchants Council dinner in New York on June 6, textile and retail businessmen vied for opportunities to make offerings: There was one pledge for $1.5 million and four for $1 million each. CJFWF began issuing daily fund-raising bulletins. On June 5, a $12,500 UJA contributor gave an additional $150,000 and a $250,000 contributor upped his gift to $1.3 million. On June 6, the first fifty-one Israel Emergency Fund gifts in Boston totaled $2.5 million. In Erie, Pennsylvania, four givers donated $95,000—which was more than the UJA campaign just concluded had raised. *Landsmanschaften* began turning over their treasuries, and in Cleveland, 150 gifts totaled $3 million.

Non-Jews caught the fever. A shipping magnate, told that his $100,000 contribution would not be tax-deductible unless it was channeled through a philanthropic organization, ordered his aide to "Send it to Tel Aviv directly." At the Hollywood Bowl, a capacity audience of 20,000, with 10,000 outside, heard Frank Sinatra read an account of the capture of the Wailing Wall. Sixteen New York city officials—Catholic, Protestant, Russian Orthodox, and Jewish—developed plans for an unofficial, nonpartisan, and nonsectarian group to assist UJA. Mayor John Lindsay presided at the first meeting.

As Israeli forces moved across the Sinai Desert, the American Council for Judaism said the emotional reaction to victory amounted to hysteria, and thereby lost most of its remaining supporters. Rabbi Elmer Berger, the tall and scholarly chief spokesman and dialectician, resigned. Anti-Zionism was erased as a factor of any consequence in Jewish communal life.

In November 1967, Pinhas Sapir announced that the war had cost Israel $750 million. Intensive campaigning raised $350 million, two-thirds of it in the United States. American Jewish businessmen had also begun attempts to spur economic growth through increased sales of

Israeli products in the United States. In late June, a group of American magnates spearheaded by Meshulim Riklis, whose McCrory Corporation included 1400 stores, and Charles Bassine, whose Spartan Industries sold about $60 million in apparel each year through E. J. Korvette stores, announced plans to establish a joint buying office in Israel. In August, sixty of the wealthiest and most influential Jewish business leaders in the world met in Jerusalem as a prelude to a larger meeting of Jewish businessmen the following year.* Sapir told them Israel's industry and agriculture could not develop maximally, unless there was a large influx of capital funds. With funds, exports could be increased 12 percent a year, doubling the 1967 figure of nearly $1 billion. In an optimistic mood, Ze'ev Sharef, Minister of Commerce and Industry, similarly saw signs of recovery from the prewar recession: a decline in unemployment, new investments from abroad, and loans from the International Bank for Reconstruction and Development.

Sapir said that the goal of self-sufficiency could be reached, but to be on the safe side, Rabbi Herbert Friedman, executive vice-chairman of UJA, announced that UJA's "Israel Emergency Fund," initiated during the conflict, would continue. "The logic behind this decision is quite clear and simple," explained the rabbi. Israel still faced "a serious military and security problem, as a result of the present political impasse. As long as the Arab world maintains its position of belligerence, the people of Israel are forced to divert all their economic strength and resources to defense at an enormous cost."

Israel's peril inspired a Jewish unity few would have predicted six months earlier. Relief that a second holocaust had been avoided accomplished what *aliyah* propaganda had failed to produce: a sizable upswing in immigration.† Thousands of volunteers remained in Israel after

* The later meeting included the "millionaires' conference" and saw the creation of the Israel Corporation, intended to promote the economy. Tax incentives were granted to spur investor interest.

† This was somewhat complicated by the question how to define Jewish. Under Jewish religious law, an individual's religion was determined by the religion of his or her mother. In January 1970, the Israeli High Court ruled that an Israeli could register his children as Jewish by nationality rather than by religion, even if their mother was not a Jewess. This amounted to saying "A Jew is anyone who says he is a Jew." The Orthodox were aghast, viewing the decision as a grave threat to Judaism and to Jewish identity. Ben-Gurion, who had a Christian daughter-in-law and wanted Jewish grandchildren, was not counted among Orthodoxy's allies on this occasion.

the war, including 225 doctors and nurses and 1800 students, professionals, and kibbutzniks. By October 1968, between 40,000 and 50,000 Jews had come from Moslem and eastern European countries. Most of Poland's 25,000 Jews either fled to Israel or melded completely into the communist bureaucracy, and the last traces of Jewish cultural life in the country disappeared.

The focus of attention next swung to the largest single group of oppressed Jews and prospective immigrants in the world, 3.5 million people in Russia. On different pretexts and with appalling chicanery, Soviet authorities denied them educational, language, and cultural rights guaranteed in the country's constitution.* It is outside the scope of this book to describe talks between American Jews and the American, Soviet, and Israeli governments. In essence, the survival of a people who nurtured Jewish culture over a 1000-year period received a great boost in the aftermath of the Six Day War. Many Russian Jews who previously tried to disguise their Jewishness began identifying openly with Israel. Worse from a communist standpoint, they began to learn Hebrew, commemorate Jewish victims of the Nazis, and reopen synagogues.

Continued agitation in the West forced action on their behalf. In 1972, the Russians announced they would permit Jews to leave, if certain "education taxes" were paid as exit fees. This amounted to ransom, but well-meaning people began to consider the possibility of raising $200 million to free Soviet Jewry. Russian Jews themselves told Western friends not to "pay this robbery." Moscow was seeking trade and credits from the United States, and American Jewish leaders prevailed on Washington to negotiate an end to the exit fees as part of agreements.† Mrs.

However, the Israeli cabinet, under pressure from religious parties, reversed the High Court decision and a Jew again became what the Orthodox said he was.

* In *The Gulag Archipelago, 1918–1956,* Aleksandr Solzhenitsyn charges that Stalin planned a mass pogrom in 1953. The first phase was the so-called "Doctors' Plot," in which Soviet authorities charged Jewish physicians with plotting the murders of Russian officials with the help of JDC. Newspapers were in the process of whipping up anti-Semitism when Stalin died. In the de-Stalinization period that followed, the total exile of the Jewish population was dropped as a serious idea.

† Citing assurances from Soviet leaders, President Nixon said that "in his opinion" the "education taxes" were removed in April 1973. By the end of the year, the Russians were doing some maneuvering of their own. A group of American executives with whom they hoped to do business fanned out to key American cities, taking their case for greater trade and less interest in Jews along with them. The Russians later cancelled a trade agreement that had provisions for Jewish emigration, protesting that no nation had the right to meddle in their internal affairs.

Meir warned American and Canadian Jewish communities that greater financial support would be necessary for Israel to absorb the expected heavy flow of immigrants; Israel bonds set higher goals; and Moscow permitted between 30,000 and 40,000 people to leave each year.

Israeli emissaries went to Latin American and English-speaking countries in new recruiting drives. Eleven absorption centers were operating in Israel by the end of 1969 as a record number of American Jews, mostly youths, arrived on summer and year-round work-study programs. By 1971, 22,900 Americans had emigrated over three years, roughly double the number between 1948 and 1967. They were encouraged by exemptions from income taxes and import duties for three years and received rental subsidies and liberal mortgages. Theoretically, newcomers from every country were entitled to these benefits, but it was only the Americans who came with enough capital to fully utilize them.*

Meanwhile, the war presaged an arms race that Egypt, Israel, Jordan, and Syria could not afford. When Golda Meir became premier in March 1969, counter-thrusts to *fedayeen* terrorist attacks included commando raids in Egypt and the destruction of passenger airplanes in Lebanon. Until 1967, Israel's weapons came through West Germany and France, and America avoided Arab hostility. With the end of German reparations and De Gaulle's about-face in French Middle East policy, Washington openly became chief purveyor of arms to Israel.

Costs skyrocketed. In 1966, 10.5 percent of Israel's gross national product was spent for arms, and in 1970, military spending took 25.1 percent of the gross national product. By 1972, weapons cost $1.5 billion, four times what they had cost in 1966. Half of a $500-million American credit in November 1971 went for purchases of F-4 Phantom fighters, which cost nearly $3 million each. Israel ranked fourteenth among world powers in its military expenditures.

To meet defense needs, Israelis paid higher taxes than the citizens of any other country in the world. Some welfare costs, particularly those for the anticipated record number of Jews from the Soviet Union, were partly covered by a novel form of government financing—"voluntary contributions" solicited by Finance Minister Sapir from wealthy in-

* The number of Americans peaked at 9500 in 1970, a disappointment to Israelis who had hoped for 10,000 a year. Between 24 and 40 percent returned to the United States, discouraged by taxes, new life styles, and the antagonism of older residents who could not obtain apartments because they were preempted by Americans.

dividuals and domestic corporations.* But at current rates of expenditures, only hopeless optimists believed that Israel could carry on its military procurement program in addition to any sizable percentage of economic development and *aliyah*. Addressing 3000 UJA leaders in December 1969, Louis Pincus, chairman of the Jewish Agency in Jerusalem, said Israel's foreign currency reserves were strained "to the breaking point." Social and economic development would have to be shifted almost completely from Israeli shoulders to Diaspora Jewry. In December 1968, nonmilitary needs were set at $365 million; the following year, Israel bond sales reached $159 million† and UJA raised $107.3 million. In 1971, bond sales were $209 million, and UJA raised $253 million. All nonessential fund-raising drives in the United States and special drives for various Israeli institutions were discouraged.

This was fund raising with a vengeance and on an order calling for the most exquisite coordination between Israeli officials and American fund-raising agencies. In late 1968, Rabbi Friedman initiated UJA's Operation Airlift, in which financial needs were demonstrated to cross-sections of American Jews, mostly big givers. Travelers left for Israel from New York's Kennedy Airport on a Sunday, paid their own way, and spent a week being briefed by military intelligence officers, mayors, police chiefs, and almost anyone else they wanted to see, including the premier. They watched immigrants arriving at Lydda Airport, visited the Bar-Lev Line along the Suez Canal, and saw kibbutzim under artillery bombardment in the Beisan Valley. Saturday afternoons were set aside for a caucus, during which each traveler considered his financial commitments. Sunday was spent flying back to Kennedy. "It's the application of modern technology to philanthropy," declared the rabbi.

Communal leaders were courted, informed, advised, flattered, cajoled, and cultivated as never before. Super-*shtadlanim* took charge. Max Fisher, a kindly, gray-haired Republican industrialist from Detroit whose fund-raising techniques were reported to be a deadly combination of card-calling and gentle persuasion, had close ties in the White House. Fisher traveled the country explaining arms and loan negotiations between

* Legislators smiled when news of these "contributions" was announced in the Knesset. Everyone knew that Sapir's approval was crucial to important business transactions. One of his friends told me he also knew "where the bodies were buried." A suggestion from him was like an order from anyone else in the government.

† $27.3 million in bonds was sold outside the United States.

Washington and Jerusalem to local big givers. Sam Rothberg, a Peoria, Illinois, distiller and close confidant of Golda Meir, regularly headed Israel bond drives. Meshulim Riklis, who made corporate mergers an art form, played a crucial role in national UJA drives. Lawrence Tisch, whose financial genius made the Loew Corporation a $500-million giant, led UJA and federation campaigns in New York. Samuel Hausman, a textile executive, was Gov. Nelson Rockefeller's tie to the New York Jewish community.

At the very top of the pyramid of prospects stood big big givers whose charitable donations, like those of other rich Americans, could actually save them money.* Great Yahudi names were missing—Schiffs, Lehmans, and Guggenheims had intermarried and their descendants had minimal interest in Jewish matters. On the other hand, defections were made up by wealthy descendants of Yidn. In addition to Fisher and Tisch, Riklis and Rothberg, there were the Bronfmans, whose progenitor, Samuel, founded Distiller's Corporation-Seagrams Ltd. and amassed a fortune conservatively estimated at $400 million before he died in 1971. In Cleveland there were the Ratners, in Los Angeles there was Bram Goldsmith, and everywhere big gifts were no longer the $50,000 and $100,000 blockbusters of the early 1950s. Big gifts were now contributions upwards of $250,000 annually.

Big big givers kept raising the sights of ordinary big givers who paid $550 a couple to attend a concert and dinner for the American-Israel Cultural Foundation. When Mrs. Moshe Dayan came to New York in 1970, their wives contributed from $500 to $2500 to hear her speak at luncheons. In regular campaigns they were irresistible solicitors. By 1971, Detroit went from $5 million to $13 million a year; Los Angeles went from less than $6 million to $26 million; and Miami went from $1.5 million to $7 million. Few potential givers could hide. Men who had made large sums through stock vehicles, but were never part of the Jewish community, were traced through research into public records by UJA's "Operation Breakthrough."

"Some federations require their president to have been a former general chairman of the campaign," said one speaker at the 1971 CJFWF As-

* When a donor in the 70 percent tax bracket gives, say $10,000 to charity, it reduces his tax by $7000. If he contributes stock, it is theoretically possible to take a deduction and also to avoid a capital gains tax on the securities.

sembly. "The best president may not be the best presiding officer or the best organized individual. He may even regretfully know little of our Jewish heritage." Paul Zuckerman, UJA's national chairman, declared that "Our task, as fund raisers, is to translate this deep concern [for Israel's survival], this growing sense of solidarity into new dimensions of giving, giving that is equal to the new dimensions of the needs." Zuckerman described the impact on prospects when "creativity, courage, and cooperation" were applied equally: "When a national leader, an Israeli, and a respected local leader call on a man, then quite literally the world Jewish community is calling on him. And the giving will be responsive. This is not theory; it is proven fact."

In Israel, from Golda Meir to the newest clerk, the bureaucracy labored to cement already solid ties with American Jews, who lived in "plaque-land," where *koved* was a way of life.* At the June–July 1969 conference of the Jewish Agency in Jerusalem, Louis Pincus unveiled a new plan "to give world Jewry, which raises funds for Israel, a direct say in the way the funds are spent." The Jewish Agency would sever formal ties with the World Zionist Organization. Fifty percent of its assembly members would be drawn from non-Zionist ranks; America, which provided the bulk of funds, would get 30 percent of the representatives. The executive would consist of eleven members, including UJA's chairman and two designees from the United Israel Appeal board. The Jewish Agency's program would be only such as might be carried on by tax-exempt organizations in the United States.

Zionists were crushed. Forty years after it was created, the Jewish Agency finally capitulated formally, legally, and totally to the big givers of America. Presiding at the founding assembly of the reconstituted Jewish Agency, Max Fisher proudly noted that "We, who came from the United States, Great Britain and all the lands represented here have never been given a greater vote of confidence."

In America, there was another reaction to the Six Day War, the implications of which were ominous. Twenty-two years after the collapse of the most anti-Semitic regime in history, anti-Semitism suddenly be-

* Israelis felt that these Americans could have made the crucial difference had they come to Israel. With a highly-trained population of 5 to 7 million, the country would have been in an immeasurably stronger position vis-à-vis Arabs and vis-à-vis industrial and agricultural development.

came part of political rhetoric. Unlike its pre-1945 manifestation, it was identified with leftist politics. Two groups raised its standard: clergymen* with missionary experience in Arab countries and the New Left, which used anti-Semitism to strengthen political positions even though many of its adherents were Jewish. Arab propagandists deliberately stoked both fires, claiming (to clerics) that Jews lost all rights to the Holy Land because "it was their ancestors who handed Christ to the Roman ruler and crucified him," and claiming (to radicals) that Israel and South Africa had formed an alliance against black and Arab populations in newly-developing nations.

The lack of supportive response from church-governing bodies concerned Jews. Even pro-Israel Christians could not grasp the feelings of American Jews who saw Israel's existence as a symbol of their own survival. There was a discrepancy between inspiring calls for brotherhood and silence in the face of Israeli peril. Christian, as well as Jewish, theologians were struck by the indifference.

Ecumenism faltered badly, but did not collapse. Relationships between Jews and the New Left, however, underwent a major crisis, causing massive rifts within the Jewish community. Since the great waves of Jewish immigration in the early years of the century, bonds between Jews and socialists were thought unbreakable; bonds between Jews and blacks were similarly considered eternal.

Jewish liberals were completely unprepared when the New Left caucus in Chicago after the Six Day War condemned Zionism and the basic validity of a Jewish homeland. Black militants, frustrated by unrealized social and economic expectations, developed an anti-Semitic ideology as part of their political strategy—but nonetheless felt Jewish money should continue to be solicited for their cause.† Although most blacks were

* In 1965, the Second Vatican Council promulgated a Declaration on the Jews denouncing anti-Semitism, affirming the "common patrimony" of Christians and Jews, and calling for "fraternal dialogue." Many theologians regretted that the declaration had not come in advance of the holocaust, but hailed it as the herald of a new era in brotherhood. Four years later, an Anti-Defamation League study still found one out of three Americans anti-Semitic, a second free from prejudice, and a third indifferent. More than one-third said that a political candidate's anti-Semitism would not bother them.

† A black client for whom I worked briefly was insistent that no stone be left unturned in the search for Jewish support. I pointed out that the particular cause had little to attract Jewish givers. My arguments made little impression. Jews were well known for their generous impulses—what difference did the cause make?

disinterested in anti-Semitism, they were equally disinclined to do much about it.* Apologists suggested that scurrilous rhetoric heard on street corners in black neighborhoods was poetic excess inspired by dishonest Jewish merchants; Jews should not become hysterical about it.

Confrontations between blacks and Jews centered in New York, which had more Jews (1.8 million) and more blacks (1.5 million) than any other city in the world. As the white middle class fled to the suburbs, it left behind a rear guard bureaucracy that was Jewish in the schools and welfare department. Blacks seeking civil service jobs came into conflict with Jews holding them.

Creatures of habit, big givers with socialist family traditions followed the lead of radical intellectuals and radical youth in supporting extremists. The black United Front of Boston, which attacked Brandeis University as racist during a black sit-in, received contributions of $300,000 through two young men, one with a Jewish name. The money was raised from local businessmen on the premise that it would assuage the feelings of alienated blacks. During the most highly publicized fund-raising party of 1970, Leonard Bernstein and perhaps thirty guests dug deep for a Black Panther Defense Fund.† When news of the soirée appeared on the front pages of newspapers, Mrs. Bernstein complained to the New York *Times* about space given to the event, similar functions were cancelled, and Maestro Bernstein hurried off to conduct concerts.

In New York, scions of great Yahudi families who lived in magnificent Manhattan apartments or Westchester estates (or both) vied with each other to head Urban Coalition drives and counsel Mayor John Lindsay on interracial problems. Big givers who would never dream of contributing to extremists were also brought into the fray, sometimes without realizing the connection. Completing a $100-million fund-raising campaign in 1967, which had seen multimillion-dollar gifts from Andre Meyer and Leon Shimkin and million-dollar gifts from Charles Bassine, K. B. Weissman, and Leah and Joseph Rubin, New York University established a Martin Luther King Afro-American Center. John Hatchett, its director,

* It made no difference whether a teacher was white or black, black parents responded in a 1968 Ford Foundation survey. Yet they preferred a sharp reduction in the number of Jewish school teachers.

† The most memorable quote of the evening: "He's a magnificent man [Ray "Masai" Hewitt, the Panther's Minister of Education], but suppose some simple-minded *schmucks* take all this business about burning down buildings seriously?"

said Jews castrated blacks and practiced genocide in black neighborhoods. Complaints to the university about Hatchett's paranoia were unavailing; President James Hester sought somehow to rationalize the anti-Semitism. Growing bolder, Hatchett called Richard Nixon, Hubert Humphrey, and George Wallace "racist bastards." This was too much, and Hatchett was fired. Jewish big givers, untuned to the implications of Hester's position, continued making pledges of $1 million and more to NYU and served as its fund-raising chairmen.*

In less exalted circles there was a noticeable sag in Jewish support of liberal causes, albeit with no corresponding increase in support of Jewish causes. A survey of Reform Jews by the Union of American Hebrew Congregations found adult respondents willing to give 68 percent of their contributions to Jewish organizations and only seven percent to three nonsectarian agencies, the National Association for the Advancement of Colored People, SANE, and the American Civil Liberties Union. Younger respondents were willing to give 43 percent of their contributions to Jewish organizations and 26 percent to the three nonsectarian agencies; 32 percent of the adults said contributions to Jewish philanthropy were essential for a Jewish life, but only four percent of the young thought so.

One Jewish radical said, "The Jewish establishment is so busy serving other people's causes that it neglects the cause of its own people." In 1969, Rabbi Arthur Hertzberg, soon to become head of the American Jewish Congress, found Jewish identity so eroded that it was only "a kind of jerry-built intellectual construct" over a foundation of anti-Semitism. Five hundred delegates to the American Jewish Congress's National Women's Division also heard Professor Martin Peretz of Harvard say Jewish youth became more alienated as "their parents and teachers are becoming . . . more accepting of and more accepted into the general culture." B'nai B'rith announced it would spend more than 42 percent of a record $15.6 million budget for teenage programs, vocational counseling services, and college campus activities. UJA continued organizing field trips by youth groups to the sites of death camps in Europe.

How much all this helped Jewish identification and philanthropy is questionable. A conference on Jewish college youth, organized and paid for by B'nai B'rith's Hillel Foundation "to diminish some of the mis-

* By 1972, all was forgiven, and Hester received B'nai B'rith's annual Gold Medallion for Humanitarian Services.

understandings, false notions and misconceptions with which the organized Jewish community and its college generation tend to interpret each other," heard from one student that organized Jewry was "too vast, too stiff, and too unhearing." A few months later, Nathan Glazer told the Conference of Jewish Social Studies that the pervasive influence of New Left ideas was turning Jewish youth away from "specifically Jewish interests," which included the fate of Israel, anti-Semitism, and openings in occupations that traditionally attracted Jews, such as finance, teaching, and retail trading.

In December, 250 students picketed CJFWF's annual conference, demanding it put more emphasis on "Jewish values" and Judaism. The council, which expected to raise $263 million in 1970, promised to consider the establishment of a $100 million foundation for "Jewish identity."* In a similar vein, Zionist students criticized the passive attitude of American Zionists to Israel and philanthropic support for institutions that "are Jewish in name only and are nonsectarian in character."†

Jewish education and financial support for yeshivas and day schools next became battle cries. Jewish youths who knew their heritage would face enemies eye-to-eye without hesitation. It was the uneducated and uncertain who vascillated, assimilated, and became radical converts. But as percentages of blacks and Puerto Ricans increased in the New York public school system, middle- and upper-class Jews transferred their children to nonsectarian private schools. Pleas from Board of Education officials to maintain a middle-class presence, and from the Orthodox for contributions and increased attendance in all-day Jewish schools combining religious and secular courses, were ignored.

By 1969, New York's 165 Hebrew day schools with 55,000 students were at the "gates of disaster," willing to join Catholic parochial schools

* The promise took form in 1972 as the Institute for Jewish Life in Wellesley, Massachusetts, but was financed at considerably less than $100 million. Some 230 local federations and welfare funds promised $350,000 in its first year, $450,000 in its second year, and $550,000 in its third year. About $900,000 was to be solicited from foundations and other sources.

† Montefiore Hospital and Medical Center, which by then got less than two percent of its income from New York Federation, was an example. By 1971, the hospital had long since done away with an exclusively kosher kitchen and an in-house synagogue and was in the process of working Jewish holidays out of the official hospital holiday schedule. The descendants of great Yahudim who sat on its board were not overly enthusiastic givers; at least one frankly preferred Harvard as a recipient of his donations.

in open demands for funds from federal and state governments. Their students came from the poorer sections of the city where Orthodox parents were frightened for the safety of their children in crime-ridden neighborhoods. Federations unwilling to become embroiled in battles over relative allocations to Reform, Conservative, and Orthodox schools did not increase grants;* major Jewish organizations were also strongly opposed to federal aid to schools on grounds that it would violate the principle of separation of church and state.

The Jewish community split into two camps on the issue. The liberal, establishment position was reaffirmed at the end of January 1971 by the Anti-Defamation League, the Central Conference of American Rabbis, and the American Jewish Congress, among others. A joint statement opposed public aid as a "grave threat to the independence of religion and the stability of government." Mrs. Charles Snitow, cochairman of the congress's national governing council and president of its women's division, announced in March a "nationwide drive of legal action and public information to oppose pressures for public funding of private and parochial schools." Mrs. Snitow, a former school teacher who lived in Scarsdale, a Westchester County community with no black-white problem of consequence, added that public schools had traditionally served as "the great ladder of upward mobility in American life." The congress encouraged groups that provided religious education for children, but felt that these groups should "look to their own constituents for support, not to the public to raise funds."

The opposing camp consisted mainly of Orthodox and a growing number of Conservative rabbis. In November, Orthodox religious leaders at the CJFWF's national conference in Pittsburgh demanded that federations and welfare funds "substitute cash for rhetoric" and allocate $100 million for Jewish education. Max Fisher, CJFWF president, urged delegates to reexamine their obligations, but no large sums were forthcoming. Four months later, the Rabbinical Council of America, the leading organization of Orthodox clergymen, flatly appealed for federal legislation to grant tax deductions to parents paying tuition in parochial schools, an action supported by Roman Catholic groups. At the 1972

* Until 1972, New York's federation channeled less than $2 per child in direct aid to Jewish day schools. As the situation worsened, it added funds for scholarships, buses, and various programs, and finally sought $20 million to construct and to rehabilitate educational facilities.

CJFWF conference in Toronto, Orthodox rabbis again said federations and welfare funds were unable to comprehend the "vital significance of Jewish education" and again came away without major commitments. By 1976, Jewish education would be in a worse state of ferment than ever, with most major Jewish agencies opposed to federal support and an accelerating decline in school enrollment owing to a lack of teachers and facilities.

On another issue, however, establishment organizations took the opposite position on the use of public funds. Jewish welfare agencies had been reluctant to participate in federal poverty programs during the early 1960s, viewing them as threats to their dominance in the Jewish community. They were also unequivocally opposed to the concept of community control of welfare funds.* When the Jewish poor were suddenly rediscovered in the early 1970s, it was too late to play leading roles on community welfare boards. Yet the president of the Jewish Federation of Metropolitan Chicago insisted to the 1971 CJFWF conference that "the primary responsibility for the cash income needs of *all the poor* [italics added] lies within the governmental sector. This is a basic principle which was established in the 1930s." By this time, Jews in the inner cities—particularly in New York—were as disenfranchised through political chicanery as blacks had been in Mississippi.

They were possibly even more disenfranchised, because no one knew how many there were. The Union of American Hebrew Congregations estimated 50,000 "invisible" Jews in Brooklyn's Brownsville and Crown Heights sections and in the East Tremont section of the Bronx. The American Jewish Committee estimated between 400,000 and 800,000 throughout the United States, about two-thirds of them over sixty-five. A research team from the New School for Social Research, working for New York's federation, estimated 272,000 in the metropolitan area, about 15.1 percent of the Jewish population. Whatever the number, tens of thousands had gone unnoticed by Jewish agencies.†

* The first inkling of change in welfare procedures occurred in 1963 with the passage of the Federal Community Mental Health Centers Construction Act, which indicated that facilities must be used "principally [by] persons residing in a particular community." Areas chosen for funding were based on such criteria as high welfare roles and delinquency rates, neither of which were characteristic of the Jewish poor.

† These findings aroused considerable interest among such journals as the *Village Voice*, but failed to stir the radical chic, still busily seeking support for more glamorous causes. The Jewish poor included a large number of elderly Jews found living in

New York's federation initiated several new programs. In 1972, $1.2 million was allocated for neighborhood centers, the total number of dwellings available for the Jewish aged was increased to 1200, and five new nursing homes were opened. Six buses were purchased to take the aged to clinics and health centers. Constituent federation agencies were said to spend nearly $500 million in private and public funds each year, of which 50 percent was for poverty programs.

And yet the fact was that until the abandonment of the Jewish poor became an issue in the press, it hardly loomed as a major item in federation's overall program. "We have cured and comforted, sheltered and cared for, counseled and trained, enlightened and enriched the lives of a great many of our friends and neighbors—and people who were strangers until they sought our help," said Lawrence Buttenwieser, president of federation, in December 1973. Unfortunately, the Jewish poor had meanwhile been swept out of sight.* In June 1971, a federation commission debated whether or not federation still had any responsibility to meet the needs of the Jewish community as an entity or whether its obligations were limited to individual Jews. Indicative of the agency's philosophical drift over a half century, a future course was to be determined on empirical grounds, as well as on commitment to *zedekah*.

While trustees tried to decide what services federation could render, about $30 million a year was raised almost by rote. And at the end of 1971, federation's big givers were solicited for a $218-million building drive to continue construction where the 1961 City of Life campaign had left off a decade before. Plaques were available, some of them in buildings used only minimally by Jews. "Donors of gifts of $100,000 or more to the Free Fund of the Building Fund, including gifts of $100,000 or more towards the overall costs of the campaign, shall have their names in-

semisqualor not far from Miami Beach's opulent oceanfront hotels. In the 1920s and 1930s, visions of a warm and graceful old age in the sun had inspired them to think about retiring to Florida when their working days were over. Savings plus social security allotments would assure modest budgets. By the end of the 1960s, inflation had wiped out their security, and many resorted to shoplifting in supermarkets to obtain food.

* The Educational Alliance was one example. It operated on a $2 million budget, much of it provided by New York Federation. But many of the few thousand old and poor Jews remaining on the Lower East Side were too frightened to use its facilities. Muggers and street gangs waited to prey on them if they ventured out at night. Rightly or wrongly, federation did not consider cutting off funds and using them for purposes more directly supportive of Jewish interests.

scribed on a Sponsors Plaque to be placed at each institution with approved Building Fund Projects," said a description of campaign plans sent to trustees. This did not mean givers were absolved from annual contributions: "The strength and stability of the Jewish community's philanthropic enterprise depends on acceptance of this two-fold responsibility, . . ." it also noted.

May 1973 marked Israel's twenty-fifth anniversary. Officials and visiting leaders from the Diaspora agreed that, come what may, the future could never be as grim as the past. The past was defined as the period before the Six Day War. In Jerusalem experts predicted that Egypt, Syria, and Jordan would need fifteen years to properly train and equip armies. Seeking detente and stability, neither America nor Russia pressed for return of occupied territories. New markets were being developed, and in 1972, exports rose 19 percent to $2.17 billion. Between 1960 and 1970, per capita income increased to $1800 a year, about the fifteenth highest in the world, and in March, foreign currency reserves reached $1.2 billion, three times their level four years before.

On the philanthropic front, there was also good news. UJA's regular campaigns and UJA's Israel Emergency Fund drives were still delivering huge amounts. In 1967, the agency received $67 million during the regular campaign and $173 million in supplementary funds. Between 1968 and the end of 1971, $311.7 million was raised in regular campaigns and $451 million in emergency funds. Net receipts from global sales of Israel bonds totaled $448 million after redemptions. United States government aid had reached about $3 billion since 1949, including $2.5 billion in loans of which nearly $800 million in principal and interest had been repaid.

The Jewish establishment in America and the Mapai establishment in Israel were confident of economic and political policies, and most of their respective populaces were confident of the establishments.* Most Israelis acted as if it were impossible to fail in peace or in war. Political leaders continued to set examples of *chutzpah*: The government led the nation in

* Among those who weren't confident were Nahum Goldmann, who made an abortive attempt to confer with Nasser in 1970, and various doves who kept saying that the occupied territories should be used to negotiate a settlement even if Israel did not get everything it wanted.

delaying repayment of debts, and purchases on the installment plan reached an all-time high.

True, all was not well with the world. In Washington, Senator Fulbright claimed that the United States was subservient to Israel, thus encouraging assorted cranks to institute a lawsuit challenging UJA's tax-exempt status.* Israel was in danger of running out of water in three to eight years and becoming increasingly dependent on Arab labor. In 1972, the national debt on a per capita basis amounted to $1125; every year it took more than $.5 billion, or 10 percent of the gross national product, just to service the debt. To get out of debt, it was necessary to export more. To export more, it was necessary to increase production. To increase production, more borrowing was necessary. "We're not worried so long as our exports and the general economy combine to expand by 10 percent or more," said Daniel Rekanti, chairman of the 129-branch Israel Discount Bank. "They say this is a country of miracles."

Israel prided itself on its socialist, egalitarian society. Yet after 1967, a military-industrial class became rich building fortifications, housing, and factories with government and private financing. So great was the shortage of professionally-trained managers that the government looked the other way rather than crack down on corrupt defense contractors. Similarly, because of the overwhelming need for capital, the misdeeds of Michael Tzur, the country's most prominent financial official, were not thoroughly investigated until after millions of dollars had been lost. Through the Israel Corporation, a government-sponsored development agency, Tzur had transferred funds to the International Credit Bank in Geneva, headed by Pinchas Rosenbaum, who was prominent in Israeli and international Jewish circles. Rosenbaum in turn transferred funds to Liechtenstein, where laws of financial secrecy were even stricter than in Switzerland.

The manager of Israel's oil company in the occupied Sinai Peninsula resigned after rumors of wrongdoing and profiteering. A pillar of the cabinet, Justice Minister Yakov Shimshon Shapiro, was forced out of the government after being charged with awarding exorbitant stipends to

* Few people paid attention to this action, with the exception of Arabs and die-hard American Council for Judaism types. The suit was dismissed in a lower court.

lawyers investigating the oil company's operations. Businessmen aware of tremendous profits in tourism concentrated on building motels and financing car rental agencies, instead of using scarce construction materials and capital for housing and welfare programs.* Important transactions continued to flow through Pinhas Sapir's office for approval; it helped to be the descendant of early Zionist pioneers. Sapir himself raised hundreds of millions throughout the world, sometimes even at the air terminals where Jewish leaders and big givers met him.

The government repeatedly turned to the army, the one group whose administrative ability was demonstrated where it counted most, on the battlefield. Former commanders did not fade away; they took top positions in industry.† Meir Amit, former chief of the army's operations branch and security service, became president of Koor Industries, a conglomerate operating one-fifth of all industrial enterprises; Dan Tokolowski, a former chief of the air force, became general manager of the powerful Discount Bank Investment Group. Generals entered political life on local and national levels, but a government spokesman contended that a military takeover "could never happen here" because the army was civilian in nature.

Life styles of the new rich‡ included heated pools, Texas-style yachts, and original Picasso, Dali, and Chagall prints hung in houses designed in informal, California styles. The Tel Aviv suburb of Savyon became Israel's Scarsdale. "You can't build a house here for less than 500,000 pounds [about $120,000], and many cost twice that," said Mordecai Ben-Horin, an architect who was popular in the area. For those who preferred living in Tel Aviv, an elegant four- or five-room penthouse cost from $125,000 to $160,000; a two-room apartment cost $30,000. A Volkswagen that cost $2000 in the United States cost about $8000 in Israel, and a $4500 Ford Mustang cost $16,000. The top 20 percent of the population were

* Many of the most luxurious dwellings and cars were purchased by rich American, British, and South African Jews who maintained homes in Israel.

† In Israel, professional military men retire in their mid-forties, giving younger men time to acquire ample experience in key posts.

‡ The number of Israeli millionnaires in 1973 was anywhere between 100 and 2000. I was given the low figure by a government minister; the head of a leading Israeli accounting firm opted for 2000, and an authentic Israeli millionaire told me the number was higher than that. It was somewhat difficult to become a millionaire, since income over $400 monthly was taxed at 72 percent.

competitive consumers: Lively purchases of homes and automobiles proved that Israel was no longer the country early Zionists had envisioned.

While some Israelis grew rich, others stayed poor. About 20 percent of the population, mostly Sephardim,* lived below the poverty line. Ruling Ashkenazim appeared in no great hurry to upgrade Oriental Jews' living standards while emigration could be encouraged from America and from Russia. Orientals were relegated to low-paying jobs and squeezed into cramped public housing developments called "black ghettos." They constituted 60 percent of the primary school population, but only 1.4 percent of university graduates. There were no Afro-Asian generals in the army, and only one Afro-Asian minister in the cabinet. "We are 1 percent in government and 96 percent in jail," said a leaflet distributed in Jerusalem by the Israeli "Black Panthers," which consisted of Oriental youths. Yitzhak Ben-Aharon, secretary-general of Histadrut, admitted to a New York meeting of the National Committee for Labor Israel that Israel was "embarrassed by the persistence of poverty in our midst." Problems could be overcome in six to eight years, continued Ben-Aharon, given concentration on new housing, expanded educational opportunities, and job training.

The poor, some of whom had been awaiting change for twenty years, were no longer patient. A wave of strikes in vital public services—hospitals, electric utilities, and docks—was suppressed by the government in June 1971 through emergency regulations,† and Black Panther demonstrations were brutally ended by club-wielding police. Strikes and demonstrations coincided with the arrival of Jewish communal leaders for the founding assembly of the reconstituted Jewish Agency, the agenda of which was heavily weighted toward fund raising. Even larger sums would be needed in the future, because Israel's foreign debt was en route to a new record, passing the $3 billion mark. The government was in no danger of falling, although conspicuous consumption, striking workers,

* Jews of North Africa or Near Eastern descent. In Israel they are called Orientals and constitute a majority of the population.

† The National Religious Party, which controlled religious education in the schools, chose this moment to threaten an end to its coalition with the ruling Mapai party. Grievances had arisen after a prospective reorganization of the Ministry of Education promised to loosen National Religious Party control.

Black Panthers, and a Histadrut rebellion* against the government's anti-inflation policies were not the best advertisements for UJA and Israel bonds.

Nor were these symptoms of basic Israeli ailments missed by American Jews living and working in Israel. Edward Geffner, an American social worker in "black ghettos" met the redoubtable Rabbi Arthur Hertzberg at a mutual friend's home. Among his dozens of responsibilities, Hertzberg served as a member of the executive of the Jewish Agency. He was in Jerusalem teaching at Hebrew University. Geffner took Hertzberg through areas as depressed as any inner city slum in New York and described attempts to force the government to make changes, utilizing tactics of the American civil rights movement. The two men decided to bring the Israeli poor to the attention of the world Jewish community.

In a lecture, "Can Israel learn from America?" given at the American Cultural Center in Jerusalem eight days before the Jewish Agency meeting, Hertzberg attacked the over-bureaucratization of Israeli life and the indifference to social justice of Israeli political, religious, and intellectual leaders. Disastrous policies that characterized American life were being repeated in Israel. Orientals, like American blacks, were expected to pull themselves up by their bootstraps. Disturbers of the peace were told "that they are not very nice boys . . ." in the hope that quiet would be restored. Meanwhile, "the American Jew as the absentee money-giver is an outworn notion because the money-givers come three or four times a year for an extended stay, and some of their kids are on kibbutzim . . . [and] there are a substantial number of American Jews increasingly . . . bi-lingual and bi-cultural. . . ." During Israel's early years, the claim for the existence of a Jewish homeland rested on a base of social justice and human dignity. Although one-fifth of the population was hopelessly poor and 70 percent of juvenile delinquents were functional illiterates, middle-class Israelis were willing to condone poverty and to overlook any strains on their conscience.

Hertzberg's lecture was reported in the American and European press.

* Histadrut was the largest single agglomeration of power in Israel and controlled some 25 percent of the country's economy in 1969. It was organized along socialist lines, but it was expected to show a profit each year along capitalist lines.

The New York Board of Rabbis denounced him, the communist press quoted him, and a high Israeli official excoriated him in private.

The opening session of the founding assembly was preceded by a Black Panther demonstration. Despite pleas for reform, its agenda remained unchanged. Edward Ginsberg, UJA's chairman, said that 1971 proved something—"It proved that we could raise more money than ever was raised before in any single year." The agency's reconstitution put Diaspora big givers into policy-making positions, Louis Pincus reminded 300 delegates from twenty-seven countries: "[In 1969] you did not bear the direct burden of responsibility. Today you do." If financial shortfalls occurred, the "bitter decisions" about which health, educational, and welfare services to cut would have to be made by big givers.

A feeling of malaise spread. "What has happened to us in the last year? What has happened to our understanding? To our good sense? To our self-discipline?" Golda Meir asked the Knesset in mid-August 1972. "We are behaving as if there were no danger ahead of us, as if we had already eliminated poverty and completed the development of the country, as if we did not have to prepare ourselves for the immigration that will arrive." With her inimitable ability to defuse issues by partially agreeing with opponents, the premier acknowledged the existence of poverty, admonished rich Israelis hell-bent on pleasure, but defended governmental economic policies. She insisted that she was not preaching for a return to the austere patterns of days past. "But I must warn against the gap between a life style imported from abroad that is taking root in Israel—especially among the higher-income strata—and our real national economic capacity. This is a dangerous and ominous gap."

Happily, another gap was rapidly increasing in Israel's favor. Israel's strategy was not to yield an inch of occupied territory until Arab countries yielded—on Israeli terms. In Washington, Defense and State Department officials agreed with Israeli officers that the balance of military power in the Middle East was, if anything, tipping in Israel's favor. In July 1972, Egypt's President Anwar el-Sadat ordered 15,000 to 20,000 Soviet military advisors and technicians to leave his country. This was interpreted as a sign of serious strain between Egyptians and Russians. Unused Soviet equipment was to rust in the desert as a result.

At an emotional meeting in early February 1973, foreign and defense ministers from eighteen Arab countries vowed they would coordinate efforts and place military forces under the overall direction of Gen. Ahmed Ismail, the Egyptian war minister. Sadat promised a great victory. In Jerusalem, this news was greeted with yawns. Sadat made a habit of promising victories that never materialized; Arabs pledged undying loyalty to each other frequently, then immediately began plotting the overthrow of newfound allies.

It was thus all the more shocking when well-equipped, well-trained Egyptian forces crossed the Suez Canal and waves of Syrian tanks backed by Iraqi and Jordanian units attacked the Golan Heights in meticulously planned operations on Yom Kippur.* Israel, which had made strategic and tactical surprise articles of its military faith, was unexpectedly assaulted by overwhelming forces.† Its air superiority was neutralized by Soviet-made SAM-6 and SAM-7 missiles. Russian 120-mm. antitank missiles directed by infrared rays wreaked havoc with Israeli armor, until countermeasures were devised. North Korean and North Vietnamese pilots, blooded in battles with American pilots, flew air cover in MIG-21s. Arab units fought with tenacity and skill under the leadership of tough, disciplined junior officers.

A major factor that saved Israel from a complete debacle in the first forty-eight hours was strict Arab adherence to classic Soviet military doctrines that called for consolidation of positions rather than rapid exploitation of breakthrough opportunities. In a series of brilliant countermoves in Sinai, Israeli armored forces knifed between Egyptian mechanized units, crossed to the west bank, established a bridgehead, and trapped the Egyptian Third Army. Missile sites were blown up; tanks flying the Star of David approached Cairo. Similarly, Syrian and Iraqi units were pushed back, and Israeli forces fanned out from the Golan Heights to approach Damascus.

After the auspicious opening round, Moscow was unwilling to see its

* A skeleton force of 700 men manned the Bar-Lev Line; about 80 tanks and 1000 Israeli troops in the north held fifty miles of front against 800 tanks and perhaps 100,000 men.

† The Israeli cabinet was less surprised, having been warned of an impending attack the night before. Rather than order pre-emptive air strikes on troop concentrations and thus take on the onus of starting the war, it decided to let events take their course. This was the official description of events, which does not explain why the northern (Golan Heights) front got advance warning while the southern (Sinai) front got no warning. Nor does it explain the slow and confused call-up of reserves.

clients snatch defeat from the jaws of victory. A massive Soviet airlift reequipped Arab forces. In Washington, the Israeli ambassador, Simcha Dinitz, conveyed a message from Golda Meir to President Richard Nixon and Secretary of State Henry Kissinger that Israel might be forced to stop fighting unless it, too, were reequipped; one-third of the air force and 800 tanks had been lost. An American airlift began, despite warnings from oil companies that aid to Israel would impair or stop the flow of Arab oil to the United States.* As Israelis pressed forward, word reached Washington that Soviet airborne divisions were in staging areas preparing to board aircraft for the Middle East. American armed forces were put on an alert, Kissinger made a statement on mutual responsibilities at a press conference, negotiated with Moscow, and the fighting stopped.

At that point, Arabs and Israelis alike were sure they had not lost the Yom Kippur War, although each side was hard-pressed to prove it had overwhelmingly won it. Sadat proved that his troops could cross the Suez Canal and retake the east bank. Israelis recovered from the defeats of the first forty-eight hours to regain the upper hand tactically. Nonetheless, for the first time in twenty-five years, Israeli generals ended a war accusing each other in public of incompetence. A five-man judicial Commission of Inquiry into the War asked, "What went wrong that left Israel so unprepared for the combined Arab attack of October 6?" An interim report answered that the chief of staff, Lt. Gen. David Elazar, bore direct responsibility.

As alarming as Arab military prowess was the new political coordination and use of oil revenues. Libyan and Saudi Arabian money flowed freely to buy Soviet weapons, which were not cheap. At the beginning of November 1973, the Israeli flag flew from only five diplomatic missions in Africa: Twenty-six countries had severed diplomatic relations in eighteen months. They included Uganda and Nigeria, both of which had received large sums in Israeli foreign aid. Western Europe and Japan were flatly told their oil imports would be cut month by month unless Israel returned territories taken in the 1967 war. Any economic counter-

* European countries were warned by Arabs that if American planes used bases in their countries, oil embargos would be imposed. They denied America the use of airfields, and embargos were imposed anyway. Only Portugal permitted huge C5-A transports, which could carry tanks, to land and refuel. Phantom fighters were flown directly to Israel.

measures risked serious consequences, and if the United States took military action, Saudi Arabians and Libyans would blow up their own oil fields.

Recognizing similarities between Nazi Germany in March 1933 and the Arab countries in November 1973, international statesmen acted accordingly. There was no coordinated policy. Whether or not Israel survived or was able to acquire weapons to defend itself was a matter of indifference.* In Western Europe, each country tried to make its own deal with oil sheiks, as it had tried to make its own deal with Hitler.

Like earlier military appraisals of Arab armies, first judgments in Jerusalem on the economic and psychological effects of the war were wrong. In the past, crises had been intense, but short. Pinhas Sapir spoke with American Jewish community leaders early in the conflict, and it was decided for the time being not to press an emergency appeal for funds. Foreign currency reserves were still at a record $1.5 billion, oil and food reserves were plentiful, and, if the conflict ended in a stalemate, no shortages were foreseen. As late as October 8 there were no plans for oil rationing.

But this crisis, although intense, was not short. Israel's political isolation produced as traumatic an effect as did Arab military success. For months, between 150,000 and 200,000 Israelis were to be on military reserve duty, crippling economic life.† Maintenance of the reserves, the drop in production, and equipment losses during the war cost $7 billion, the extrapolated United States equivalent of $1.3 trillion. Western Europe supplied 60 percent of Israel's commodity imports and absorbed two-fifths of its exports; how far it would go in currying favor with Arabs was anybody's guess.

A sober Israel began to reassess itself. In December, General Amit stated that "everything in the last five years led to the Yom Kippur War. It was the outcome of a kind of overconfidence, overeating, overdrinking, over everything except overworking. We thought, 'Nothing can

* Except for the United States, which made available $2.2 billion for arms purchases, $300 million in "regular" military credits, $50 million in "supporting assistance," and $36.5 million to resettle Russian emigrants. No less than $1.5 billion was given in outright grants. The appropriations were overwhelmingly approved 66–9 in the Senate and 364–52 in the House.

† Israel's socialist and egalitarian ideals bar exemptions from military service for key individuals in business and industry. Highly satisfying as a social achievement, this can work to the detriment of the economy.

happen to us.' That was true not only in defense but in economic, social —any sector of our life."

Austerity measures included cancellations of government subsidies on bread, milk, and other foods. New voluntary and involuntary war loans were instituted. Neither defeatist nor despairing at first, the populace approved the measures. There were few doves left in Israel,* although the cocksure attitude of prewar days was also gone. A survey conducted by the Communications Institute of Hebrew University found 84 percent of those questioned believed cuts in standards of living were acceptable, and 20 percent believed they were necessary.

By early February 1974, however, Israeli consumers were taking a different view of government economic policies† designed to roll back the standard of living. Prices of oil and electricity doubled, bread went up by 70 percent, milk by 64 percent, sugar by 57 percent, and eggs by 61 percent. The poor were hardest hit because food items constituted a larger part of their budget. Histadrut demanded workers get immediate raises, and the Black Panthers staged a violent demonstration in Tel Aviv. Public opinion polls found one out of five young Israelis willing to consider moving elsewhere.‡

At that point, the government said it could not spare the Israeli equivalent of $225 million a year for price supports because defense expenditures were approaching 45 percent of the gross national product. Taxes and compulsory loan payments increased revenues by nearly 30 percent, but a greater deficit was predicted in the following year's budget.§

* Their ranks, incidentally, had included Sapir and Ben-Aharon, who called for unilateral Israeli withdrawal from part of the west bank of the Jordan.

† Views about Israel's political policies were also changing. Golda Meir was among the last of the Israeli Old Guard, whose sparkplug had been Ben-Gurion and whose base was the Mapai party. How much longer this group—its survivors were now in their mid-seventies—could go on ruling was hotly debated. At the end of December, the Mapai party won the most seats in a general election, but its strength in a coalition government was tenuous. In mid-April 1974, Golda Meir announced her resignation and brought down the government.

‡ Eighteen thousand Israelis actually packed up and left in 1974.

§ In July 1974, the Israeli cabinet proposed that more than $200 million be taken out of circulation through a five percent tax on payrolls and the diversion of cost of living allowances to the state. In November, the pound was devalued 43 percent, imports of twenty-nine luxury products, including autos, were banned for six months, and Orientals rioted in Tel Aviv. Israelis were told that they would have to depend on their own resources more than ever, and the standard of living dropped by 10 percent as measured by prices and income.

Scarcely ten months after the twenty-fifth anniversary parade, Israeli and American communal leaders feared they had further misjudged: It *was* possible for the future to be grim.

The chief observation to be made about American Jews after the Yom Kippur War is that a course initiated during World War I, confirmed by the holocaust, further strengthened in 1948, and put to the test in June 1967, received its final confirmation in October 1973. Support of a Jewish state now included not only contributions, but unprecedented campaigns in Washington for arms and federal funds. No matter that the 1973 setback stemmed partly from an unrealistic reliance by Israelis on American-Jewish influence in the sphere of American foreign policy. Nor that the war and its aftermath were positive demonstrations that Israel could not protect Diaspora Jewries, and was, in fact, utterly dependent on the 80 percent of world Jewry that lived outside Israel. The United Jewish Appeal spoke openly of "taxation," and the Jewish Agency's National Committee on Control and Authorization of Campaigns exercised even tighter control over Israeli fund raising in the United States.

These developments were made inevitable by the shattering possibility that Arabs had succeeded in the first stage of a two-stage plan for Israel's destruction. While executing the first stage of the plan—Israel's isolation—Arabs were careful to avoid saying Jews would be thrown into the sea, as they had said in 1967. Euphemisms like "an end to racist colonial presence in Palestine" were substituted for open Jew-hatred.* Ancient history was rewritten: Hebrews, said an Arab full-page ad in the New York *Times*, had lived in the Holy Land for only 100 years while "Palestinians kept their continuous residence in Palestine [sic] until they were expelled by Zionists in 1948." It was argued that aid to Israel—both governmental and private—was draining the American economy, preventing allocations of funds to blacks and to other minorities.

Arab propaganda and the lure Arab oil money held in a recession economy increased Jewish malaise. The Southern Conference of Black Mayors, a group of seventy elected officials from Southern towns and cities, planned a Middle Eastern trip to seek Arab investments and

* The American communist party spearheaded the anti-Israel campaign on the Left; the Washington-based Liberty Lobby spearheaded it on the Right.

markets for local products. It was feared that early publicity would cause hard feelings in the Jewish community, but it was hoped that concern could be headed off through meetings with American Jewish leaders. Gen. George Brown, chairman of the Joint Chiefs of Staff, remarked publicly that Jews control banking and newspapers; this gave comfort to writers like Rowland Evans and Robert Novak, busy proving that there was a Zionist plot against the country in general and against them in particular.

If American Jews stood by and did nothing, the sinister twentieth century anti-Semitic dream of a *judenrein* world might be realized by Arabs in a second-phase military assault, after czarist Russians, Nazis, and Stalinist Russians had failed at the task.* "Israel matters to me in precisely the way, I imagine, that it matters to many [Jews]," wrote Irving Howe, editor of *Dissent.* "Not as a fulfillment of the Zionist idea, nor even as the negation of *galut* (exile), but as . . . the home of our survivors."

At the CJFWF conference in New Orleans that followed the war, people spoke as if they themselves were living in a country threatened by imminent conquest. "For if we Jews are now an endangered species, as has been suggested, we are not polar bears nor bald eagles," said one speaker. "We are Jews, with both a millennial experience in dealing with a hostile world and with immense new capabilities for forging our own destiny rather than being, as we were for centuries, puppets of history, manipulated by others. . . . Does anyone think at this heart-stopping moment that there is a separation, for example, between Jewish fund-raising and Jewish identity? Fund raising *is* profound Jewish expression. It *is* Jewish culture. Jewish responsibility is indivisible. And that is why the agenda for war and for peace are obverse sides of a single agenda."

The only tangible help most people could offer was money, and the overwhelming outpouring of funds indicated American Jewish concern. Over the Yom Kippur weekend, $4 million was collected as people

* Despite renewed hostility from the extreme Right and the extreme Left, there was more Christian support for Israel in the immediate aftermath of the 1973 war than in the aftermath of the 1967 war. One exception was Father Daniel Berrigan, whose speech before the Association of Arab University Graduates describing Israel as a "criminal community" further discredited him to the American public. Gallop polls showed that sympathy grew for Israel, from 47 percent in mid-October 1973 to 54 percent in mid-December.

learned what had happened; five synagogues in Long Island and Brooklyn raised $700,000. By Monday, October 8, $10 million had been collected, including two cash donations of $1 million each at a luncheon in New York. State of Israel bonds announced it had sold $35 million in securities since the crisis began.

By Tuesday, UJA's Greater New York chapter had set a $50-million goal for the metropolitan area and raised $25 million toward it. At a rally in Memphis, Tennessee—which had the largest Orthodox congregation in the United States—$1 million had been raised; and at rallies in Cincinnati and Columbus nearly $1.4 million was raised. Additional rallies were planned in Philadelphia, Dallas, Atlanta, and Chattanooga. Five hundred Jewish leaders prepared to meet in Washington, and UJA said it was aiming to raise $100 million by the end of the week.

United Press International reported various Jewish organizations had raised at least $130 million by Wednesday. In New York, a Great Neck synagogue sent $2 million, and $15.9 million in bonds was sold at a Plaza Hotel dinner. Next day Israel bonds reported it had sold $128 million in bonds, and UJA was past the $100-million mark. Within ten days, Six Day War results had been exceeded. Within three weeks, UJA raised $175 million and announced a campaign to raise a total of $750 million in 1974, of which $250 million would be sought in the Greater New York area.* There had been two gifts of $5 million each, and Meyer Lansky, alleged to be organized crime's chief financial brain, was among several $1-million contributors. Israel bonds, which normally raised $25 million during the High Holy Days each year, was competing fiercely with UJA and was on its way to $502 million in sales by the end of the year.

Washington, D.C., was typical of cities throughout the country. On October 8, area Jews set a $2-million goal. Eleven days later, more money was pledged and contributed to UJA than in all of 1967, including the post-Six Day War period. Area residents also purchased $7.7 million in Israel bonds, $4 million of it after the outbreak of the October war. The Jewish community became an "extended family"; normal fund-raising

* In addition, CJFWF set a $150-million goal for local and national agencies and institutions. In Boston, the Combined Jewish Philanthropies campaign raised a record $17.2 million in 1974. The Allied Jewish Appeal-Israel Emergency Fund in Philadelphia raised $22 million.

procedures were abandoned as telephone calls and telegrams replaced letters and formal invitations to banquets. Dimensions of needs, not previous giving patterns, determined donations. Gifts that failed to meet expectations were refused. By the end of 1973, $12 million was raised in Washington and precedent had been set for future goals.

In New York, federation and UJA launched a joint, coordinated campaign for the first time in local history. "We are one," read the headline in a full-page ad. "The time is now to preserve the worldwide Jewish community and our Jewish community here at home. The time is now to nurture the Jewish spirit. The time is now to assure the Jewish future." Similar themes were taken up in ads throughout the country: Jewish solidarity, Jewish identification with Israel, the worldwide oneness of Jews. And in a less philosophical area, $125 million was raised in New York, compared to $67 million in 1967.

In a sense this is similar to the beginning of the American Jewish experience, with Jews seeking a haven from enemies sworn to make the world *judenrein* and with established, albeit insecure, Jewish communities oceans away seeking to deliver them. I submit that other peoples do not behave similarly. True, during critical periods, for example the Battle of Britain in 1940, a great national unity develops and self-sacrifice becomes the rule rather than the exception. At such times, however, whole peoples are directly involved in the crisis. The puny response by wealthy Arab countries and the black American upper and middle classes to the Sahel drought in the 1960s is more often the rule. Similarly, incredible 1971 massacres in Bangladesh failed to move 700 million Moslems to great philanthropic exertion. In 1974, Arab countries contributed a meager $1,810,000 to the United Nations Aid Agency for Palestinian Refugees.*

If this is a correct conclusion to draw, can we say that Jews have

* With the influx of new revenues, the oil-exporting countries began allotting funds to Third World countries for loans, investments, and humanitarian aid. They appeared to be inspired less by disinterested philanthropy than by a need to counter the charge that 400 percent increases in oil prices ruined development hopes in poor countries. Stories about sheiks gambling away millions in Las Vegas while starving millions in Asia cried out for food were considered poor public relations, but no remedial action was taken. In 1974, the Organization of Petroleum Exporting Countries promised poor countries $10 billion in aid and delivered less than 25 percent of that amount.

also devised more efficient means than other peoples to finance philanthropic efforts? The United Jewish Appeal has been called the "most successful nongovernmental money-raising organization in the world." By 1974, Jews had greater experience than they wanted in philanthropy. UJA and CJFWF run extremely smooth operations. Office furnishings are spartan (under no circumstances should contributors think money goes for staff luxuries), but key personnel are uniquely able to gauge community strengths and do not ordinarily waste time on poseurs who take time and don't give money.*

On the other hand, this does not mean that internal stress is lacking. No matter how much one hears about unity and card calling, the fact is that few people have the big money that can make a real dent in any campaign, Jewish or nonsectarian. Without them, chances for success are bleak. As a result, many Jews are not so much put off by the intellectual emptiness of American Jewish philanthropy as they are excluded from it. "America can be described as an unequal society that would like to think of itself as egalitarian," Herbert Gans wrote somewhere. It is a truism with which few Jewish agencies would argue. Jews also like to think of their philanthropies as egalitarian. The problem is that in philanthropy some people are always going to be more equal than others.

This brings us to the Jewish establishment and to the community leaders we have encountered: Sephardic elders soliciting contributions in the West Indies for Shearith Israel; Yahudim holding dinners to raise funds for New York's Mount Sinai Hospital; *shtadlanim* using Hirsch money for New Jersey colonies; Weizmann on the campaign trail with *nouveaux riches* Yidn; and Zionists, Yahudim, and Israelis all concerned about big givers. Quite a variety of types, and it does not include all those we have encountered. My own favorites are the Yidn on the Lower East Side who created *landsmanschaften*, strike funds, and welfare agencies with their pennies, thus making possible social experiments that in turn led to the great welfare programs of the 1930s. Their names are buried in the minutes books of organizations long defunct, unknown even to historians. In the truest sense, these men and women were part of an establishment.

* Efficient, yes, but unfortunately not always successful. Because of the business recession and a reaction to revelations of corruption in Israel, UJA contributions in 1974 dipped by 42.8 percent to $300 million; bond sales dipped from 1973 highs by 54.7 percent, to $275 million.

There is quite a difference between those plain Yidn, whose favorite sport indoors and outdoors was alternately lambasting and helping each other, and their elegant, soft-spoken sons, grandsons, and great-grandsons in Great Neck, Scarsdale, and Southfield. The fathers knew at first hand about persecution, tenements, miserable hospitals, and abject hopelessness on the Lower East Side; events further away could be ascertained by reading the *Forward.* Modern community leaders are at home in New York, Washington, and Jerusalem, do business throughout the world, play golf on the finest links, and get their news through the worldwide offices of the New York *Times.* Most cannot read in Yiddish.

Why *do* they give? Of course, the need for recognition is a driving force. I can't help thinking of a philanthropist whose moment of glory was dinner with Mayor Robert Wagner; another whose appointment as an assistant Police Athletic League commissioner called for a standing ovation at a board meeting; a third who confided that Mayor John Lindsay often consulted him for the final word on race relations; and a fourth who wouldn't attend certain committee meetings unless assured beforehand that Gov. Nelson Rockefeller would be present. And who can forget the big giver who reduced his contributions to Yale because the university cut its paint purchases from a company he owned?

And yet, something more basic than a need for recognition must sustain a tradition that began thousands of years ago in the Holy Land and achieved its greatest flowering in twentieth-century America. On the face of it, the reasons are self-evident. Colonial Sephardim gave to preserve a tiny Jewish outpost in the New World, and Yahudim of the 1870s gave because they wanted Jews to be self-reliant and not call attention to themselves as Jews. East European immigrants gave because they could turn with some dignity only to each other, and Yidn and Yahudim gave to federations because there was no other way to organize givers and receivers. Finally, everyone gave to overseas relief—and gives to Israel today—because Jews beset by anti-Semites inevitably turn for help to more fortunate coreligionists.

No, more than that is involved. If one pattern is clear, it is that in times of crisis Jews respond not only by seeking to preserve each other but by seeking to preserve Judaism, however vaguely practiced or understood. The same incredible determination to survive that characterizes Jewish history characterizes a willingness to give mountains of money when the threat of eradication presents itself. After standard cries of financial exhaustion and disinterest, somehow, someway, givers appear on the scene. They need no reasons to give after they comprehend the scope of the problem.

Bibliography

GENERAL REFERENCE WORKS AND ANNUAL PUBLICATIONS

American Jewish Year Book. Philadelphia: Jewish Publication Society, 1899–1974.
Ausubel, Nathan. *The Book of Jewish Knowledge*. New York: Crown, 1964.
Dictionary of American Biography, 20 vols. and supplements. New York: Scribner, 1928–1958.
Encyclopedia Judaica, 15 vols. Jerusalem: Keter, 1971.
Finkelstein, Louis, ed. *The Jews*, 2 vols. 3rd ed. New York: Harper, 1960.
Herzl Year Book. New York: Herzl Press, 1958–1971.
The Jewish People Past and Present, 4 vols. New York: Encyclopedia Handbooks, 1955.
YIVO Annual of Jewish Social Science. New York: YIVO Institute, 1946–1969.

PERIODICALS

American Hebrew. New York, 1905–1918.
Answer. New York, 1948.
Herald. New York, 1914–1924.
Herald-Tribune. New York, 1924–1950.
Jewish Messenger. New York, 1881–1883.
Jewish Spectator. New York, 1950–1970.
National Observer. New York, 1970–1972.
New Palestine. New York, 1925–1929.
Times. New York, 1882–1975.

ARCHIVAL SOURCES

American Jewish Committee
Survey Committee: Educational Department Survey, 1933–1941.

Joint Distribution Committee
Folders (1914–1918):
1. "Joint Distribution Committee, General."
26–28. "Commissioners, Members, and Representatives of JDC."
29–32. "Fund Raising; Meetings; Conferences."
50. "Central Committee for the Relief of Jews Suffering Through the War, N.Y."
136. "Persecutions and Pogroms of Jews."

Folders (1919–1921)
1. "Joint Distribution Committee, General."

30, 39, 40. "Administrative Personnel."
48. "[Fund-raising] Campaigns."
256b. "Pogroms."

Franklin D. Roosevelt Library
Lehman, Herbert H. "Papers as Lieutenant Governor of the State of New York," 1929–1932.
Morgenthau, Henry M., "Papers," 1943–1945.
U.S. War Refugee Board, "Records," 1944–1945.
YIVO Archives
"Minutes of the Board of Directors of the Educational Alliance" (microfilm), 1889–1900.

ANNUAL REPORTS, COMMITTEE REPORTS, MINUTES OF MEETINGS

American Jewish Committee
"Minutes of the Conference on Organization," February 3 and 4, 1906.
"Annual Reports," 1907–1973.
"Minutes of Special Conference," November 9, 1930.
"Survey Committee [Reports]," 1933–1941.
Council of Jewish Federations and Welfare Funds
"Council Reports" [June 5, 1967–July 3, 1967].
"40th General Assembly: Assembly Papers," 1971.
"41st General Assembly: Assembly Papers," 1972.
"42nd General Assembly: Assembly Papers," 1973.
"43rd General Assembly: Assembly Papers," 1974.
Federation of Jewish Philanthropies of New York
"Minutes of the Meetings of the Special Federation Committee Held at the Residence of Mr. Felix M. Warburg," March 29, 1916; April 1, 1916; April 11, 1916; April 16, 1916; April 25, 1916.

Friedman, H. G. "Report of the Organization Committee to the Committee on the Plan of Canvass," [n.d.].

"Report of the Finances of Federation," July 1, 1917.

"Mr. William Goldman's Report to the Meeting of the Board of Trustees and the Executive Membership Council of September 27, 1917."

Perlstein, Benjamin. "Summer Membership Campaigns," December 16, 1917.

"Minutes, Board Meeting," February 25, 1918.

"Minutes, Executive Committee Meetings," August 13, 1918; September 30, 1918.

"Annual reports, Federation for the Support of the Jewish Philanthropies of New York City, 1921–1929.
Jewish Agency
"Report of the American Section of the Jewish Agency for Palestine to the Zionist General Council," 1950.

"Meeting of the Planning Committee for the Reconstitution of the Jewish Agency for Israel," 1970.

"Founding Assembly of the Reconstituted Jewish Agency," 1971.

Joint Distribution Committee

"Annual Reports," 1933–1945.

Montefiore Hospital and Medical Center

"Annual Reports," 1885–1912.

"Minutes of Board Meetings," 1908–1909.

Union of American Hebrew Congregations

Fein, Leonard, *et al.* "Reform Is A Verb." New York: Long Range Planning Committee of the Union of American Hebrew Congregations, 1972.

PAMPHLETS

The American Jewish Joint Distribution Committee in Russia. New York: Joint Distribution Committee, 1924.

Berlin, Isaiah. *Zionist Politics in Wartime Washington: A Fragment of Personal Reminiscence.* Jerusalem: Jerusalem Post Press, 1972.

Campaign Manual of the 1935 United Jewish Appeal for Publicity and for Information of Speakers. New York: United Jewish Appeal of Joint Distribution Committee and American Palestine Campaign, n.d.

Commission of the American Jewish Relief Funds. New York: American Jewish Relief Committee, 1917.

Cowan, Paul. *Jews Without Money, Revisited.* New York: Village Voice, 1972.

Dissolution of the National United Jewish Appeal. New York: American Jewish Joint Distribution Committee, 1945.

Five Years of the United Jewish Appeal for Refugees, Overseas Needs and Palestine: An Accounting of Stewardship. New York: United Jewish Appeal, 1944.

Friedman, Elisha M. *Inquiry of the United Jewish Appeal.* New York: United Jewish Appeal, 1941.

Goldberg, S. P. *The American Jewish Community.* New York: Ort, 1968.

Glanz, Rudolf. *Jews in Relation to the Cultural Milieu of the Germans in America up to the Eighteen-Eighties.* New York: 1947.

Higham, John. *Anti-semitism in the Gilded Age.* New York: Anti-Defamation League, n.d.

The Jewish Congress vs. the American Jewish Committee. New York: Jewish Congress Organizing Committee, 1915.

Jewish Construction Work in Germany Since 1936. Paris: American Jewish Joint Distribution Committee, 1937.

The Jewish Poor and the War Against Poverty: Report and Recommendations. New York: American Jewish Congress Commission on Urban Affairs, n.d.

The Jewish Situation in Germany. New York: American Jewish Committee, 1934.

Karigal, Rabbi Haym Isaac. *A Sermon Preached at the Synagogue in Newport, Rhode Island called "The Salvation of Israel."* Newport: Southwick, 1773.

The Kishinev Massacre, Proceedings of a Meeting of Citizens of New York. New York: American Hebrew, 1903.

Korn, Bertram W. *German-Jewish Intellectual Influences on American Jewish Life, 1824–1972.* Syracuse, NY: Syracuse University, 1972.

Lasky, Moses. *Between Truth and Repose.* New York: American Council for Judaism, 1956.

Liptzin, Sol. *Ben Hecht and Waldo Frank: Flaming Wrath and Olympian Detachment.* New York: Yiddish Scientific Institute, 1945.

Marcus, Jacob R. *The American Colonial Jew.* Syracuse, NY: Syracuse University, 1967.

Pincus, Louis A. *A New World Partnership for Israel's Needs and Progress.* New York: Council of Jewish Federations and Welfare Funds, 1971.

Report of Mr. Morris Wolf and Mr. M. J. Roseneau to the Special Commission, American Jewish Relief Committee. Vienna: American Jewish Relief Committee, 1922.

Reports Received by the Joint Distribution Committee of Funds for Jewish War Sufferers. New York: American Jewish Joint Distribution Committee, 1916.

Rosenwald, Lessing J. *The UJA Funds' "Reorganization."* New York: American Council for Judaism, n.d.

Schmid, John W. and Childe, Cromwell. *American Jews and the War.* New York: Joint Distribution Committee of the funds for Jewish war sufferers, 1917.

Schoener, Allon. *The Lower East Side.* New York: Jewish Museum, 1966.

Sixty Million Dollars and Eleven Years. Address by Felix M. Warburg at the National Conference of the United Jewish Campaign. Philadelphia: American Jewish Joint Distribution Committee, 1925.

Staff Conference of National Field Representatives of UJA Held at National Headquarters, July 8–12, 1940. New York: United Jewish Appeal, 1940.

Twenty-five years—Jewish National Fund (5662–5687). Report of the Head Office of the Keren Kayemeth. Jerusalem: Keren Kayemeth, 1927.

ARTICLES

"The American Jew Today." *Newsweek* (March 1, 1971): 56–64.

Astor, Gerald. "The Agonized American Jews." *Look* (April 20, 1971): 17–19.

Berlin, George. "The Brandeis-Weizmann Dispute." *American Jewish Historical Quarterly* (September 1970): 37–68.

Best, Gary Dean. "Financing a Foreign War: Jacob H. Schiff and Japan, 1904–05." *American Jewish Historical Quarterly* (June 1972): 313–324.

Bierbrier, Doreen. "The American Zionist Emergency Council: An Analysis of a Pressure Group." *American Jewish Historical Quarterly* (September 1970): 82–105.

Brown, Michael. "All, all alone: The Hebrew Press in America from 1914 to 1924." *American Jewish Historical Quarterly* (December 1969): 139–178.

Diamond, Sander. "The Years of Waiting: National Socialism in the United States, 1922–1933." *American Jewish Historical Quarterly* (March 1970): 256–271.

"Eichmann Tells His Own Damning Story." *Life* (November 28 and December 5, 1960): 19–25, 101–112; 146–158.

Fein, Isaac. "Israel Zangwill and American Jewry." *American Jewish Historical Quarterly* (September 1970): 12–36.

Feuer, Leon. "Abba Hillel Silver: A Personal Memoir." *American Jewish Archives* (November 1967): 107–126.

Geffen, Joel. "Whither: To Palestine or to America in the Pages of the Russian Hebrew Press *Ha-Melitz* and *Ha-Yom* (1880–1890)." *American Jewish Historical Quarterly* (December 1969): 179–200.

Glanz, Rudolph. "The German Jewish Mass Emigration 1820–1880." *American Jewish Archives* (April 1970): 49–66.

Ginzberg, Eli. "The Economics of Jewish Belonging." *Jewish Digest* (February 1970): 29–32.

Glazer, Nathan. "Herbert H. Lehman of New York." *Commentary* (May 1963): 403–409.

Gottlieb, Moshe. "The Berlin Riots of 1935 and Their Repercussions in America." *American Jewish Historical Quarterly* (March 1970): 302–328.

————. "In the Shadow of War; The American Anti-Nazi Boycott Movement in 1939–1941." *American Jewish Historical Quarterly* (December 1972): 146–161.

Hirsh, Ze'ev. "Israel's Economic Miracle." *Times of Israel* (October 1973): 18–19.

"The Jews: Next year in Which Jerusalem?" *Time* (April 10, 1972): 54–64.

Lurie, Walter. "Jewish Philanthropy as a Pattern of Jewish Affiliation." *Jewish Digest* (April 1971): 41–44.

Lipset, Seymour. "The Socialism of Fools." *The New York Times Magazine* (January 3, 1971): 6–7, 26–27, 34.

Mandel, Irving. "The Attitude of the American Jewish Community Toward East European Immigration." *American Jewish Archives* (June 1950): 11–35.

Norden, Margaret K. "American Editorial Response to the Rise of Adolf Hitler: A Preliminary Consideration." *American Jewish Historical Quarterly* (March 1970): 290–301.

Novick, Julius. "Rich Jews." *Village Voice* (November 5, 1970), 46, 50.

Robinson, Solomon F. "The Saga of America's 'Russian' Jews." *Commentary* (February 1946): 1–7.

Rossman, Evelyn. "A Fund-raiser Comes to Northrup." *Commentary* (March 1962): 218–225.

Sanders, Marion. "The Several Worlds of American Jews." *Harper's* (April 1966): 53–62.

Shapiro, Judah. "The Non-Zionists Inherit Zionism." *Jewish Digest* (February 1970): 13–18.

Shulman, Charles. "The Wizard of Jewish Fund Raising." *Jewish Digest* (November 1969): 39–43.

Sklare, Marshall. "Forces Shaping American Jewry." *Jewish Digest* (November 1969): 1–6.

————. "The Future of Jewish Giving." *Commentary* (November 1962): 416–426.

————. "The Trouble with 'Our Crowd'." *Commentary* (January 1968): 57–62.

Szajkowski, Zosa. "The Attitude of American Jews to Refugees from Germany in the 1930s." *American Jewish Historical Quarterly* (December 1971): 101–143.

————. "Budgeting American Jewish Overseas Relief (1919–1939)." *American Jewish Historical Quarterly* (September 1969): 83–113.

————. "The Impact of Jewish Overseas Relief on American Jewish and Non-Jewish Philanthropy, 1914–1927." *American Jewish Archives* (April 1970): 67–90.

————. "A Note on the American-Jewish Struggle Against Nazism and Communism in the 1930s." *American Jewish Historical Quarterly* (March 1970): 272–289.

————. "Private American Jewish Overseas Relief (1919–1938): Problems and Attempted Solutions." *American Jewish Historical Quarterly* (March 1968): 285–350.

————. "Private and Organized American Jewish Overseas Relief (1914–1938)." *American Jewish Historical Quarterly* (September 1967): 52–106.

————. "Private and Organized American Jewish Overseas Relief and Immigration." *American Jewish Historical Quarterly* (December 1967): 191–253.

————. "Relief for German Jewry: Problems of American Involvement." *American Jewish Historical Quarterly* (December 1972): 111–145.

Teller, Judd. "Is This the Reality of American Jewry?" *Jewish Digest* (March 1970): 1–7.

Wise, Isaac Mayer. "The World of My Books." *American Jewish Archives* (June 1954): 107–148.

Zion, Sidney. "Once a Jew, Sometimes a Jew." *Harper's Magazine* (August 1972): 70–78.

Ziegler, Mel. "Jewish Poverty amid Jewish Affluence." *Jewish Digest* (March 1969): 1–7.

BOOKS

Abrahams, Israel. *Jewish Life in the Middle Ages.* New York: Meridian, 1958.

Adler, Cyrus. *Jacob H. Schiff: His Life and Letters*, 2 vols. New York: Doubleday, 1929.

Agar, Herbert. *The Saving Remnant.* New York: Viking, 1960.

Aleichem, Sholom. *Some Laughter, Some Tears.* Trans. from the Yiddish and with an introduction by Curt Leviant. New York: Paperback Library, 1968.

Amory, Cleveland. *Who Killed Society?* New York: Cardinal, 1962.

Arendt, Hannah. *Eichmann in Jerusalem: A Report on the Banality of Evil.* New York: Viking, 1963.

Balabkins, Nicholas. *West German Reparations to Israel.* New Brunswick, NJ: Rutgers University, 1971.

Baron, Salo. *The Jewish Community*, 3 vols. Philadelphia: Jewish Publication Society, 1942.

Baron, Salo and Blau, Joseph, eds. *The Jews of the United States 1790–1840: A Documentary History.* New York: Columbia University, 1963.

Baron, Salo W. *The Russian Jew Under Tsars and Soviets.* New York: Macmillan, 1964.

———. *Steeled by Adversity.* Philadelphia: Jewish Publication Society, 1971.

Bauer, Yehuda. *Flight and Rescue: Brichah.* New York: Random House, 1970.

Bendix, Reinhard and Lipset, Seymour Martin. *Class, Status, and Power*, 2d ed. New York: Free Press, 1966.

Ben-Gurion, David. *Israel; A Personal History.* New York: Funk & Wagnalls, 1971.

———. *Letters to Paula.* Pittsburgh: University of Pittsburgh, 1971.

———. *Memoirs.* Thomas R. Bransten, comp. New York: World, 1970.

———. *The Jews in Their Land.* Garden City: Doubleday, 1966.

———. *Ben-Gurion Looks Back in Talks with Moshe Pearlman.* London: Weidenfeld and Nicholson, 1965.

Benjamin, I. J. *Three Years in America 1859–1862.* Trans. from the German by Charles Reznikoff, with an introduction by Oscar Handlin. Philadelphia: Jewish Publication Society, 1956.

Birmingham, Stephen. *Our Crowd.* New York: Harper, 1967.

Bisgyer, Maurice. *Challenge and Encounter.* New York: Crown, 1967.

Blau, Joseph L., *et al.*, eds. *Essays on Jewish Life and Thought.* New York: Columbia University, 1959.

Blum, John Morton. *From the Morgenthau Diaries*, 3 vols. Boston: Houghton Mifflin, 1959–1967.

Bogen, Boris. *Jewish Philanthropy.* New York: Macmillan, 1917.

Brandeis, Louis. *Brandeis on Zionism.* Washington: Zionist Organization of America, 1942.

Bridenbaugh, Carl. *Cities in the Wilderness.* New York: Knopf, 1955.

———. *Cities in Revolt.* New York: Capricorn, 1964.

Cantor, Norman F. and Werthman, Michael S. *The History of Popular Culture.* New York: Macmillan, 1968.

Churchill, Allen. *The Upper Crust.* Englewood Cliffs, NJ: Prentice-Hall, 1970.

Cohen, Naomi. *A Dual Heritage: The Public Career of Oscar S. Straus.* Philadelphia: Jewish Publication Society, 1969.

———. *Not Free to Desist.* Philadelphia: Jewish Publication Society, 1972.

Cordaso, F., ed. *Jacob Riis Revisited.* New York: Doubleday Anchor, 1968.

Danish, Max D. *The World of David Dubinsky.* New York: World, 1957.

Dawidowicz, Lucy S. *The War Against the Jews, 1933–1945.* New York: Holt, 1975.

Dimont, Max I. *Jews, God and History.* New York: Signet, 1962.

Doroshkin, Milton. *Yiddish in America.* Rutherford, NJ: Fairleigh Dickinson University, 1969.

Eban, Abba. *My People: The Story of the Jews.* New York: Random House, 1968.

Ellis, Edward Robb. *The Epic of New York City.* New York: Coward-McCann, 1966.

Elon, Amos. *The Israelis: Founders and Sons.* New York: Holt, 1971.

Feingold, Henry L. *The Politics of Rescue.* New Brunswick, NJ: Rutgers University, 1970.

Feuer, Lewis S. *The Conflict of Generations.* New York: Basic Books, 1969.

Frankfurter, Felix. *Felix Frankfurter Reminisces.* New York: Reynal, 1960.

Freid, Jacobs, ed. *Jews in the Modern World.* New York: Twayne, 1962.

Friedlander, Saul. *Pius XII and the Third Reich.* New York: Knopf, 1966.

————. *Prelude to Downfall: Hitler and the United States, 1939–1940.* New York: Knopf, 1967.

Friedman, Saul. *No Haven for the Oppressed.* Detroit: Wayne State University, 1973.

Friedmann, Georges. *The End of the Jewish People.* Trans. from the French by Eric Mosbacher. Garden City: Doubleday, 1967.

Frisch, Ephraim. *Historical Survey of Jewish Philanthropy.* New York: Macmillan, 1924.

Gans, H. J. *The Levittowners.* New York: Pantheon, 1967.

Gerassi, John. *The Coming of the New International.* New York: World, 1971.

Gersh, Harry. *Minority Report.* New York: Collier, 1961.

Gilbert, Arthur. *A Jew in Christian America.* New York: Sheed and Ward, 1966.

Ginzberg, E. *Report to American Jews.* New York: Harper, 1942.

Glazer, Nathan. *American Judaism.* Chicago: University of Chicago, 1957.

Gold, Michael. *Jews Without Money* [*1930*]. New York: Avon, 1965.

Golden, Harry. *Forgotten Pioneer.* New York: World, 1963.

————. *The Greatest Jewish City in the World.* New York: Doubleday, 1972.

————. *Only in America.* Foreword by Carl Sandburg. New York: Pocket Books, 1959.

————, ed. *The Spirit of the Ghetto: Studies of the Jewish Quarter of New York by Hutchins Hapgood* [*1902*]. New York: Funk & Wagnalls, 1965.

————. *For 2¢ Plain.* Foreword by Carl Sandburg. New York: Pocket Books, 1960.

Golden, Harry L. and Martin Rywell. *Jews in American History.* Charlotte, NC: Henry Lewis Martin Co., 1950.

Goldin, Judah, ed. *The Jewish Expression.* New York: Bantam, 1970.

Goldmann, Nahum. *The Autobiography of Nahum Goldmann.* New York: Holt, 1969.

Goldstein, Israel. *Israel at Home and Abroad.* Jerusalem: Rubin Mass, 1973.

Goodman, Abram Vossen. *American Overture.* Philadelphia: Jewish Publication Society, 1947.

Goren, Arthur A. *New York's Jews and the Quest for Community.* New York: Columbia University, 1970.

Grayzel, Solomon. *A History of the Jews.* New York: Mentor, 1968.

Grunberger, Richard. *The Twelve-Year Reich.* New York: Holt, 1971.

Grusd, Edward E. *B'nai B'rith: The Story of a Covenant.* New York: Appleton-Century, 1966.

Gutstein, Morris A. *To Bigotry No Sanction.* New York: Bloch, 1958.

Handlin, Oscar. *Adventure in Freedom.* New York: McGraw-Hill, 1954.

———. *Continuing Task: The American Jewish Joint Distribution Committee, 1914–1964.* New York: Random House, 1964.

Hecht, Ben. *A Child of the Century.* New York: Signet, 1954.

Heller, Celia, ed. *Structured Social Inequality.* New York: Macmillan, 1969.

Heller, James G. *Isaac M. Wise.* New York: Union of American Hebrew Congregations, 1965.

Hentoff, Nat, ed. *Black Anti-Semitism and Jewish Racism.* New York: Baron, 1969.

Herberg, Will. *Protestant-Catholic-Jew.* New York: Doubleday Anchor, 1960.

Hertzberg, Arthur. *The French Enlightenment and the Jews.* New York: Columbia University, 1968.

Herzl, Theodor. *Zionist Writings.* Vol. I, 1896–1898. Trans. by Harry Zohn. New York: Herzl Press, 1973.

Hilberg, Raul, ed. *Documents of Destruction.* Chicago: Quadrangle, 1971.

Hindus, Milton. *The Old East Side.* Philadelphia: Jewish Publication Society, 1971.

Hirschman, Ira A. *Life Line to a Promised Land.* New York: Jewish Book Guild, 1946.

Höhne, Heinz. *The Order of the Death's Head.* New York: Ballantine, 1971.

Hoyt, Edwin P. *The Guggenheims and the American Dream.* New York: Funk & Wagnalls, 1967.

Hurwitz, Maximilian. *The Workmen's Circle.* New York: Workmen's Circle, 1936.

Janowsky, Oscar I., ed. *The American Jew: A Reappraisal.* Philadelphia: Jewish Publication Society, 1964.

Jennings, Walter. *Twenty Giants of American Business.* New York: Exposition, 1953.

Joseph, Samuel. *The History of the Baron de Hirsch Fund: The Americanization of the Jewish Immigrant.* Philadelphia: Jewish Publication Society, 1935.

Kahn, Roger. *The Passionate People: What It Means to Be a Jew in America.* New York: Morrow, 1968.

Kanovsky, Eliyahu. *The Economic Impact of the Six-Day War.* New York: Praeger, 1970.

Karp, Abraham J., ed. *The Jewish Experience in America,* 5 vols. New York: KTAV Publishing House, 1969.

Katz, Robert. *Black Sabbath.* New York: Macmillan, 1969.

Katz, Samuel. *Days of Fire.* Garden City: Doubleday, 1968.

Keller, Werner. *Diaspora.* Trans. from German by Richard and Clara Winston. New York: Harcourt, 1969.

Kertzer, Morris N. *Today's American Jew.* New York: McGraw-Hill, 1967.

Kessler, Henry H. and Rachlis Eugene. *Peter Stuyvesant and His New York.* New York: Random House, 1959.

Klaperman, Gilbert. *The Story of Yeshiva University.* New York: Macmillan, 1969.

Klutznick, Philip M. *No Easy Answers.* New York: Farrar, Straus, 1961.

Kochan, Lionel. *The Jews in Soviet Russia Since 1917.* London: Oxford University, 1970.

Korn, Bertram W. *The Early Jews of New Orleans.* Waltham, MA: American Jewish Historical Society, 1969.

Kramer, Judith R., and Leventman, Seymour. *Children of the Gilded Ghetto.* New Haven: Yale University, 1961.

Krausnick, Helmut; Buchheim, Hans; Broszat, Martin; and Jacobsen, Hans-Adolf. *Anatomy of the SS State.* Trans. from the German by Richard Barry, Marian Jackson, and Dorothy Long. Intro. by Elizabeth Wiskemann. New York: Walker, 1968.

Kurzman, Dan. *Genesis 1948.* New York: World, 1970.

Landesman, Alter E. *Brownsville.* New York: Bloch, 1969.

Laqueur, Walter. *A History of Zionism.* New York: Holt, 1972.

———. *The Israel-Arab Reader.* New York: Bantam, 1969.

———. *The Road to War.* Harmondsworth, England: Penguin, 1968.

Learsi, Rufus. *The Jews in America.* New York: World, 1954.

Lendvai, Paul. *Anti-Semitism Without Jews.* Garden City: Doubleday, 1971.

Levai, Eugene. *Black Book on the Martyrdom of Hungarian Jewry.* Zurich: Central European Times Publishing, 1948.

Levin, Nora. *The Holocaust: The Destruction of European Jewry 1933–1945.* New York: Crowell, 1968.

Levin, Shmarya. *Forward from Exile.* Trans. by Maurice Samuel. Philadelphia: Jewish Publication Society, 1967.

Levine, Naomi and Hochbaum, Martin, eds. *Poor Jews: An American Awakening.* New Brunswick, NJ: Transaction Books, 1974.

Liebman, Charles. *The Ambivalent American Jew.* Philadelphia: Jewish Publication Society, 1973.

Lipsky, Louis. *A Gallery of Zionist Profiles.* New York: Farrar, Straus, 1956.

Litvinoff, Barnet. *A Peculiar People.* New York: Weybright and Talley, 1969.

Lomask, Milton. *Seed Money: The Guggenheim Story.* New York: Farrar, Straus, 1964.

Longworth, Philip, ed. *Confrontations with Judaism.* London: Blond, 1967.

Lurie, Harry L. *A Heritage Affirmed: The Jewish Federation Movement in America.* Philadelphia: Jewish Publication Society, 1961.

McWilliams, Carey. *A Mask for Privilege: Anti-Semitism in America.* Boston: Little, Brown, 1948.

Manners, Ande. *Poor Cousins.* New York: Coward, McCann, 1972.

Manvell, Roger and Fraenkel, Heinrich. *The Incomparable Crime.* New York: Putnam, 1967.

Marcus, Jacob R. *American Jewry: Documents, Eighteenth Century.* Cincinnati: Hebrew Union College Press, 1959.

————. *Early American Jewry*, 2 vols. Philadelphia: Jewish Publication Society, 1953.

————. *Essays on American Jewish History.* Cincinnati: Hebrew Union College, 1958.

————. *The Colonial American Jew. 1492–1776*, 3 vols. Detroit: Wayne State University, 1970.

————. *The Jew in the Medieval World.* New York: Atheneum, 1969.

————. *Memoirs of American Jews, 1775–1865*, 2 vols. Philadelphia: Jewish Publication Society, 1955.

Matz, Mary Jane. *The Many Lives of Otto Kahn.* New York: Macmillan, 1963.

Meir, Golda. *A Land of Our Own: An Oral Autobiography.* Marie Syrkin, ed. New York: Putnam, 1973.

Metzker, Isaac, ed. *A Bintel Brief.* New York: Ballantine, 1971.

Meyer, Isidore S., ed. *Early History of Zionism in America.* New York: American Jewish Historical Society and Theodor Herzl Foundation, 1968.

Miller, Alan W. *God of Daniel S.* New York: Macmillan, 1969.

Morgenstern, Julian. *As a Mighty Stream.* Philadelphia: Jewish Publication Society, 1949.

Morris, Robert and Freund, Michael. *Trends and Issues in Jewish Social Welfare in the United States, 1899–1958.* Philadelphia: Jewish Publication Society, 1966.

Morse, Arthur D. *While Six Million Died.* New York: Ace, 1968.

Morton, Frederic. *The Rothschilds: A Family Portrait.* New York: Crest, 1963.

Myers, Gustavus. *History of Bigotry in the United States.* Ed. and rev. by Henry M. Christman. New York: Capricorn, 1960.

————. *History of the Great American Fortunes.* New York: Modern Library, 1937.

Nevins, Allan. *Herbert H. Lehman and His Era.* New York: Scribner, 1963.

Noveck, Simon, ed. *Great Jewish Personalities in Modern Times*, 2 vols. New York: B'nai B'rith, 1960.

Packard, Vance. *The Status Seekers.* New York: Cardinal, 1962.

Patai, Raphael, ed. *The Complete Diaries of Theodor Herzl.* Harry Zohn, trans., 5 vols. New York. Herzl Press and Thomas Yoseloff, 1960.

Phillips, Cabell. *From the Crash to the Blitz, 1929–1939.* New York: Macmillan, 1969.

Pool, David De Sola. *Portraits Etched in Stone: Early Jewish Settlers, 1682–1831.* New York: Columbia University, 1952.

Pool, David De Sola and Tamar. *An Old Faith in the New World.* New York: Columbia University, 1955.

Postal, Bernard and Levy, Henry W. *And the Hills Shouted for Joy: The Day Israel Was Born.* New York: McKay, 1973.

Postal, Bernard and Koppman, Lionel. *Jewish Landmarks in New York.* New York: Hill and Wang, 1964.

Presser, Jacob. *The Destruction of the Dutch Jews.* Trans. from the Dutch by Arnold Pomerans. New York: Dutton, 1969.

Raphael, Chaim. *The Walls of Jerusalem.* New York: Knopf, 1968.

Reznikoff, Charles. *Louis Marshall: Champion of Liberty*, 2 vols. Intro. by Oscar Handlin. Philadelphia: Jewish Publication Society, 1957.

Ribalow, Harold, ed. *Autobiographies of American Jews.* Philadelphia: Jewish Publication Society, 1968.

Riis, Jacob A. *The Making of an American.* New ed., with epilogue by his grandson, J. Riis Owre. New York: Macmillan, 1970.

Rischin, Moses, ed. *The Spirit of the Ghetto by Hutchins Hapgood.* Cambridge, MA: Belknap, Harvard University, 1967.

———. *The Promised City.* Cambridge, MA: Harvard University, 1954.

Rosenberg, Stuart E. *The Search for Jewish Identity in America.* New York: Doubleday Anchor, 1963.

Rosenblatt, B. A. *Two Generations of Zionism.* Tel Aviv: Shengold, 1967.

Rosenfelt, Henry H. *This Thing of Giving.* New York: Plymouth, 1924.

Rosenthal, A. M. and Gelb, Arthur. *One More Victim; The Life and Death of an American-Jewish Nazi.* New York: Signet, 1967.

Roth, Cecil. *The Jewish Contribution to Civilization.* Cincinnati: Union of American Hebrew Congregations, 1940.

———. *Personalities and Events in Jewish History.* Philadelphia: Jewish Publication Society, 1953.

Roth, Henry. *Call It Sleep.* New York: Avon, 1964.

Rothman, David J. *The Discovery of the Asylum.* Boston: Little, Brown, 1971.

Rubenstein, Richard L. *After Auschwitz: Radical Theology and Contemporary Judaism.* New York: Bobbs-Merrill, 1966.

Rubin, Jacob A. *Partners in State-Building.* New York: M. P. Press, 1969.

St. John, Robert. *Jews, Justice and Judaism.* New York: Doubleday, 1969.

———. *They Came from Everywhere.* New York: Coward-McCann, 1962.

Sachar, Howard M. *The Emergence of the Middle East, 1914–1924.* New York: Knopf, 1969.

Samuel, Maurice. *Level Sunlight.* New York: Knopf, 1953.

———. *The World of Sholom Aleichem.* New York: Knopf, 1969.

Sanders, Ronald. *The Downtown Jews.* New York: Harper, 1969.

Schappes, Morris U. *A Documentary History of the Jews in the United States, 1654–1875.* New York: Citadel, 1952.

———. *The Jews in the United States.* New York: Citadel, 1958.

Schwartz, Leo, ed. *Great Ages and Ideas of the Jewish People.* New York: Modern Library, 1956.

Selzer, Michael. *The Wineskin and the Lizard.* New York: Macmillan, 1970.

———, ed. *Zionism Reconsidered.* New York: Macmillan, 1970.

Silverberg, Robert. *If I Forget Thee, O Jerusalem.* New York: Morrow, 1970.

Simonhoff, Harry. *Jewish Participants in the Civil War.* New York: Arco, 1963.

Sklare, Marshall. *America's Jews.* New York: Random House, 1971.

———. *The Jews: Social Patterns of an American Group.* New York: Free Press, 1958.

Stember, Charles Herbert, *et al. Jews in the Mind of America.* New York: Basic Books, 1966.

Stewart, Desmond. *The Middle East: Temple of Janus.* New York: Doubleday, 1971.

Still, Bayrd. *Mirror for Gotham.* New York: New York University, 1956.

Stokes, Phelps I. N. *The Iconography of Manhattan Island, 1498–1909.* New York: Dodd, 1926.

Strauss, Herbert A. and Reissner, Hanns G. *Jubilee Volume Dedicated to Curt C. Silberman.* New York: American Federation of Jews from Central Europe, 1969.

Strauss, Lewis L. *Men and Decisions.* New York: Doubleday, 1962.

Syrkin, Marie. *Golda Meir.* New York: Putnam, 1963.

Talese, Gay. *The Kingdom and the Power.* New York: Bantam, 1970.

Teller, Judd L. *Strangers and Natives: The Evolution of the American Jew from 1921 to the Present.* New York: Delacorte, 1968.

Tobias, Thomas J. *The Hebrew Benevolent Society of Charleston, S.C.* Charleston, S.C.: 1965.

Urofsky, Melvin I. *American Zionism from Herzl to the Holocaust.* New York: Doubleday Anchor, 1975.

Urofsky, Melvin I. and Levy, David W. *Letters of Louis D. Brandeis*, vols. I and II. Albany: State University of New York, 1971.

Vorspan, Albert. *Giants of Justice.* New York: Union of American Hebrew Congregations, 1960.

Voss, Carl, ed. *Stephen S. Wise: Servant of the People.* Philadelphia: Jewish Publication Society, 1969.

Wechsberg, Joseph. *The Merchant Bankers.* New York: Pocket Books, 1966.

Weizmann, Chaim. *Trial and Error.* New York: Schocken, 1966.

Werner, M. R. *It Happened in New York.* New York: Coward-McCann, 1957.

Wirth, Louis. *The Ghetto.* Chicago: University of Chicago, 1956.

Wischnitzer, Mark. *To Dwell in Safety: The Story of Jewish Migration Since 1800.* Philadelphia: Jewish Publication Society, 1948.

———. *Visas to Freedom: The History of HIAS.* New York: World, 1956.

Wise, Stephen. *Challenging Years.* New York: Putnam, 1949.

Wolfe, Tom. *Radical Chic & Mau-mauing the Flak Catchers.* New York: Bantam, 1971.

Wyman, David S. *Paper Walls: America and the Refugee Crisis, 1938–1941.* Amherst: University of Massachusetts, 1968.

Yaffe, James. *The American Jews.* New York: Paperback Library, 1969.

Zborowski, Mark and Herzog, Elizabeth. *Life Is With People.* New York: International Universities, 1952.

Zuckerman, William. *Voice of Dissent.* New York: Bookman Assocs., 1964.

Index

Temple Israel

Minneapolis, Minnesota

In Honor of the Bat Mitzvah of
JUDITH LYNN HYMES

by
Mr. & Mrs. Harvey Hymes

February 26, 1977